As I Go

As I Go

BOB VERNON

His Life Story ... In His Own Words

FROM TV'S "HOMESTEAD USA" AND THE VERNON BROTHERS

Published by CHRISTELL

As I Go by Bob Vernon

© 2018 by Bob Vernon. All rights reserved.

Scripture marked (KJV) is from the King James Version of the Bible.

Scripture marked (ASV) is from the American Standard Version of the Bible.

Scripture marked (NASB) taken from the NEW AMERICAN STANDARD BIBLE®, Copyright © 1960, 1962, 1963, 1968, 1971, 1972, 1973, 1975, 1977, 1995 by the Lockman Foundation. Used by permission.

Scripture marked (Phillips) taken from The New Testament in Modern English by J.B. Phillips copyright © 1960, 1972 J. B. Phillips. Administered by The Archbishops' Council of the Church of England. Used by Permission.

Scripture quotations marked (RSV) are from the Revised Standard Version of the Bible, copyright © 1946, 1952, and 1971 the Division of Christian Education of the National Council of the Churches of Christ in the United States of America. Used by permission. All rights reserved.

Scripture marked (NKJV) taken from the New King James Version®. Copyright © 1982 by Thomas Nelson. Used by permission. All rights reserved.

Scripture quotations marked (NEB) taken from the New English Bible, copyright © Cambridge University Press and Oxford University Press 1961, 1970. All rights reserved.

Cover and Graphics by Judy Gilmore, *www.GilmoreGraphics.org*

LCCN: 2017917210

ISBN-13: 9781977739773
ISBN-10: 1977739776

Autobiography / Memoir / Church / Christianity / Ministry / Religion

Published by CHRISTELL
Printed in the United States of America

As I Go

As I go along life's road,
I don't have a heavy load,
For there's one who goes with me,
Taking all anxiety.

But I cannot help but feel
Pain and anguish so real,
For humanity downtrod,
Without hope and without God.

Bound and in darkness,
The light they will not see,
Until someone goes to guide them
To faith and purity.

So let's pledge ourselves today
To help people find the way,
That brings faith and hope and love,
And God's blessings from above.

I've but one life I may give,
So for God above I'll live.
I'll be faithful every day,
And His Word I will obey.

Tho' I suffer pain and wrong,
In my heart I'll sing a song
Of the Saviour's strength divine,
That all nations need to find.

-Words and Music Bob Vernon
Copyright 1967 Lexicon Music, Inc.

Dedication & Gratitudes

I lovingly dedicate this book to my beautiful, queenly, and recently departed wife, Patricia Ann, my co-partner in ministry and life who stepped so easily into her role as a young first lady in the churches we began and served. And then the many years of evangelizing, filming, traveling for rallies and concerts, and raising our children. She is to be lauded for her patient endurance and faith, even though suffering some years in broken health before finally being made whole to perform more service for her Lord and others. I also dedicate this account of my life story to our three loving and talented children Rebecca, Gregg, and Deborah, all of whom minister and are so very gifted in music and ministry. I could not have completed this book without Becky's countless hours transforming an old-fashioned typed first draft into this book. And her husband, Stephen, who has invested months of his time in numerous details and took the bull by the horns and made it happen. And gratitude for my son, Gregg, who went over a thousand photos and selected and edited ones for this book. And the love and support from Debbie and her family always encouraging me. Loving honor to our baby, Karen Elizabeth, taken to Heaven when we were filming our first television series in Hollywood. All my children played themselves in our *Homestead USA* television series.

I can't thank my niece, Judy Vernon Gilmore, enough for her magnificent graphics and artwork on the book cover. She and her husband, Gary, continue their ministry in South Africa. Special thanks to the many people who through the years have inspired me to tell my life's story. This includes my family, brothers, friends, and a host of supporters, co-laborers, missionaries, and congregations across the world.

And, of course, I give thanks and all the praise to our Heavenly Father who has done far more "exceeding abundantly above all that we ask or think, according to the power that works within us, unto Him be the Glory in the Church and in Christ Jesus unto all generations forever and ever. Amen."

-Bob Vernon

Table of Contents

Introduction

FOR YEARS, PEOPLE have asked my father, Bob Vernon, when he was going to write a book about his life and how he and the Vernon Family landed in Hollywood pioneering the new medium of television by filming the trailblazing weekly television program *Homestead USA* at Universal Studios. And how all the music, albums, church planting, crusades, films, and television programs came to be for seven decades (and counting). And how his wife Patricia (my mother) became his lifelong partner in all these endeavors along with the extended Vernon Family.

It was only natural that this book should be titled "As I Go." One of my father's albums of sacred music which he recorded for Word Records was titled "As I Go," and which was also the theme song for this album which he wrote. And one of the films which my father filmed in the former Soviet Union and Africa was titled "As I Go." My father was one of the first westerners to go to the restricted areas of the former Soviet Union and actually film and preach!

And the words "As I Go" truly reflect the theme of my father's remarkable life, adventures, ministry, and approach to the life God gives each of us while we travel our journey for the brief time we have here. Jesus told us to "GO!" Go into the entire world and share the good news with everyone that we can while we can. That's my dad all right! Now you can go with him as he takes you on his adventure in this book. Enjoy the journey!

-Gregg Vernon, July 2017

Ancestry And A Surprise Birth!

CHAPTER 1

Birth And Ancestry

IT WAS A cold and snowy early evening hour when Dr. J.C. Benage arrived in his shiny black Ford coupe at the Dallas and Beulah Vernon two-story farm house on January 4th, 1927. He had driven the nine miles of narrow, country roads from the little town of Lebanon, Missouri, to oversee the birth of an expected Vernon baby. Of course, all these details were related to me when I was a child and intrigued me greatly! Mother had been in labor for some time, prompting my father to hurriedly crank the large wall telephone in the kitchen, calling "Central" to ring up the doctor.

Mother's labor pain was harder this time, unexpectedly, having already given birth over the previous eight years to three babies, J.P., Ward T., and Dallas Jr. Dallas, five years old at the time, later told me that curiosity had gotten the best of him, and he sneaked up to the ground-floor window to peek in where the birth was taking place. Mother spotted him and was frantically waving to him and crying out, "Get away, get away!!"

The handsome face of a little brown-eyed, dark-haired baby soon appeared in the rugged but tender hands of the good doctor, who exclaimed, "It's a boy!"

Dr. Benage tended to the needs of the happy but relieved mother and healthy babe, cutting the umbilical cord, while our proud father fairly beamed at the birth of his fourth son. The scene took a sudden and unexpected turn when fifteen minutes later, the doctor said, "Well, what do you know? I'm going in after another one!" And that was me, a blue-eyed, blond-haired tyke, two inches shorter but a bit chubbier than my twin brother they named Billy Dean Vernon. And the name scribbled on my birth certificate is Bobby Gene Vernon, but that is scratched out rather messily by a somewhat unschooled neighbor and replaced with "Bobby Jean Vernon." Maybe that was an omen for some messes I got into later!

As to my ancestry, I was born on the farm homesteaded by Obadiah and Sarah Sally Wyatt Vernon. They had traveled in 1844 with their young boy, Joe, from the East in a caravan of oxen-pulled covered wagons, settling on 160 wooded acres of back Indian country called "Blackfoot," situated in the hills of Spring Hollow in Southwest Missouri. The original Homestead had been granted to James Lynch, a Private in the Infantry, who had fought in the War of 1812. Upon his death, it was returned to the Federal Land Office. Obadiah felled trees, built a log house and log barn, and farmed the land, being granted the 160 Homestead acreage signed by President James Buchanan May 15, 1857. Obadiah and Sarah had seven more children, including my Grandpa James Polk Vernon, making a total of eight for Sarah to raise alone after her husband died at age 39 in 1860.

What brave, hardy, and God-fearing souls these pioneering great-grandparents of mine were, facing such difficult challenges as they carved out a new beginning in this new land! With the overcoming spirit they demonstrated, together with the legacy of love, faith, and courage they left for me and my kin who follow in their footsteps, how could I fail in my quest for meaning and success in life!

My fraternal grandfather, James Polk Vernon, was born on Valentine's Day February 14, 1847, and died on October 6th in 1920. He was the third child of Obadiah Vernon (8/19/1821 – 6/15/1860) and Sarah Sally Wyatt Vernon (1/25/1825 – 9/15/1901). He was a Veteran of the Civil War, serving in the 16ᵗʰ Regiment of the Missouri Cavalry Volunteers from August 11, 1864, to June 30, 1865. His discharge described him as being "18 years of age, five feet 10 inches high, sallow complexion, blue eyes, light hair, and by occupation, when enrolled, a Farmer."

I never knew my Grandpa Jim, for he passed away seven years before I was born. But from my father, I learned that he was a successful farmer, saw mill owner on the farm, and threshing machine operator during every harvest season. I was so delighted not too long ago to discover the obituary in the news after his funeral, and I am quoting it in full as recorded:

"James P. Vernon, a lifelong resident of Laclede County, passed away very suddenly Wednesday evening of last week. Mr. Vernon had been in his usual health and had attended to the chores about the place during the afternoon as was his custom. He and Mrs. Vernon had just finished their supper when she saw him sink forward in his chair. She went to him, thinking he had strangled, but he died instantly it is supposed from a stroke of paralysis. Funeral services were held at the home Friday at 2:30, conducted by Rev. I.P. Langley, former pastor of the Lebanon, Missouri Baptist Church. An unusually large crowd of relatives, old friends and neighbors were present to share the sorrow of this wife and children who were so crushed by the loss that had come to them like lightning from a clear sky. The three sons, E.A. 'Ed' Vernon, Dallas Vernon, and Owen Vernon, two sons-in-law, Oscar Welch and Robert Bolles, and a nephew, J.W. Vernon, were the pall bearers. He was buried in the Atchley Cemetery. James P. Vernon was born in Laclede County near the Blackfoot schoolhouse February 14, 1847. He was a son of Mr. and Mrs. Obadiah Vernon, pioneer citizens, who settled on the homestead. Mr. Vernon has spent his entire life on that farm or a farm nearby. He was married in young life to Miss Eliza Smith, and to them were born two children, W.A. Vernon of Tulsa, Oklahoma, and Mrs. Ruth Vernon Kelsey of Miami, Oklahoma. The wife passed away about forty years ago. Several years later he was married to Miss Etta Beckner. Four children were born to them: Mrs. Lena Vernon Welch, Dallas Vernon, Owen Vernon, all living in the neighborhood, and a daughter, Mrs. Oda Vernon Bolles, who passed away about two years ago. All the other children were present for the funeral. He also is survived by fourteen grandchildren and two great-grandchildren. A brother, W.A. Vernon, and a sister, Mrs. Irene Vernon Adkins, also survive him. What greater heritage can a man leave to the world than a family of stalwart sons and dutiful daughters, who follow the paths of good fellowship and right living as pointed out by him? Mr. Vernon will be greatly missed in the neighborhood where he spent nearly seventy-four years."

Grandpa Jim's first wife, Eliza Smith Vernon, was only 24 years of age when she died. They had two children, Ruth and Alfred A. Vernon (called Ed). Records at the Laclede County Recorder's Office in Lebanon, Missouri, show that on August 19, 1884, a wedding is recorded that took place between Grandfather and Etta Adeline Beckner (7/4/1867 – 2/5/1950) some time before. Grandma Ettie, which is what we called her, always said she was 16 years old when she got married, so it must have been a traditional June wedding. She had been hired to help with the small children, so she must have fallen in love and helped herself to a man as well! What a nice love story and a smart lady!! As to her parents, her father's name was Eli Beckner, and I believe her mother's maiden name was Hoke.

Grandma had inherited the Homestead of 139 acres when Grandpa Jim died in 1920. Of the original 160 acres, twenty had been sold to a neighbor, and one acre had been donated to build a schoolhouse a quarter mile from the Vernon home.

Among some ancient letters I came across, I found one dated November 5, 1884, that Grandma Etta, my father's mother, had written to Grandpa Jim just two months after their first child had been born. This would have been six years before my father, Dallas, was born in 1890. The letter was written from North Springfield, Missouri, addressed to James P. Vernon at the Homestead, Laclede County, Lebanon, Missouri, as follows:

"Mr. James P. Vernon: My dear Jim, I got your letter just a few minutes ago. I never was so proud to hear from anybody in my life! Ruth [Jim's little girl by his first wife who had died] went to the Post Office and got it. She is in a big way to go home. We will be going just as soon as we can after the 10th. I don't know what Pa [Eli Beckner, her father, a builder] wants me to stay for, but I will find out, then I can hardly wait for the time to come for us to go home. I want to see you all so bad! I am glad that Martha is better, but I am sorry that George and Iwanace got throwed. I would of liked to of been to [all] the Speaking they have had in the two big Raleys [sic], one Republican, and one Democrat. I tell you, they had a big time. We was all to see it, it was a big sight for Ruth as she never saw one before. Pa is building a house at Strafford, he started this morning. It is between here and Lebanon. He will not be at home until next Saturday. I am sorry that Iris' folks are not well.

"The next time you see Mattie Barber, you can tell her my baby beats her's agrowing, it is just two months old today. Weighs 14 pounds and is nearly big enough to sit alone. Mamie and Willie [Grandma's sister and brother] are at school. I guess there will be a big fuss when I start home and leave them, they want to go so bad! Fannie is getting dinner while I write this.

"Well, I believe I have written all I can think of now. My cold still hangs on, and I guess it will last all winter.

"I will write and tell you when I will be there. You answer this so we will get it before we go, for I always love to hear from you. Now write soon.

"I remain as ever, yours, Etta."

The baby Grandma Etta refers to in her letter was her first, my Aunt Lena; her second child Oda, to whom I have earlier referred, died as a young mother; then my father Dallas, born in 1890; and the last child in the family was my Uncle Owen.

I thought it important to include this letter, for it is so old and in Grandmother's own handwriting telling about her life.

Grandma was the owner of our place until my father was elected County Assessor in 1936, and in 1941 he bought the Homestead for $2,900.00! He later purchased 200 more adjacent acres, bringing the total to 340 acres. By that time a large consolidated rural school building had been erected at a different location. The old two-story school house that I had walked to and that had been donated to the school district was returned to the Vernon Homestead Estate.

Grandma Etta used a cane, but she was a sturdy, active soul, strong willed, but very loving and good to us grandchildren. I recall one evening she was standing at the old kitchen range preparing a meal for us boys, weeping heavily and so concerned for my oldest brother, J.P., hospitalized and not expected to live because of a ruptured appendix. Mother and Dad had carried him, so desperately ill, out to our '28 Model A Ford to rush the nine rugged miles to the hospital in Lebanon for emergency surgery. My brother did survive, after three critical weeks in the hospital. Another example of Grandma's love was when she made eighty plate-sized pancakes for us seven boys to see how many we could eat. I think she was at the stove a full hour. I ate ten!

My dad, Dallas Vernon (2/23/1890 – 12/7/1975), was the third of four children. Oda, as a young wife and mother, died in the "flu" epidemic of 1919. And my mother, who had just given birth to her first child, J.P., also was near death with the "flu" but thankfully survived. A year earlier, Dad had married my Mom, Beulah Ida Tribble Vernon (8/24/1891 – 11/17/1975), on Easter Sunday, March 31, 1918. Their wedding song was "The End of a Perfect Day."

My mother's maiden name was Tribble. My great grandfather was Robert James Tribble (1834 – 1924). He married Rebecca Ellen Bilderback, born in 1835, date of death unknown. Through the influence of his wife, he gave up alcohol and became a devout Christian and dedicated minister. My mother told me how dearly she loved him and how much he influenced her life.

My grandfather was Anderson Ward Tribble (1869 – 1930), who was the fourth of seven children, and his wife was Minnie Miller (1870 – 1949). One of my first memories is when I was not quite four years old, with my mother and twin brother Bill, as my grandfather was drawing his last breath. Grandmother and other family members lovingly surrounded him in his bed, and my Uncle Homer Tribble spoke quietly, "Well, he's gone," and he tenderly placed a coin over each of his eyes. I remember the next morning asking my mother to lift Bill and me up so we could look into the casket to see our grandfather. Later, at the cemetery on that windy winter day of December, I recall so vividly my folks in their overcoats, my dad with his arm around my mom, both of them weeping softly.

My maternal great grandfather was Henry Fletcher Miller (9/17/1849 – 1/1/1937), and I remember him quite well as a gentle, loving man, as I was ten years old three days after he died. His wife was Ida Rowena McNeely (1/23/1851 – 3/7/1929). They had eight children, my Grandma Minnie being the oldest. You talk about a sweet grandmother in every respect, she fit the bill in every way! Though we lived about twelve miles away, a few times each year Mother would load us little boys up in the 1928 Model A Ford to go see Gramma. I can see now that huge old dead tree with one giant limb slanting up that Bill and I would slowly inch up and sit on, pretending that we were in a plane flying to New York or California! And oh, the sweet pickled beets, cole slaw and fruit salad that Granny fixed for us, plus those luscious pies! I recall one time when I was only four or five being out in the yard with a large soap box in front of me, preaching up a storm! Grandma Minnie came by, laughing and lovingly teasing me. I guess we had been to Sunday services, and I had "gotten religion." Grandma was very fun-loving, but she was devout in her faith, never missing church. I never dreamed that I would ever think about being a preacher, but when I was in the Navy Submarine Service during World War II and atomic bombs were dropped, I began to think seriously about it. I wrote Grandma a letter about that "preaching" experience I had as a child at her place and about which she had teased me. She quickly wrote back a nice letter of encouragement, saying, "Oh Bobby! I'm so sorry if by teasing you I hurt or discouraged you. I was laughing because it was so cute!"

CHAPTER 2

My Wonderful Parents

SINCE MY LIFE and character have been greatly influenced and shaped by my parents, I want in the next few pages to show you what kind of people they were by using words from their own writings describing their own lives. First, from my dear handsome father who had impeccable character, neither drinking alcohol nor smoking, and who enjoyed life to the fullest; then, from my darling mother, such a bright light to all who knew her, so loving, so intelligent, and so attractive.

The following is from a chapter entitled "The Homestead," written by my father, Dallas Vernon Sr., in a booklet called "Our Seven Sons":

"While I was born near Lebanon [Missouri], I was not born here on the homestead. My birth place was about three miles to the southeast [in a log cabin we called 'Horn Hollow']. My dad owned 80 acres there. While I was not born here on the homestead, I have lived all my life in this section of Missouri. The school district which I attended was called the Blackfoot School District and I graduated from high school in Lebanon, Missouri, where I pitched on the baseball team [and later on the team in college at Springfield]. I had an offer to join one of the major league teams then in existence. However, my mother described the type of life I would have to live and I felt that it would be much better for me to continue working [the] farm, living with my family and having friends and neighbors in the Lebanon, Missouri area and letting fame and perhaps fortune go to other men. I do not regret that decision. My life has been deeply blessed.

"I met my wife, Beulah, in 1914 or 1915, at the picture show in Springfield, Missouri. The name of the theatre was the Jefferson. As she was walking up the aisle to leave, she passed a note to me and asked in effect, 'Aren't you Dallas Vernon?' I read the note very quickly, looked up and said, 'Yes I am. Won't you sit down?' She had coal black hair and beautiful brown eyes. Beulah was attending [college] at Southwest Missouri State University in Springfield at that time, although the name of the school was Missouri Normal. I was [in college] staying with a friend, the son of a doctor. When Beulah sat down beside me in the Jefferson Theatre in Springfield, my life took a marked change! I married her three years later.

"I have always been active in the Church, as was my father [and mother]. We were members of the Oak Grove Baptist Church [about a mile from home]. I was raised in that church. In fact, that is the first Sunday School I remember. I was baptized in 1916 and the place of my baptism was the Bennett Springs Branch. The name has been changed to the Bennett Springs State Park and it is one of the oldest State Parks in Missouri. The man's name who baptized me was Amos, who later married my cousin, Opha Garland.

"Most of my life I had spent working the farm. When I was a child I would get up at six o'clock in the morning, and we would begin our chores. I would go to school, come home at night and once again do my chores. I would go to bed between the hours of eight and ten o'clock.

"I left the area for a brief time as a telegrapher for the Frisco Railroad in Marionville, Missouri, and later for the Union Pacific Railroad in the State of Nebraska. At that time it ran from Omaha, Nebraska to the West Coast. After being married, Beulah and I, together with our first three little boys who had been born, moved to Tulsa, Oklahoma. Although I was injured a couple of times working for both the Union Pacific and the Frisco Railroad in Tulsa, I was never injured seriously. I did return to Lebanon after working on the railroads in the very early years of this century, and I have not left Lebanon since.

"I was defeated by just a few votes in both the primary and general elections in campaigns running for County Assessor in 1928 and 1932. In 1933, we had a seventh son, so I was determined and knew that in the midst of the Great Depression, I had to improve our family's financial situation. So I ran again in 1936 and finally won. I was elected and served as Laclede County Assessor for sixteen years, and Beulah was my Deputy [and secretary, keeping and updating the books of the County]. After I turned 65, she and I with an attorney, started the Vernon-Dillard Co., an Abstract and Tax service. My membership in the Oak Grove Baptist Church was changed in the early 1950's when I joined Beulah and the boys placing my membership in the Christian Church at Phillipsburg, Missouri.

"Later we became charter members of Southern Heights Christian Church in Lebanon, started by our sons preaching in a revival. My life has been centered around the farm, around my family, and around the Lord's work."

That is the end of my father's description of his long and successful life as a hard-working, faithful husband and father. He used to occasionally say, "You'll miss me when I'm gone." He couldn't have been more right!

We four brothers were privileged to help start the Southern Heights Christian Church in Lebanon along with our cousin, Roger Tribble, and our older brother, Dallas Jr. Today it is one of the prominent churches in Lebanon.

My mother, at the age of ten, attended a tent revival near Phillipsburg held by evangelist John Stovall in 1901. She went forward at the invitation to confess her faith in Jesus. That same night, they went out in the cold to a nearby stream where the ice was cut for her to be baptized!

Now in order for you to know how blessed and privileged we brothers were to have such a sweet, intelligent and talented mother as we had, I want you to be aware of some of the hardships she endured and overcame.

Mother was quite a writer. After her very busy life of raising us seven boys, she wrote for a column in the *Springfield Daily News* called "Over the Ozarks." Her articles were subtitled, "Happenings from the Homestead." The following is a classic, describing her feelings right after her marriage on March 31, 1918, when they moved into the dilapidated old log cabin situated on 80 acres that Obadiah Vernon had bought in 1859. My father had been born there, as well as my two oldest brothers, J.P., and Ward in 1919 and 1920. The article is entitled "Horn Hollow," which follows in its entirety:

"It was such a forlorn looking place. The porch was gone. The cattle that grazed on its wooded slopes came up at noon to stand lazily under the big walnut tree, overspreading the well and the watering trough in one corner of the yard. The house was log with a lean-to kitchen and a big fireplace. One window on the South and two half-windows on the North let in the shifting shadows of the little valley.

"'Horn Hollow' we called it, my husband and I, when we went there to make a home. To me, it was the most impossible situation I had ever found myself in; to my husband, it was next to Heaven itself! You see, he had played there when a boy. He had waded in its creeks, had showered the old granary door with rocks, had leaped its rail fences in 'fox and hound,' and had played marbles in the shade of its great white oaks. And he had nestled in the trundle-bed that rolled under the big double bed that stood in one corner of the front room.

"But the rustling of the leaves on the trees that came right up the front door whispered no comforting words to me. The trickle of the water as it washed over the pebbles, wearing them round and smooth, made no music in my ears. The giant oaks with their spreading branches held no sheltering arms for me.

"All I could see was the tired fences, lying here and there as if to rest, the oldness of the house with its huge beams that supported the floor of the attic, the funny little barn that was only a stone's throw from the kitchen door, the proximity of the cattle when they came to drink the clear, sparkling water pumped from the well, the flies that persisted in getting into the house in spite of screens.

"Yes, we fixed screens, we fixed the porch, we made more windows, we built a picket fence to keep our little boy and his dog from wandering into the hills and fields. We polished up the walnut doors and facings, we hung gleaming white curtains at the windows. We had a garden of the richest black soil, and the greenest vegetables, only six feet from our kitchen door, we had rich milk and thick cream, chickens and pigs, calves and lambs, geese and turkeys, and two of the prettiest horses that I have ever seen anywhere, a black and a bay, high spirited with arching necks, and we called them Bally and Black Beauty. We had flowers, and we had another baby. We lived and we had fun!

"But we also had droughts and floods. We watched our corn brown and sour in the scorching sun, and we watched those same fields, fat with long green ears, drown in the raging torrents of a 'gully-washer.' We watched our debts double and our savings dwindle, 'til we could take it no longer. So the little Valley became only a memory."

That is the end of my mother's graphic and moving account of her "honeymoon" and two years following.

Mother was not only a great writer and speaker, but extraordinarily fabulous as a mom and a gifted woman in so many ways. She was conservative, but progressive, keeping up with the times. She played the piano. By riding the train to California as a young single woman to pick oranges, she had earned enough money to buy our family piano and silverware. She taught school, was active in the P.T.A., church, business, politics, the Professional Women's Club, and War Mothers. And finally, for her distinction as a mother and participant in public affairs, she was nominated to be Missouri Mother of the Year. What a mother, and what a woman!

Dad and Mom lived first at "Horn Hollow," as she has described. Over the next fifteen years, beginning with the influenza epidemic of 1919 which almost took Mother's life, then the lean times and hardships of the twenties, and followed by the crashing and crushing period of the Great Depression, Mother and Dad endured it all with faith, grit, and a loving spirit. They presented us seven sons, who were born during this time, a household of joy and laughter, a reverence for God, and a deep love for our parents, our neighbors, and each other. They took us to church. They taught us to work hard, live right, and since they were both college-educated school teachers, to do well in school. Of course, boys will be boys, and I'm not about to say we always lived up to their teachings! But it really motivated us as it was their practice to compliment us with a job well done when we did the chores, plowed the fields, washed the dishes, helped mom with the housework, put in the crops, or milked the cows. We had no electricity, no indoor bathroom or toilet, no tractor, and no bright, shiny, new farm implements. Yes, we were poor, but we either didn't know it or didn't let on like we knew it. Hard times? Yes! But good times? YES!! Mother quit teaching school to have babies. Dad not only farmed but kept on teaching school until our family's fortunes changed when he was elected Laclede County Assessor in 1936. But until then, in my early childhood I remember very well him going out to the barn on cold winter days to saddle up our pony and ride down the miles of the hollows and woods to the Flatwoods School.

CHAPTER 3

Origin Of The Name "Vernon"

I WAS so stunned when I learned that there is ancient history concerning the Vernons, and how our name originated, that I would like to tell you about it. Several years ago, I made a trip to Europe, specifically to the town of Vernon, France, to see if I could learn anything concerning our origins. I stayed in a nice, quaint hostel for a few days and walked the clean cobblestone streets of "my" town, meeting people, and with my tiny French-English book of translated words and phrases, had fun exploring the village. I visited the library, museums, historic sites, and every place I could think of to gain information about "who we were." But all to no avail. Finally, on the last day, I packed my small satchel at the hostel (I always traveled light on such trips), grabbed it and my briefcase, and walked down the street toward the train station, intending disappointedly to take the thirty-mile trip back to Paris and fly home. But as good fortune would have it, I noticed the sign on a building I was about to pass that read, "Vernon Newspaper Office." I paused and to myself said, "Hmm, just maybe!" I opened the door and went in, hoping against hope that at least I could get some of the valuable information I was seeking. I introduced myself to a very nice Frenchman, the owner, who spoke perfect English. Quickly, I explained my dilemma. It was nearly closing time for businesses, so he said,

"Please wait here, and let me walk over to City Hall nearby and see if they're open. There's something there I want you to see." In a few minutes, he came back and said, "Come on, let's go over. They're still open." Hurriedly, we walked the two blocks to the aged but well preserved, architecturally sound and impressive building. We rushed up the spiral stairway to the second floor into a huge, high-ceilinged room. I couldn't believe my eyes! There on one side of the room, covering the entire wall from floor to ceiling, was imprinted in color a huge chart headed with the bold letters, "GENEALOGICAL TABLE OF THE VERNON FAMILY." I gasped in disbelief! To me, it was like fastening my eyes on the Magna Carta of 1215. I was over-awed, almost in a trance at this chance good fortune. The first date is 942 – 996 of either the father or ancestor of the first Vernon mentioned, but who had a different last name. This was puzzling to me. The first Vernon listed was Richard de Vernon, who had changed his last name from de Vieres to de Vernon, which I learned from further research on the web in an article entitled, "History of the Vernon Family." (source: *http:// www.geocities.com / Heartland / Valley / 7825 / vernhist.html*)

I am including this entire article on the ancient history of the Vernon Family. I won't belabor you with all the dukes, barons, and no doubt scoundrels listed in that chart of Vernon names I found in France, the last date being 1965:

"The 'Vernon Family' story begins back around 888 – 906 when the Vikings under 'Marching Rollo' invaded and conquered Normandy, including the ancient town of Vernon. The town dates back to Gallo-Roman times and is located in a beautiful valley on both sides of the Seine River, thirty miles northwest of Paris.

"Rollo's son, William Longsword, became Duke of Normandy in 925. The family became very powerful and wealthy holding many large estates in Normandy.

"Richard de Reviers, the first Vernon, was a good and loyal officer serving the Duke of Normandy, William the Bastard, future William the Conqueror. He was such a good and loyal officer that, in 1050, he was given the little town of Vernon-sur-Seine as a reward. From then on, Richard de Reviers and all his descendants to come, took the name of their town for their name. The VERNON family was born. Richard de Reviers changed his name to Richard de Vernon. Sixteen years later, William the Conqueror invaded England in 1066, and at least two of his high-ranking officers were Vernons. Richard de Vernon definitely took part in the invasion. Many others of the family also accompanied him. For the service, more great estates in Normandy and England were granted to the Vernon family, and its members were ranked among the wealthiest and most powerful in both countries. Several members became barons and were knighted.

"Shortly following the Battle of Hastings, the area around Chester County, England became a Norman stronghold. William the Conqueror awarded Chester to his nephew, Hugh Lupus, in 1070. Hugh immediately appointed four great barons, one of them being Sir Richard de Vernon, Baron de Shipbrook. He and his brother, Sir Walter, were both at the Battle of Hastings. Their father was Sir William de Vernon of Vernon Castle in Normandy.

"The Quaker Vernons descended from Sir Richard de Vernon, Baron de Shipbrook. They not only were friends of the Quaker, William Penn, they were related to him through marriage. William Penn's father was owed a great deal of money by the King of England, and to settle that debt, he gave the area of Pennsylvania to William Penn. Thomas Vernon made the surveying voyage to Pennsylvania with William Penn in 1681 and returned later that year to England. He and his brothers were among the first to obtain property in the newly-acquired land. Land titles in Delaware County records the three Vernon Brothers' purchase of 625 acres each in March 1681. Randall Vernon purchased a further 829 acres in 1711 and 1712. Robert Vernon purchased a further 330 acres in 1684. The three Quaker brothers came to America, arriving on a Liverpool ship, the 'Friendship,' Robert Crossman, Master, which is presumed to have arrived 14 August 1682 at Upland, Pennsylvania. The 'Friendship of Liverpool' was one of the twenty-four known ships that sailed from England, arriving December 1681 through December 1682 with passengers to establish William Penn's 'Holy Experiment' in Pennsylvania. Thomas Vernon of Stanithorne, near Middlewick, County Palatine, Chester, England, was the eldest of the three brothers and had been persecuted for being a Quaker in 1678 and 1679.

"This was the beginning of the Vernon Family in America. During the next one hundred years, the brothers prospered and their families grew and spread throughout several states."

That is the end of that account of the history of, and the origin of the name of, our family. I am presuming that one or more of my particular ancestors could have been on that good ship "Friendship," but I am not certain of that at all. Persecution and martyrdom was rife in Europe and England during and following the Protestant Reformation, and, of course, shiploads of immigrants were coming across the sea to this new land for conscience sake to escape the harsh reality of anti-Scriptural, Ecclesiastical domination and authority:

> "As early as 1606, King James I, who had succeeded Elizabeth on the English throne, was persuaded to issue a charter to some London and Plymouth merchants who had in mind the establishment of new outposts of trade in Virginia … The London merchants were the first to take advantage of this grant. In December 1606, they sent out three shiploads of colonists, who the next spring founded Jamestown at a point thirty miles inland from the mouth of the James River." (*A Short History of American Democracy* by John D. Hicks, 1946, page 11)

Perhaps some of my forebears were on one of those ships, or maybe on a later voyage of Pilgrims or Puritans seeking religious freedom and a land where they were not ruled by the monarchy or papacy. No Vernon was on the "Mayflower," I know, for the "Mayflower Compact" specifically lists the forty-one named passengers and signers, as I recall.

Early Years And Approaching War

CHAPTER 4

A Young Man And A Love For Music

NOW THAT I have told you about my birth, my parents, my ancestors, and the origin of our family name, let me tell you about my boyhood and adolescent years. It was absolutely a wonderful and happy time, so much so that I didn't want to grow up and leave it!

It was such great fun being part of a big family! I had a deep love for my parents and all my brothers. And being a twin was extra special, as it still is to this day. We were Billy and Bobby, being dressed alike and doing everything together. That is until we started to school! Billy wanted to start when he was only four years old, and being more shy than he, I certainly didn't want to. But since we were so close and he was always the leader when we were young, I tagged along that first day. But for me it was a frightful experience, and at noon I left and walked the dusty quarter of a mile back to the safety and security of my home sweet home! I remember when I got there, I took my little toy car outside to the barn lot and had so much fun playing with it. So for the eight years of elementary school, we were separated by one grade. Then Bill repeated the eighth grade so we could be in high school together.

When I started to school the following year, I was a slow learner. I recall that first day how difficult it was for me as my teacher, Miss Gala Singleton (who boarded at our home), was explaining how to take a page of paper, fold it, and print our name at the top -- something as simple as that. And learning to read was so hard for me. My dad, who was teaching at a country school at Flatwoods, some miles away, would come home and bring a little reader called "Dumbo the Elephant." There was a nice picture of Dumbo which I liked, and Dumbo and my dad helped me learn how to read! I finally did well in my studies, except for those terrible written problems in my arithmetic book I couldn't figure out. But I especially excelled in spelling, music, art, mathematical tables, and ciphering matches, as well as penmanship. I never got in trouble while in elementary school except two times. There were two Billy Vernons and two Bobby Vernons in our Blackfoot school, and most of the time we were well-behaved kids. Really!! But on this occasion when I was in the second grade, we and perhaps one or two classmates decided that during recess we would leave the school grounds and climb the fence into adjoining woods of our Vernon Homestead. We made our way through the underbrush to the sinkhole lake about a half-quarter mile away. We didn't go skinny-dipping, but we sat there for a while enjoying our getaway and Mother Nature, then returned very sheepishly and very late as classes were in session. What was our punishment -- standing in a row in a corner of the schoolroom before all the other students with opened school books balanced on top of our heads!

The other reprimand and punishment came when I was in the sixth grade on the upper floor of the two-story schoolhouse. Four grades were on the bottom floor, four on the upper. This incident was for something that really was not my fault. Really! I shared a seat with a classmate, William Franklin. It was a cold winter day, and I had on heavy laced boots with a small pocket near the top of each boot. William kept on pushing a pocket knife down into one of those spaces, and all the time I was trying to get him to stop. We got tickled and it was causing a disturbance in the classroom. Finally, the teacher came to our seat and gave us a mild warning, all to no avail, for now it was too late. We covered our mouths and tried to stop laughing but couldn't. She walked over to the corner of the room, grabbed a long hickory stick, and marched over to our seat. "Stand up, William," she fumed, and gave him a few whacks on the lower back side. "You're next, Bobby, get out of that seat," she exclaimed! Totally embarrassed, I rose and got five or six good blows. But it hurt my pride more than it hurt me physically 'cause I had on long underwear and thick bib overalls!

All in all, those school years were fun times, not only the learning but also softball and dodgeball, and the making of good friends. Speaking of fun, Mother and Dad bought us autograph books when I was ten years old, and at school kids wrote some of the funniest and craziest little verses in my book, which I still have. I was 'kinda smitten' on a pretty blond classmate named Bonnie Jean Clayton. But apparently she didn't have the same feeling for me! She wrote, "Love is sweet, but oh how bitter, to kiss an old tobacco spitter." So much for that young romance! I was humiliated and horrified. But another classmate, Nellie Sharp, for whom I had no special feelings whatsoever, wrote, "Kiss me quick and let me go, here comes pappy with the old shotgun." I was even more embarrassed and downright disgusted. She didn't even know how to make it rhyme! But my cousin, Jean Tribble, wrote a verse that made a lot of sense and that I have used in my messages as good advice, "If she ain't got nothin', and you ain't got nothin', don't be in a hurry to wed; for nothin' plus nothin' will always be nothin', and nothin' don't chew like bread!"

But my dear mother, in presenting the book to me, topped all that had been written. She had penned on one page these verses from the Bible, "Remember now thy Creator in the days of thy youth … Study to show thyself approved unto God … The Lord is my shepherd, I shall not want." On the other page is written,

"Apr. 16, 1937, My dear Bobby Boy: You are such a dear little blue-eyed boy. I want you to be always manly and honest. It is such a pleasure to see you and Billy grow up so thoughtful of each other. 'Politeness is to do and say the kindest things in the kindest way.'"

At home during all these young years, Mother and Dad were both loving and tolerant, I would say, when we boys would get a little out of hand in our behavior. But Dad kept a wide razor strap hanging in the kitchen corner, which rarely had to be used, thankfully. Mother's favorite was a very thin switch from a tiny tree limb. It never really hurt except in the summertime heat when, as little boys, we were wearing shorts. But I remember only two times that happened, and even then it stung slightly on our bare legs. It served its purpose, and I'm sure we deserved what we got!

In the first ten years of my life, the Depression hit my folks hard and money was scarce. It didn't affect our happiness as a family, and we boys "made do" with homemade toys for the most part. For example, we made our own "beanie-flippers" by sawing and shaping them out of a board and cutting strips from an old inner tube, or finding a forked tree limb and sawing it at the two forked limbs above and the bottom below the fork, then attaching the two cut rubber strips and the pouch to hold a rock. It made a nice flipper. What fun! And for a wheeled toy, which we called a "guider," we would saw a board about four feet long and two inches wide, find an old can and hammer it flat in the middle, leaving the top and bottom in an upright position (it had to be that kind of a can), nail the middle of the flattened can to one end of the board which served as the handle, and we had a nice "instrument" to guide a wheel in front of us as we would run along. For the wheel, we used a "rim" that easily came off a milk can. That's a long and difficult description, but it worked.

On Christmas Eve, the folks would hang stockings, and if we got an orange, a packet of marbles, a pocket knife, a small toy, a candy bar, or a banana, we were happy! How different it is today.

I have already written about the chores and the work assignments we had around the place. But there are two or three that I want to mention specifically. I'll never forget when Dad taught me how to bridle our pony and to harness the work horses; or when he took Bill and me down to the valley field with the team of horses, Pet and Tops, hooked up, and taught us how to plow with the single-bladed, two-handled implement. At one end of the field, he said:

> "See that post at the other end of the field? Now with the horses positioned to pull the plow, lift the handles up so the sharp and pointed blade will gently thrust into the earth as you say 'get up' and as you start to move, you'll see the plow blade automatically dig about eight inches into the ground, turning that rich, black earth over as you go along. But keep your eyes on that post so you can plow a straight furrow."

Wow! It worked, and what a feeling that gave me. We were about eleven years old. We eventually learned to use the riding disc, the homemade drag, and the A-harrow, made out of railroad ties bolted together, as well as the corn planter, the wide spiraling hay rake, and the mower.

We always milked ten cows inside the barn with their heads in stanchions. One jersey named "Old Tippy" was fidgety and sometimes kicked, so we had to put "kickers" around the bottom of her legs. We always had cats when I was growing up, and when they came into the barn, sometimes we would squirt milk into their mouths. Or better still, we might squirt at one another in a milk fight. More fun!

We were instructed to always do the chores first when we got home from school, then we could play. On one occasion, I guess we "forgot." Yeah! Well anyway, this day getting home, we got involved in a good, tight baseball game. It was our favorite sport, which we learned from our father, who had been a star pitcher in his day and who often played with us at the schoolyard after Sunday church and Mom's luscious Sunday cookin' and pie. We got so caught up in our ballgame that darkness started settling, and our chores were still waiting to be done. Suddenly, we saw the lights of a car on the road across the field and thought, "Uh-oh, that's probably Mom and Dad returning home from work in town, and we're in big trouble!" You never saw a bunch of boys get "with it" so fast in your life! One ran out and got the cows herded into the milk barn. Another one rushed into the house and fired up the cook stove, as a brother grabbed milk buckets to start the milking. One started mixing up the ingredients for the cornbread. Another exclaimed, "I'll peel the potatoes," while someone else went to feed the hogs. The last and smallest brother ran out to the henhouse to gather the eggs. Well, what do you know, the folks drove up the driveway, and we barely managed to escape any repercussions. But I think we learned a lesson!

Oh, how fortunate and blessed we seven brothers were to grow up on the farm, our HOMESTEAD USA! It really was fun. I can honestly say that I even made hard work on the farm fun. It made me feel good, and that I had an important part in accomplishing things that had to be done. And, aside from work, we had ample time for the sheer joy of recreation: swimming in the pond; ice skating on the sink hole lake in the corner of the woods; riding bareback on our pony, "Old Fly," at breakneck speed (she wasn't old and how she could "fly"); playing ball and croquet; playing checkers and dominoes; playing Tarzan up in the big oaks and swinging on the grapevines; fishing and happily picnicking at Bennett's Spring; tripping to 100-foot-high White Bluff and the "Tunnel," a block long and huge enough for two side by side trains to pass through; and finally, when our family's means allowed and we got our Zenith radio, listening to *The Lone Ranger* right after school, with his "hi-yo-Silver" and the electrifying theme music as the program started. And on Sunday evenings just before church, sponsored by "J-E-L-L-O," was the *Jack Benny Show* with Rochester. On Tuesday night, it was *Fibber McGee and Molly*, while on Thursday night we couldn't miss and felt related to *One Man's Family*. Another favorite was *Lum and Abner* and their "Jot 'em Down" store!

As to music in our family, our father played the harmonica, and Mother, the piano. In our country church, she played the old pump organ and Dad led the singing. One of my first memories is when I was four years old standing on a piano bench with Bill, Mother beside us and accompanying us as we sang "Jesus Wants Me for a Sunbeam" in church. I recall when I was nine, I sang in a mixed quartet with my brother Dallas Jr. (we called him Junior in those days), five years older than I, at his graduation from the eighth grade. Then when I was thirteen, I guess I was a "big hit" at my Blackfoot country school eighth grade graduation exercises, even though I wasn't there! The teacher brought a radio to school that day so all the students could listen to me singing duets with my brother J.P., accompanied by the Country Ozark Band, on the radio in Springfield, sixty miles away. I remember the announcer, Bill Bailey, kept referring to me as "little 13-year-old Bobby Vernon." My voice hadn't changed yet and I sang high. The songs we sang were "Home on the Range," "Beautiful Texas," and "My Little Girl." J.P. had a great voice and, as a teenager, he managed somehow to earn enough money to purchase a guitar. From playing the notes to me as I sat at the piano, he taught me how to play "by ear" the chords on the piano, which I do to this day. As I remember, Dallas Jr.

collected enough coupons to send off in the mail to get a ukulele which he would play and teach us smaller boys some silly songs. He and J.P. got some black liquid Shinola Shoe Polish, and we dabbed on white sheets these words, "VOTE FOR OUR DAD, DALLAS VERNON!" Then we attached the two signs on either side of the car, and all of us piled into our '28 Model A Ford and rode around the whole countryside singing our hearts out. That was in 1936, and we got our father elected! Later, in two more campaigns, Bill, B.J., and I (Don was too young) harmonized in a trio for those memorable events. We belted out, "Put Your Arms Around Me, Honey," "Water That's Hot," "Home on the Range," "Down in the Valley," and "The More We Get Together." I'll never forget the late afternoon when Mother drove up the driveway at the Homestead when I was a sophomore in high school. Dad had been elected as County Assessor by then, and money was available for Mom to bring out on trial four shiny musical instruments: a trombone, a saxophone, a clarinet, and a trumpet. Wow! Immediately, I eyed and chose the saxophone; Bill, the trombone; B.J., the clarinet; and little Donnie, only 9 years old, the trumpet. I practiced and worked my way up to first chair in the band by the time I was a senior. How I enjoyed playing the marches, the pop songs, and the Jitterbug music like "Dark Town Strutters Ball." And as a soloist, I won a vocal musical meet contest by singing "Jeanie With the Light Brown Hair." I loved being in the glee club, and since World War II was raging, my two favorite songs were "Give Me Some Men Who are Stouthearted Men," and "This is Worth Fighting For." I had one brother, Dallas Jr., in the Air Force. After graduating from high school and getting in one semester at Drury College, Bill and I, then in the Navy, were honored by singing in a thousand-voice choir and orchestra on all three radio networks as a birthday tribute to our Commander-in-Chief, President Franklin D. Roosevelt. I went on to serve on a submarine, sometimes singing with the crew, and

Bill on an aircraft carrier. How grateful to God we were that the war ended and we didn't have to invade Japan. We dedicated our lives to the Lord's service, and how fulfilling it was in 1948 for five of us brothers, J.P., Dallas Jr., Bill, B.J., and I, to sing together each week on our hometown radio station. Don was too young, and Ward who had cerebral palsy would hum along with us. How he always inspired us!

And speaking of inspiration and music, I will forever be grateful that my son, Gregg, and I got to be backstage with Ronald Reagan at the Shrine Auditorium in Springfield for a political rally. There I sang two songs I had written and recorded on Capitol Records: "Tell America" followed by "Freedom Prayer." How great to meet and sing for him!

CHAPTER 5

High School And The Approaching War

IN HIGH SCHOOL, I was somewhat shy and withdrawn, especially the first two years. I was afflicted with a terrible plague of pimples that lasted for years, and regardless of all the remedies and medications I tried, nothing seemed to work. It embarrassed me greatly. But my music classes and playing some basketball and football helped bring me out of my shell. And being a twin seemed to give me some special recognition in causing my classmates to overlook my facial problem. I guess being blue-eyed and blond (all my brothers had brown eyes and dark hair) helped! But I'll never forget how nervous I was when Bill and I attended our first dance as farm boys and freshmen. It was held in town at the spacious residence of Major and Mrs. Armstrong, hosted by their two lovely daughters, Georgina and Patsy. Major Armstrong was stationed at newly built Ft. Leonard Wood, some thirty miles away, but lived in Lebanon as one of its most prominent citizens. You talk about two "hillbilly" boys feeling out of place, and besides, in our day, good Christian boys weren't supposed to go to dances! But our mother, though quite devout, saw through that and wanted her boys to learn social graces as well as having Christian character. And our dad, since we only had an "out-house" on the farm, prepared and prompted us to "flush the toilet" if we had to use the bathroom. We were only 13 and had to be driven in, and when we arrived we were graciously welcomed and blended in with the other some fifty kids.

I stood by myself on one side of the huge, well-decorated living room for the first twenty minutes or so. Then Georgina glided over, took my hand and said, "You look so forlorn and unhappy. C'mon, let's dance." I quickly replied with emphasis, "I don't know how to dance!" "Oh, that's no problem. I'll teach you," she answered as she discreetly placed my right hand behind her waist and gently held and led me with the other hand. At first, I was nervous as a kitten. But you know what? I very quickly caught on because I'd always been musically inclined and piano playing had taught me rhythm. So that broke the ice, and not only did I enjoy the evening, it really helped my self-confidence and self-esteem. I had no special feeling for Georgina except gratitude for her thoughtfulness, plus the fact that she was two years older than I. In fact, I never dated in high school except one more time when I was a freshman. And that was a total disaster. One of my best friends, John Dudley Perrey, invited Bill and me to a Western style party and barn dance. His father was to open a Firestone store in Lebanon, but before they had built any counters or had an opening, it was totally vacant. So they had hay bales, straw, and Western décor to carry out the theme for the occasion. And you had to bring a date. Oh my! Who to ask? I sheepishly asked Betty Ewing, whose folks lived at an oil company pumping station three miles from our farm home. Since Bill and I were not old enough to drive, my older brother Dallas Jr. and his girlfriend, Mabel, (later his wife) drove us to pick up our dates and then on into town to the party. It is such a blur now that all I remember is hanging out with the guys and not dancing with Betty or anyone else. Apparently it was a dull evening for her, and I was a dud, which I guess I was. On the way to drop her off at her house after the party, in the back seat, I nervously slipped my left arm around her shoulders. And just as quickly, she reached my arm behind her shoulders and gently slid it back over into my lap and spoke not a word. Oh, how embarrassed and humiliated I felt! I couldn't wait till we got to her home. Without either of us uttering anything at all, I walked her to the door and returned to the car and on home in stunned silence. So much for dating anymore!

But things do change, don't they. Two years later, the whole summer between my junior and senior years in high school, I lived with my oldest brother, J.P., eight years older than I, and his wife, Oleta, at the Homestead farm. By this time, my folks had bought a large doctor's home in Lebanon (for $2,000.00) and had moved there. Despite our age difference, J.P. had great influence on my young life. We had a wonderful time during that period, doing the farm work, putting up twenty large stacks of hay, playing and singing music, and studying the Bible. Oleta's father was a minister of the non-instrumental Church of Christ, and J.P. had been baptized, so each Sunday I especially enjoyed the teaching and a cappella four-part harmonious singing of that congregation. Well, guess what? Oleta had a beautiful sister, Lois, and the love bug bit me bad.

I was still quite shy, but one evening as we slowly got acquainted, J.P. and Oleta were taking us home and they put Lois and me in the back seat. I worked up nerve enough to slip my arm around her and, surprise of surprises, she didn't mind at all! So all the way home, I softly sang *Hit Parade* songs in her ear, and I was in seventh Heaven! A week or two later, on our first real date after which we returned to her home, I did it. Under the high, bright yard light just outside her door, I swooped her up in my arms, gave my very first kiss to a very sweet girl, and stars exploded all around me! From then on, it was a secret love, I guess, because we attended different high schools. But my feelings and respect for her never changed. After my discharge from the Navy and a year at Drury College, I did have one last wonderful time with her after church when we were driven around in the back seat of a convertible owned by Harold King and his wife, Helen, through the countryside of the "Shepherd of the Hills" winding roads. We kissed a sad goodbye, for I had dedicated my life to serving the Lord and would shortly enter training at Ozark Christian College. Besides, we were in totally different churches, she in the very strict non-instrumental Church of Christ, and I in the Christian Church believing there is no prohibition of musical instruments taught in the Bible. Plus, I was going to convert the whole wide world and not get married! That is, not until two years later when I met the very gorgeous young woman who became my wife, Patricia Ann Anderson!

In my last two years of high school, music was my great love. We now lived in town, so I was able to give more time to practicing both vocal and instrumental music, as well as concentrating on my studies. I did take a job washing milk bottles at 30 cents an hour in the Bahr Dairy Bar, and then, during my senior year, was promoted to milkman, getting up at 4:00 a.m. to deliver milk. I was our senior class president, and Bill served as student body president. I did well enough in all my classes (algebra was difficult) to make the National Honor Society. Because of the war, I took a course in aeronautics, which I really liked. An Air Force officer came to our school and administered a test which I passed, qualifying me after graduation to be inducted into the Navy's Flight Officers Unit. I received a very nice certificate from the Civil Aeronautics Board in Washington, D.C. I turned that down and later went into the Submarine Service. At our graduation, Bill and I sang a duet entitled, "By the Bend of the River," and we had the great honor of listening to our mother deliver a wonderful speech to the graduates on the subject, "The Importance of the Home." How proud we were when she got a rousing, standing ovation. After we graduated, J.P. got us both a job at Detroit Tool and Engineering Co. in Lebanon where he worked, and where, after the War, Dallas Jr. was employed, working his way up to becoming president. Bill and I earned enough, with a scholarship and job at the college, to enter Drury that fall.

Prior to leaving for college, there were two incidents at the tool and engineering company that are noteworthy. I started out on the lathe and was soon promoted to running a machine called a "Shaper." With a small tool sharp at one end and clamped into a conveyer, I would lower it ever so slightly to cut into a secured piece of steel to shape it as the back and forth motion of the tool cut it as desired. One day, the owner came by looking over my moving machine. After a couple of minutes, he said rather gruffly, "Bobby, you're not cutting deep enough." He wheeled the tool up out of its clamp, re-set it deeper, started the machine, and I almost laughed under my breath as that big metal piece came crashing down to the floor. "You had it right in the first place," he muttered and walked off in a huff! The second occasion was quite scary. I was tending to my work at the shaper when, without any warning, the back of the brick building started crashing down with a fierce, whistling gale and debris was whipping fast towards me and the other workers. "It's a tornado!" someone yelled. Some headed toward a side door as I quickly turned my machine off and ran as fast as I could towards the larger front door, with others scampering to do the same. As I fled the building into the howling and roaring wind and rain, parts of the tin roof were flying in every direction, which I managed to dodge. I dived into the ditch at the side of the highway and held on for dear life to a little sapling. I lay there for several crucial moments, getting drenched and fervently praying, until the black tornado lifted. I think God used that close encounter with nature to deepen my faith. Maybe He had special plans for my life!

CHAPTER 6

World War II And Submarine Service

IT WAS AN unusually hot day on December the 7th, 1941. Our mother, as usual, fixed us a nice, hot breakfast of oatmeal, fried eggs, bacon, and homemade hot biscuits and gravy. All this after we had done the milking and other morning chores. We dressed in our Sunday best, went to Sunday school and church, came home to hot rolls and a scrumptious dinner (for us country people it was breakfast, dinner, and supper), and then went out in the yard to play croquet. About mid-afternoon, Dad rushed out to the front porch, and with a deep concern in his voice said, "Boys, I've got bad news. The Japanese have attacked Pearl Harbor in Hawaii, and they've sunk a lot of our ships." We quit our game and talked among ourselves about what it meant. No doubt, war, we agreed. But I thought to myself, "I won't have to be in the war. I'm too young." How wrong I was!

After high school and a summer of work, Bill and I got in one semester at Drury College before we had to go. I really enjoyed my studies and college activities, including singing in the choir, playing six-man football, joining Lambda-Chi-Alpha, and meeting a nice girl, Norma Williams, with whom I had a couple of dates. But Uncle Sam was calling, and Bill and I were about to be drafted. To beat that, we twins, and a couple of other classmates who were close friends, Don Threlkeld and Robert Lillard, went downtown to the Navy Recruiting Center and enlisted in that branch of the Service. We were able to spend the next few days finishing the semester and then went home for the Christmas holidays. Dallas Jr., in the Air Force, was home on furlough. Our dear, sad mom would soon have three sons in the War. It was a great but bittersweet time for us all before we had to leave.

We took our first train ride to St. Louis and checked in at the Navy Induction Center. They put us up in a nearby hotel, which was just a block away from a church where they were holding a service. I thought it would be an appropriate time to get some special inspiration and strength from "on High," so we went and it was a deeply spiritual experience. The next morning we were sworn in and inducted, affirming our allegiance to and support of the Constitution of the United States of America. Then, along with hundreds of other recruits standing in long lines for hours, we got our physical examinations, our shots, and our orders. With all of that done, we boarded a train for Milwaukee, then on to the Great Lakes Naval Training Center and into our assigned barracks. I'll never forget how shocked I was upon arriving there how "blue" and raw the air turned with all the cussing in the conversations taking place. I certainly wasn't used to that. The old adage, "He swears like a sailor," was true and happening right in my face. But Bill and I, and a few others, weren't typical sailors and didn't take up that bad habit.

Ooh! The cold blasts of below zero weather hit our faces as we marched in platoons out in the icy wind! How nice, though, to attend all the classes and watch all the training films in the warm and comfortable rooms. We learned about ships, planes, guns, and submarines, and how to tie different kinds of knots in ropes. It was fun doing calisthenics, nice going to chapel and singing in the choir, as well as having a great feeling playing my sax in the band. And a couple of times near the end of our training at Great Lakes, we got to go on weekend leave to the welcoming city of Milwaukee.

On that first visit, we found a boarding house room downtown not far from the train station. We checked to see what was going on and discovered that Spike Jones and his orchestra would be putting on a show. And what a show it was! The only seats left were a couple perched high in the back row of the tiered theater seating. The music played was not my "cup of tea," musically speaking, what with improvised tooting horns, tuba, crazy instruments, and acrobatic antics. But that's what he was famous for.

The next trip turned out to be more than wonderful. We stayed at the same boarding house and found out that in honor of all the sailors in town, popular World War II music was going to be played at a local music and dance hall. We thought, "Great! Maybe we'll meet some girls!" Sure enough, after standing on the sidelines for a while, I spotted a pretty young woman seated with others on the opposite side of the hall. I took a deep breath, nervously walked over, and introduced myself to her. She smiled and said, "Nice to meet you. I'm Ila Faye Jackson." I replied, "I'm not a very good dancer, but would you like to dance? She answered, "I'm not too good either, but sure." I took her hand, guided her out on the floor, and thought to myself, "Wow! How lucky can a guy get!" We really hit it off and did more talking than dancing. After a couple of hours, it was time to catch our train. She gave me her address, walked me arm in arm to the boarding area, we paused and embraced, and had a long, sad goodbye kiss.

I boarded the train and never saw her again, because the very next week we ended our training at Great Lakes and were on our way to our next assignment. I kicked myself several times for not writing to this wonderful and thoughtful person. But it was wartime. Some of my buddies got assignments to ships headed directly to the war zone in the Pacific. It was an uncertain time. While at Great Lakes, I'll never forget when a fellow mate and friend, Smitty, got the terrible news that his brother had been killed in action. Yes, we were human and had some fun and memorable times. But it was a very sober and serious wartime effort on behalf of Freedom, Faith, and Future for America and our Way of Life.

Bill and I were fortunate in that we were selected, along with a few others, to head toward Gulfport, Mississippi, for twenty weeks of Radioman training. But oh! Going from the bitter cold of Great Lakes to the hot and humid weather of Gulfport, right on the Gulf of Mexico, was not so easy to take. I recall some of the men, dressed in lily white uniforms and standing erect in perfect order of all the platoons, would keel over during inspections out in the extreme heat of the Mississippi sun. And, with our earphones on and sitting at our typewriters, learning and typing Morse code in the hot Quonset huts with no air conditioning was almost unbearable. That, together with instruction classes and building radio sets, was what we did for twenty long weeks. But it was character building, as well as important preparation for tasks that would follow in our line of duty.

I am proud but humbled by a Certificate I still possess, dated 17 July, 1945, that states the following:

"This certifies that Bobby J. Vernon has made a perfect copy of Fox Code Messages selected at random during a 4 hour Fox Watch and consisting of a total of 600 characters. The copy was made directly from Navy Radio Station NPM under actual circuit conditions at a speed of 18 code groups per minute." It is signed by Examining Officer John D. Layton, Chief Radio Elect., USN (Ret.), and Officer-in-Charge J.L. Rhodemyre, Lt. Comdr., USNR.

Not too long into our training at Gulfport, an officer from the Submarine Service came on base seeking volunteers for that Navy Force. Bill said, "C'mon Bob. Let's sign up!" I replied, "No way, Bill. I'd like to be on top of the water and not under it." But since we were twins so close, and I didn't want us to be separated, I reluctantly agreed, and we both signed up. Well, guess what? My hero twin brother, two inches taller, ten pounds heavier, and a healthy tall, dark, and handsome specimen of the human race, came down with a serious health problem a few days later and was soon undergoing emergency surgery. I know what you're thinking. You're right. I was the one after graduation from Radio Training to go on, ALONE, to New London, Connecticut, to become a Submariner! Thank God, Bill recovered, but for him, Company D became Company F, and he was assigned to an aircraft carrier, the USS *Lexington*.

While Bill was on that operating table being prepared for surgery, I was fearful that he might not even survive, and I prayed fervently that all would go well. I remember saying to the Lord, "If you see to it that Bill's life is spared and he gets well, I'll try real hard to live for you and even try to serve you in a full-time way, if possible." That was very difficult for me, what with all the "Thou shalt nots" I had heard in the "countrified" preaching as a lad. And besides, there had never been a preacher on either side of our family except a great-grandfather on the Tribble side. But I'm sure God used that experience and the memory of it as I advanced in my faith, although music was still my first love as a career. I yearned to get back to my saxophone and just knew that I was destined to become a great singer.

But I was still under Uncle Sam's calling and charge, on the train again, excited and anticipating my role as a submariner in the "Silent Service." It was a select group, and one had to meet qualifications and endure all kinds of psychological, physical, mental, and claustrophobic tests, as well as written tests on material we learned in classes: tests in the water; tests in a diving bell; and tests on board the submarine as to whether we had properly learned the dozen operational positions we might have to manage in an emergency. It was a challenge, but I passed them all successfully and graduated with excellent scores and high honors.

When recently looking at my military record, I noted that it was on June 25, 1945, that I passed with flying colors my first physical exam, and it states "qualified for submarine duty." Then, of course, in due time came all the other strict requirements and tests. It was thought in June that an invasion of Japan was going to be necessary, and we would be training and preparing as a part of that invasion force. Bitter and ferocious kamikaze attacks were taking place, and Japan's military commanders, as well as their fighting men, had a "do or die" attitude. Our military leaders estimated that an invasion of Japan would cost two million lives. So it was still a very critical and dangerous time. The submarine to which I was eventually assigned, the USS *Piper*, had just made a secret and very perilous incursion into the Sea of Japan, but had returned safely.

Of course, the dropping of the atomic bombs on Hiroshima and Nagasaki changed everything. It proved to be a catastrophe and humiliating defeat for Japan as they reluctantly but necessarily surrendered. When I heard on the radio that a bomb, so powerful and destructive, had been dropped on and obliterated the city of Hiroshima, I was stunned and could hardly believe it! I had to get to myself and weep for the thousands of innocent lives that were snuffed out in an instant. I was so deeply moved that I breathed a prayer of thanksgiving that the war would end, and a prayer of dedicating my life to the Lord and to His service.

Estimates are that the bomb dropped on Hiroshima left almost 130,000 people dead or wounded and leveled ninety percent of the city. The Nagasaki bomb left about 75,000 casualties. But it probably saved hundreds of thousands of American and Japanese lives. It could have saved mine and Bill's, as well as our brother Dallas Jr.'s: me on a submarine, Bill on an aircraft carrier, and Dallas on a fighter plane or bomber.

An intriguing and potentially perilous incident happened shortly before the end of the war that neither we in the military nor the public knew about. The documents describing and affirming it were not declassified for Americans to learn about until long after the war. In an article written by Richard Benke of the Associated Press, appearing in the *Los Angeles Times* on Sunday, June 1, 1997, I quote:

"When a captured U-boat arrived at Portsmouth, N.H., toward the end of World War II, the American public was never told the significance of what was on board. The German submarine was carrying 1,200 pounds of uranium oxide, ingredients for an atomic bomb, bound for Japan. Two Japanese officers were allowed to commit suicide. Two months later, in the New Mexican desert, the United States detonated the first atomic bomb, a prelude to the obliteration of two Japanese cities. Unknown to many of the people who built those bombs, not to mention the public, Japan was scrambling to build its own nuclear weapon. Some of the evidence was the uranium aboard the U-boat that surrendered in the North Atlantic on May 19, 1945, shortly after Adolph Hitler committed suicide on April 30th. Documents, now declassified, including the sub's manifest, show there were 560 kilograms of uranium oxide in 10 cases destined for the Japanese army and two Japanese officers were aboard, accompanying the cargo ... The Japanese officers insisted on being given the right to commit suicide."

This incident bears out the fact that timing is so important in everything! We sing "God Bless America." Perhaps it was the providence and blessing of Almighty God to lead America to beat both Germany and Japan in developing the atomic bomb. Otherwise, what a different world we would be living in!

So my submarine activity and service consisted of maneuvering and moving on assigned missions and patrols on the USS *Piper*, but thankfully, not having to be part of a deadly invasion force. On one such time at sea, an ill wind suddenly became a hurricane-like storm. Although I was a radioman, as I explained before, we had to be "at ready" to man every position or post on the sub. I was at the helm on this occasion, and we were cruising along on the surface when huge and high waves started tossing us around like a toy. I noticed the gauge on the panel in front of me, and oh my!! The marker was way over in the red, signifying that we were dangerously close to turning sideways. I spun that wheel in lightning speed, pressed the warning signal, the sub leveled, and down we went to the sweet, noiseless sound of the silent sea below the surface. No waves, no storm, just peace. No wonder it is called the "Silent Service!"

Things were very relaxed at the news of Japan's surrender, and there were celebrations everywhere. You can't imagine the load that was taken off our shoulders knowing that we didn't have to invade Japan, and that at long last the fighting had stopped. Not too long afterwards, I got a long weekend pass and traveled to Springfield, Massachusetts, to see my brother Dallas. He was on an Air Force Base there and would soon be discharged. What a great reunion and time we had. He, a war-time buddy Clem, and I hitchhiked to New York City. Not too long on the highway after we started walking, someone in a convertible stopped and picked us up. Hitchhiking was very common and safe back in those good old days, but not anymore. How times have changed. Anyway, what a beautiful drive it was on that nice, sunny day with not a care in the world and our hair blowing in the breeze. And the brightly-colored autumn leaves of the forests along the way added to the serenity of our feelings. I can't recall the name of that nice person who befriended us, but he dropped us off right at Times Square. The hotels all seemed to be full, but at one, I believe it was the famous Knickerbocker, we paused and then went in to the front desk. "I'm sorry," said the check-in clerk, "but all the regular rooms are taken." Oh my. What to do? "Wait," the clerk exclaimed! "We do have the very spacious penthouse honeymoon suite vacant, and since the three of you are in the military, we'll let you have it at the regular rate." We thanked her profusely, checked in, went up, and WOW!! We could hardly believe our eyes at the lavishness and beauty of the décor and furnishings. There were two huge rooms, two bathrooms, a kitchenette, lush sofas, plush chairs, and more than enough sleeping accommodations. And we three were "the honeymooners!" What a great and relaxing time we had, seeing all the sights of Times Square, "shooting the breeze," visiting 'til the wee hours, and then getting a very comfortable night's sleep. The next morning, we had a late waffle and eggs benedict brunch, after which we got tickets to see a Broadway matinee. It was a stage production by the famous English Playwright, Noel Coward, but it was too elitist, too British, and too dull for me to really enjoy.

Back at New London for Submarine duty, as fall turned into a bitter, cold winter, it was a freezing experience, especially handling cables and ropes at dockside. I developed bad colds which eventually turned into pneumonia. In late February of 1946, I spent several days in the dispensary on base being treated for deep lung congestion. In looking now at my medical records while in the Navy, I see that on 3 March 1946, I was so sick again that I checked back in to that same Navy hospital at the Submarine Base. I quote from the record: "Diagnosis, Catarrhal Fever, Acute, Not misconduct but in the line of duty. Chilliness and fever, general aching and malaise. Was in the dispensary this past month for Catarrhal Fever, being discharged 4 days ago. Temp 103.4." They admitted me as a bed patient, but the next day I was feeling worse, so some changes were immediately made. I again quote from the record: "X-ray shows patchy consolidation in right lower lobe. Diagnosis changed to Pneumonia. Reason, error." The recovery was slow, and I didn't return to duty until March 18th. But by this time, my submarine was on its way to the Panama Canal, with my seabag full of uniforms and all my belongings. Soon I got transferred to the submarine base at Portsmouth, New Hampshire, on board the huge USS *Proteus*, a Submarine Tender being reconditioned in dry dock. I never did get my seabag back! Being on the *Proteus* for the last three months of my military service turned out to be providential and advantageous. It was there that I was introduced by a shipmate to the Navigators Club on board. They gave me some fifty small cards printed with a Scripture verse on one side and the Bible book, chapter, and verse location on the other. I memorized all the verses, which got me started memorizing much of the New Testament as I went on to Ozark Christian College. It was from the learning I did on the ship that, while in the Navy, I delivered my first public message on the subject "temptation." I started by quoting First Corinthians 10:13, one of the verses on my little card: "There hath no temptation taken you but such as is common to man: but God is faithful, who will not suffer you to be tempted above that ye are able; but will with the temptation also make a way to escape, that ye may be able to bear it" (I Cor. 10:13, KJV). The New American Standard

Bible puts it this way: "No temptation has overtaken you but such as is common to man; and God is faithful, who will not *allow* you to be tempted beyond what you are able, but with the temptation will provide the way of escape also, so that you will be able to endure it" (I Cor. 10:13, NASB, italics added). I made it plain then, as I do now, that it is the influence and guidance of the Lord and of my dear parents that led me to respect the Bible, and to try to follow its teachings in living right and going to Chapel when possible.

And besides the Worship and Communion of the Chapel services I got to appreciate on base, I must mention two families I met at churches in the towns of New London and Portsmouth: The Morrisons of New London and the Procters of Portsmouth. They took me in as one of their own, and, on several weekends, I was invited to stay in their respective homes. With Mrs. Morrison accompanying me on the piano, I made my first phonograph recording. It was near Christmas, and the songs were "White Christmas" and "I'll Be Home for Christmas." A few days after the holidays, I got to go home on a fifteen-day leave, and I took the little record with me as a gift to my mother. The Procters' church minister had a son away in the Navy, and they said I looked just like a twin to him, so Mrs. Procter really "mothered" me. Mr. Procter was a dentist and expert photographer, so he took a lot of pictures of me in my uniform, which I still have. The Procters and their family were members of the "Christian Advent" church.

On July 28, 1946, I boarded the train at Portsmouth bound for St. Louis, where on the 29th I went through the process of being honorably discharged from my military service. I was proud to have served and came out a better young man at the still tender age of 19. But I said "goodbye" to my Navy days and hitchhiked from St. Louis on the famous Route 66 to my "home sweet home" in Lebanon, Missouri. It looked so good, and what a reunion our family had!!

In a little over two weeks after my discharge, I was deeply humbled and honored to receive a letter of gratitude for service from the Secretary of the Navy.

CHAPTER 7

Dedicating Life To Ministry

IT WAS SO easy and pleasant to make the transition back to civilian life, and Mother enjoyed spoiling us with her good home cooking and baking of homemade light bread, hot cinnamon rolls, cakes, and pies! But re-entrance and enrollment in college, interrupted by the war, would soon be upon us. My first cousin, Roger Tribble, together with his father, made trips to a few Bible colleges to see which one he would choose to attend. He had made the decision to study for the ministry. He finally chose a new, very small one, Ozark Bible College, which had just relocated to Joplin, Missouri. I thought seriously about enrolling there with him that fall. But again, as twins and so close to each other, Bill wanted to go back to Drury College and study to become a basketball coach and be on the basketball team. So I listened to my heart instead of my soul and returned to Drury in the fall of 1946. (By the way, Bob Barker, who became famous, was a classmate there!) I played a little basketball, studied hard, and tried to enjoy myself immersed in the campus social whirl, but I was miserable! I tried to but just couldn't forget my pledge to God. Then toward the end of the spring semester, I got mononucleosis and that did it! Bernie Bleich, a Jewish classmate, said to me after I poured out my heart to him, "Bob, if you're so unhappy, why don't you make plans to go to that Bible college you told me about?" That summer, my cousin Roger came to our home in Lebanon and tried to persuade me to lead the singing in a revival meeting he was to preach in August. I said, "Roger, you know I love music, but I'm certainly not qualified to do that." But he wouldn't take no for an answer. Finally, I agreed when he said he would teach me a song leader's hand motions for 4/4, 3/4, and 6/8 time in which most hymns are written. We stood at an elongated mirror in one of the rooms at our house, and I watched myself catch on right away doing all the motions. Roger then took me to a photography shop where I had my picture taken in my one and only suit and tie. When that was ready, Roger said, "Now we'll go get a cut made." I said, "What's a cut?" He answered, "That's a metal image of your picture mounted on a small two-inch by four-inch piece of wood that the printer uses to print some handbills to publicize our meeting." In a few days, we picked up the 100 8½ x 11 handbills. I grabbed one and there it was, along with the date, time, and place of the meeting, a picture of Roger as the evangelist, and my picture under which he had ordered to be printed, "BOB VERNON, OUTSTANDING SONG EVANGELIST." I thought to myself, "What they don't know won't hurt 'em!" But when the time came to start the revival, I must say it was a wonderful experience. Roger preached great sermons, we made several converts, and I really got into the swing of things leading the music, singing a special song each night, and meeting the good people at that little country church in Cato, Kansas. Roger and I prayed together, called on homes in the community together, and laughed together. On one occasion, we put a P.A. system between us on the front seat of the car. As we drove around the country roads announcing on the loud speaker about the revival we were holding, it was so loud that we drew quite an audience as the cows came running to the fences by the road!

Roger had also taken the student minister position at the small congregation in Phillipsburg, Missouri, which he had grown up in and which was our mother's old home church. The congregation was starting to grow in attendance and, prior to our meeting at Cato, Dr. F.W. Strong, founder of Ozark Bible College, was conducting a two-week revival there. We boys attended every service, and my brother B.J., who had been a basketball star and had just graduated from high school at Lebanon, confessed Christ as his Savior and was baptized during that meeting. (I had been baptized during my senior year of high school.) It was amazing how God used this sequence of events to lead the four of us youngest brothers in the Vernon family into the service of God. And to show this even more, a Christian service camp of two weeks was to be held the last of August at Strong's Ranch near Joplin. Dr. Strong had come to our home in Lebanon to invite us to the camp and encourage us to consider full-time service to Christ. At that time, Bill was planning to return to Drury to play basketball and study coaching as a career, and B.J. had the University of Missouri and other colleges calling on him with a basketball scholarship. But I had definitely decided to go to Ozark, and Don, only 13 at the time, knew that when he got to be an adult, he wanted to raise cattle and preach. It took some "tall talking" and persuasion, almost at the last minute, to get Bill and B.J. to go to that camp with Don and me.

Our cousin, Roger Tribble, became like a brother to the four of us, and it was under his church's sponsorship that we went with their other kids to the camp. While we were there, it was like a bit of "Heaven on earth!" How we enjoyed the Bible classes, the competition and fun of the different recreational teams, the swimming, the volleyball and softball games, the inspiring vesper services, the "quiet times" with just our Bible, the evening preaching and invitational messages, and finally just the deep friendship and fellowship we found with other campers. At the closing service, a huge friendship circle was formed and we clasped hands and hearts and prayed silently. Then, very quietly, we were asked that if we wanted to publicly make our decision to enter full-time Christian service to step forward and form an inner circle of dedication. Immediately, I stepped forward and, out of the corner of my eye, I was overjoyed to see that my other three brothers had done the same. To God be the glory!

Bill, B.J., and I enrolled in Ozark Bible College a few days later. At that time, the college owned only three buildings. The main building was a three-story mansion with the president's office, a large classroom that also served as the chapel, a class/dining room, and a kitchen on the ground floor. In the basement, there were two more classrooms, and the top two floors housed the girls. As I recall, we had only about two dozen full-time students, plus a few part-time students from the city, so we didn't need many classrooms. Across the street was a two-story residence building which housed one of the faculty members and his wife on the lower floor, and the second floor rooms were used as the boys' dormitory. The third building was a two-story brick residence which housed the president and his family on the first floor, and on the second floor they put Roger, Bill, B.J., me, and a couple other students. So the college wasn't at all that impressive when it came to buildings, a campus, a large student body, or facilities. But it had Seth Wilson, a little man with a big heart and a big mind chock full of exceptional knowledge about the life of Christ, the Greek language, Biblical backgrounds, logic, the New Testament Church, Christian ethics, and an awareness of and familiarity with about everything under the sun. Yet he was so humble and so passionate in his desire to impart that knowledge to his students in an understandable way. Yes, we had other good, qualified professors, but Dean Seth Wilson was the heart and soul of Ozark during my college years. He encouraged, but didn't require, the memorization of the assigned text in his classes. But as I explained before, I had begun memorizing Scripture while I was in the Navy, so I dug in and continued the habit. Bill, B.J., Roger, and I would get up early and walk back and forth in the hall of our dorm, Bible in hand, memorizing.

A few weeks into our schooling, Brother Maurice Strater, who had been one of the speakers at camp and who was the father of one of our professors, Floyd Strater, invited Bill and me to preach our first sermon. It would be at the evening service of the First Christian Church in Carthage, where he was the minister. I prepared my message, studied and memorized the Scriptures I would use, and was quite comfortable and confident preaching for about twenty minutes on the subject of "The Eternal Word." It seemed to go over well. After a song, it was Bill's turn. I don't remember his subject, but he was a little nervous and spoke just eight to ten minutes. Unfortunately, Bill's old health problem during his time in the Navy recurred. He had to drop out of college that first semester and go to the Veterans Hospital in Fayetteville, Arkansas, to undergo a repeat surgery. Thank God he recovered and was able to return to his studies the next semester.

I was soon hired to conduct weekend student ministries two Sundays each month at Conway, Missouri, and two at Louisburg, Missouri. The first time I ever baptized anyone, I baptized twenty-six converts. I loved it! We didn't have classes on Mondays. The towns were about 120 miles from Joplin, so I would leave on a bus Friday evening or Saturday and return to college on Monday. It was a workable schedule, and I continued it for two years. Besides, Bill, B.J., and I were in a college quartet, and, for the school's public relations, we sang sometimes on the radio or on tours. Eventually, Bill, B.J., Willis Harrison, and I, as the college quartet, sang for lots of functions and programs.

Another activity that really added to our enjoyment and feeling of fulfillment, besides our studies and weekend ministries, was the fact that Roger, Bill, B.J., and I were four of the first five on the college basketball team. We were in a local league plus a challenging and outstanding Christian college league of teams scattered all over the nation. If I do say so, and I proudly do, we had a great team. But so did Lincoln, Cincinnati, Atlanta, Milligan, Johnson, Manhattan, and Kentucky Christian Colleges. Some thirty such colleges sprang up in the last century, but, as I recall, the ones I mentioned are the ones we played. On one such basketball tour, we traveled in two cars and played five successive nights, leaving early on a Monday and driving back on Saturday so we could get to our preaching points on Sunday. Many times our quartet got to sing the following morning at chapel before heading to our next game that night. We got widely acquainted with a lot of the future leaders of the Brotherhood, and this proved very advantageous later when we started our television and evangelistic mission. I think two of the greatest highs in all our basketball years were when we beat Milligan's hot, top-notch team on their own home court, and when we played against Mickey Mantle in a winter league game! And, oh yes, there was another special thrill, when I was the high point scorer in one of our local league games!

SECTION III

Love, Marriage, And Revivals

CHAPTER 8

Falling Madly In Love

In January of 1949, our college quartet, accompanied by the public relations director, James Redmon, traveled on a week's promotional tour. The school's enrollment was increasing, and on such trips we were attracting more and more students. We would sing several spirituals, hymns, and Gospel hits. Then the director, a good speaker and great fun guy, would give a speech about the college. On the very last day, we traveled from Shreveport, Louisiana, where we had presented a program the night before, to the small town of DeWitt, Arkansas. It rained cats and dogs all the way and was storming ferociously when we arrived at the church. The fields and ditches alongside the narrow highway were flooded as we passed, and we thought hardly anyone would be present at the service. But to our surprise, the place was packed. On the very first song that our quartet opened with, I spotted a knock-your-eyes-out gorgeous young brunette sitting on the third row, slightly to my right. My heart almost stopped! I could hardly believe my eyes that someone could be that beautiful. She took my breath away as I collected my wits to finish the song. I was barely able to complete our concert and hoped the speech that followed wouldn't be long so I could meet that angel. Well, wouldn't you know, the storm outside was raging so badly with torrents of rain falling that the people rushed to the door and out to their cars hoping to get home safely. I didn't even get to meet this beautiful mystery girl!

I wasn't quite myself on the trip back to Joplin or in the classes the next few days. But about three months later, I noticed on the school bulletin board a posting that read, "The First Christian Church of DeWitt, Arkansas, needs a student to come and teach in a two-week vacation Bible school to be held the first two weeks of June." Then the church telephone number was listed with a request that they be contacted as soon as possible. You know, of course, that simply out of "religious duty" and not because of any other motive, I yanked the notice off the bulletin board, went to a telephone, and volunteered my services. Ha-ha, oh yeah!! Some people call it fate. I call it God! I was one happy young man in my classes and weekend services for the next month and a half, just waiting for the day I would leave for DeWitt. We brothers had bought a car and I had use of it, so when that day arrived, I drove through the rolling hills on the winding highway, then on the flat rice-country roads past Little Rock, and finally on that narrow strip of pavement to my destination. The church had arranged for me to stay at Mrs. Roy's boarding house, so I checked in the evening before VBS was to start. I was excited, but somewhat anxious, because I had no clue as to whether that "angel" would even be at the church or whether I would be able to meet her at all. But I prayed about it and knew I'd give it my best shot.

The next morning, I got up rather early, dressed, had a few moments of devotions, and then had a hot, delicious breakfast which Mrs. Roy, a member of the church, had fixed. I drove to the stately brick church building, walked in, and glory hallelujah … there she was, fresh and resplendent in all her youthful beauty! My knees almost buckled. How lucky could a guy get, I thought, as I nervously walked over and introduced myself to her and the others. I got my assignment for the classes I was to teach and enjoyed the whole morning of teaching and mingling with the kids. But you know where my heart was. Well, lo and behold, at noon here comes Patricia (Trish she was called) walking up to me and saying, "Come with me. My mother is preparing lunch, and you're invited." Under my breath, I thought, "Wow, this is too good to be true!" We walked out to her car, and she drove us from town past all the levied and irrigated rice fields to her farm home, about seven miles out in the country. "Good," I thought, "a farm girl." We walked into the house and I met her mother and father, as well as her little brother, Jake. We visited over a table laden with delicious varieties of good country dishes, and we got quickly and easily acquainted. They all made me feel right at home. That afternoon, Trish and I just had such a nice, easy time of talking and laughing together. Then she drove me to the boarding house where I spent the rest of the day relaxing and studying for my classes.

That evening, and all the following noon and evening meals, I was invited to different homes, and Patricia was invited to be present also. All the couples of the church were having fun teasing us, as they noticed a romance definitely starting to bud. By the time of the fourth evening meal at the home of Mr. and Mrs. J.C. Stamp, I was so "out-of-it" and lovesick, I could hardly eat. But I went through the motions, taking small bites and trying to hide the queasiness of my churning stomach. After taking a few bites of the delicious strawberry shortcake dessert, I felt that I was about to lose everything. I lurched up from my chair, ran out the door to the back yard, hung my head over the fence, and out of my mouth and quivering lips poured the whole meal! Oh I was so sick and embarrassed! But I composed myself after a few minutes and returned to the table of people hysterically laughing their heads off. That was it. The cat was out of the bag and everyone knew that I had it bad. Patricia took me by the hand, and she and Mrs. Stamp consoled and controlled me, and the rest of the evening was pleasant. We started dating the remainder of that and the next week, and the romance was on. Oh, how I hated to leave and return to my home in Lebanon. But the love letters, which we still have, flowed back and forth, that is, until the middle of August. Her letters suddenly stopped. My heart was crushed! I told my twin brother, Bill, "I'm afraid I've lost her." "Maybe not, Bob. Don't give up so easily," Bill said.

He knew, though I was deeply troubled, that it hadn't been my nature ever since I had gotten home from the Navy to lose my new-found confidence as a winner and leader. But his word of encouragement helped. There was no way, though, that I could drop everything and make a trip down to DeWitt. I was busy with my ministries at Louisburg and Conway. Plus, I had two revivals scheduled, one for a week in Conway and then a week at Cato, Kansas, where I was to do the preaching and Bill the song leading. Towards the end of that latter meeting, I got a telegram from Patricia's mother saying that Patricia was quite ill in the hospital having just had an appendectomy. I spoke that night, then told Bill to please get a sermon and take my place for the last night because I had to head down to DeWitt. He agreed and off I went, arriving at the Anderson home at 3:30 in the morning. Her mother, Beulah (the same Bible name as my mother), was overjoyed to see me and made a bed up for me to sleep a few hours. I got up about 7:30, we had breakfast, and we both expressed our concern about Patricia's health as well as where she stood regarding any possibility of our getting back together again. I said, "Of course that's very important to me, but right now her recovery is the main thing." She replied, "You plan to stay here with us all week, and we'll see how things go." I drove into town, bought a nice bouquet and hurried to the hospital before noon. I walked into Patricia's room with the flowers in hand and surprised her as I said "Hi" and kissed her on the cheek. I told her how worried and concerned I was when I heard from her mother about her emergency surgery, and that I just had to jump in the car and drive all night to see her. That seemed to impress her. She teared up a little and reached out to take my hand. That was a welcome sign to me that she was glad to see me. I didn't stay too long, for she was in a lot of pain and I didn't want to overdo what seemed to be a good, new beginning for us. (What I didn't know at the time, which she later told me, was that just before the nurse ushered me into her room, another Navy man, Billy, had been there to see her and had just walked out the back door to where his car was parked! So that was why the letters had stopped!)

Patricia was able to go home a couple of days later, and we were both comfortable talking things out. She said that she had seen Billy a few times, but that he was pressuring her greatly and she had told him it was over. She added, "I'm so glad you're here, and I do care for you." Wow, those were the magic words I so wanted to hear! She healed nicely, and every day we would read from the Bible and pray, but also just have fun as we got closer and closer. By the end of the week, things had gotten so good, I knew we were meant for each other. We were sitting in a double-seated swinging rocker on the front porch late one afternoon, just talking and relaxing. Suddenly, big trouble came calling! Down the dirt road a hundred yards or so from her house came a speeding car with the dust flying behind it. The brakes screeched wildly as it swerved and made a sharp turn into the driveway just a few yards in front of us. Out of the car jumped a pudgy, five-foot-seven-inch young man, and here he came like a raging bull, marching right up to the screen door, opening it and just standing there, staring me down. "I've come to get my girl," he blared. I kept my cool and softly but firmly replied, "I'm sorry, but she's not your girl." He yelled back, "Yes she is, and I know she really loves me," and looking toward Patricia said, "Don't you, Patricia?" Not wanting to make a scene or escalate the situation, she simply but forcefully shook her head a few times in a definite "no" motion. He mumbled something awful about me even being there anyway and got totally out of control. I tried to calm him down and said, "All right, I tell you what I'm going to do now. You're standing there, Patricia's seated here, and I'm going to stand here by the door. Let's let her decide who she loves and wants to be with. Who she gets up and goes to will be the answer." The situation was volatile and tense. But without any hesitation at all, Patricia got up and walked toward me, tears flooding her eyes, and threw her arms around me in a tight embrace. Billy turned on his heels, stormed out to his car, revved up the engine, backed up almost to the ditch, and off he zoomed like a bat out of hell, clouds of dust trailing him 'til he got out of sight!

CHAPTER 9

Courting, Outlandish Rules, And Marriage

PATRICIA WAS NOT quite seventeen years old, but she was so mature in every way: raised in and active in church, an attendee the last two summers in a Christian service camp, an accomplished pianist, and a member of her high school band and chorus. She had completed two years of a course in home economics and homemaking and was planning on attending Atlanta Christian College after she graduated from high school. Despite her young age (I guess like me in the Navy when I was only 17), she certainly had all the qualifications to be my wife and partner in ministry. Besides, she was beautiful inside and out, loved and respected by everyone, and I was madly in love with her! The start of her senior year in high school was near, but I wasn't about to leave her in DeWitt in a vulnerable position of possible pressure and influence from this other guy or the amorous desires and intentions of anyone else. So on Sunday, I went to church with the family, and that afternoon, Patricia and I had a good long talk about the possibility of her enrolling along with me at Ozark Bible College in just a week and a half when the college semester would begin. "I'll be a junior there, you'll be a freshman, but you can also complete your high school credits for graduation," I said. She immediately replied, "That sounds good to me!" Relieved that she agreed, I looked right into her blue eyes and said, "I love you so much, my darling! Will you marry me?" With moist eyes and a big smile, she replied, "Oh Bob, yes, yes!"

The following day, we traveled over to Pine Bluff and picked out an engagement ring with a very tiny diamond in it. It was all I could afford, but to both of us it meant as much as if it had been a 10-carat ring. Since time was now breathing down our necks with our newly laid plans, the next day I kissed my love goodbye and headed for Missouri. She would take a bus up and meet me in Joplin a few days later. She arrived safely at the college, had been assigned a dorm room, and was enjoying herself with a group of welcoming girls when I walked in. There she was, radiant and fresh as a daisy, happily mingling with her new-found friends, among whom happened to be Joy, Bill's future wife, and Lorraine (called Lodi), who later became B.J.'s bride. So far, so good. But it didn't last long. When it came time to enroll, all of us were presented with an outrageous "Rules of Agreement" document that every student had to sign. It contained a set of twenty-one of the most outlandish and unreasonable demands one could imagine for college students. One was that an unmarried couple could not be seen holding hands inside class or out. Another was that a couple could not attend a prayer meeting together. Still another was a single boy and girl could not visit the home of a parent together. On and on the list read. Students were in an uproar and outraged and didn't know what to do in protest.

Bill, B.J., Roger, and I talked it over, and finally I said, "I'm going in to talk to President Strong (a son of the founder of the college, Dr. F.W. Strong), and I think he'll surely cancel the whole document, or at least rescind several of the most offensive and ridiculous rules." So I went in, we had a few pleasantries, and I explained my dilemma to him, stating, "President Strong, here I've brought my fiancé up from DeWitt, and according to these rules, we can't even go to prayer meeting together, and I can't take her on weekends to see my parents or have her go with me on Sundays where I preach." To my astonishment and shock, he was adamant and almost belligerent! I couldn't believe it. He said, "Bob, if you can't accept these rules, you should quit and get married." He showed me to the door, and I left, extremely disappointed and dejected. I told my brothers and Roger what he had said. We mulled it over briefly and agreed we'd all quit. Then I said to B.J., "No, you need to stay," which he did. I went to tell Patricia what had happened and to pack her bags, which the rest of us also did, and off we went, Roger and Bill in one car and Patricia and me in mine. We made two or three stops on the 120-mile trip to our homes, and instead of being downhearted, we all were high as kites, feeling that we had been freed from a cage. (We later learned that the administration, faculty, and trustees had been badly shaken, and that the so-called "Rules of Agreement" were cancelled. We all returned as heroes the next semester!)

Roger stopped at his home in Phillipsburg, Bill joined Patricia and me in our car, and we finished the twelve miles to my parents' home in Lebanon. I introduced Patricia to them and told them the whole story of what had happened. Mother hugged Patricia, graciously welcomed her, and since it was quite late, put her in one of the freshly-made beds and said, "This will be your room." We spent a couple of wonderful weeks, with Patricia being so warmly received by the family, meeting my friends, and being shown around town, out at the Homestead farm, and various scenic places. It was a fun time, very enjoyable for us all. But soon, I realized we had a real dilemma. Here I was, responsible for bringing a lovely girl, my sweetheart, from her home in Arkansas to Missouri for college, but now that was null and void. WHAT TO DO? That was a big and nagging question. It's true we were engaged, but we certainly weren't planning to get married for another couple of years. I definitely would never, I mean NEVER, think of sending her back to her home in DeWitt! That was the farthest thing from my mind. Yes, I had a job preaching half-time at two different churches, but they were small, paying me only $15.00 a week. I told myself, "Bob, you've got a huge problem staring you in the face, and you've simply got to do something fast." I went to the Conway Christian Church leaders and asked if I could go full time there at $35.00 per week. They agreed, so then I went to the good and kind folks at Louisburg, preached my last sermon, and had a wonderful farewell send-off there. Now I was getting somewhere. Next, I kissed Patricia and said, "Honey, let's get married!" I carefully and lovingly explained what I had done and why I felt that the changed circumstances we faced met with God's approval and favor. I said, "That's the most important thing anyway, to have God's blessing in our marriage, regardless of what others might think." Bless her heart, she totally and wholeheartedly agreed and said, "Yes, let's do it!" We told my folks and called her parents to give them the good news. Her mother especially was overjoyed, and all the ladies of her church who had been helping our romance along, when they got word that we were coming to be married, started making big plans for the wedding and reception. So on the evening of September 30, 1949, we were married in a beautiful candlelight ceremony, performed by my cousin, Roger Tribble. Both of our mothers were beaming and shedding a few tears of joy. My twin brother, Bill, was my best man, and B.J. was the head usher. The whole congregation turned out, as well as a lot of students and townspeople. The society editor of the DeWitt Era-Enterprise described the nuptials this way: "The bride wore white slipper satin fashioned with princess bodice, long sleeves, lace yoke with sweetheart neckline." And if I say so myself, her long, flowing, pure white wedding gown, provided by one of the ladies of her church, was spectacular. Continuing with the article in the paper, it reads: "Her fingertip veil of illusion fell down a heart-shaped tiara and she carried a Bible topped with white carnations. Her only ornament was a single strand of pearls." What a beautiful bride I got to marry!

CHAPTER 10

Early Ministry And Looking For Home

AFTER THE CEREMONY and receiving well wishes and congratulations at the door, the guys got a wheelbarrow and loaded Patricia, still attired in her wedding gown, into it and had me push her all the way around the town square! We took the traditional pictures, had a very nice reception, and then in a hail of rice with "JUST MARRIED" on the window and tin cans tied to the back bumper of our '48 Ford, we rode off into the night for our honeymoon!

Our first home was a comfortable little one-bedroom house at 508 Harrison Street in Lebanon, Missouri, my hometown. We rented it for $35.00 per month. Patricia (I now called her Pat) stepped so easily into the role of homemaker as a good cook, and she was loved and highly esteemed as my wife and partner in the ministry. We commuted on the weekends to Conway to carry on our ministry there, and as I recall, over the next three months we also conducted two revivals, she playing the piano and me singing a solo and preaching each night. The first was at the Christian Church in Halltown, and the second was at the Ohio, Missouri, Christian Church where Bill was the minister. Besides that, Pat and I hosted a revival at our full-time church in Conway with Carol and Donna Lankford as the evangelistic team.

When January rolled around, we enrolled in Ozark Bible College at Joplin, traveling on weekends back to Conway for our ministerial duties there. I'll say this, President Edwin Strong, to his credit, couldn't have been nicer to both of us. We were welcomed with open arms. Shortly thereafter, it looked like misfortune had overtaken us. The elder with the most influence at the Conway church felt they couldn't afford to keep paying $35.00 a week, even though the congregation was growing and the people loved us. He wanted instead to start a fund for a "rainy day" and go back to having preaching two times a month. I said, "I'm married now, and I simply cannot stay here then as your minister." So I resigned. Back at school, I went in to President Strong's office to talk with him about my predicament. He listened carefully and said, "Bob, there's a good church without a minister down at Cassville, Missouri. Why don't you contact them now and see if you could schedule a 'trial' sermon?" I did and we agreed on a date. Pat and I drove down on a Sunday morning, greeted the very nice congregants, I preached, they liked it and loved Pat, and they hired us on the spot! Praise the Lord! They paid $50.00 a week, provided us with a parsonage (home for the minister), gave us a furniture shower, helped us buy a new 1950 Ford, and agreed to let me continue my college studies that year and the next until I graduated. Who could ask for anything more? We got a nice little two-room apartment in Joplin and commuted there through the week for our college studies. One course that Pat loved was so advantageous to us later in our years of full-time evangelism. It was an art class that specialized in chalk art. Another was evangelistic-style piano playing. Me? I took Biblical books, Greek, psychology, logic, hermeneutics, apologetics, church history, restoration history, personal evangelism, voice culture, and homiletics. I excelled in all of them, but I especially thrived on every Bible course the college offered, as well as being on the basketball team. But back home in Cassville, shortly after we moved there, we had a real scary brush with death. They had freshly painted every room in the parsonage, and Pat got deathly ill.

Lead was still used in paint back in those days, and the deadly effect of it was that it nearly took Pat's life! I rushed her to the hospital where she spent a few critical days before recovering.

A joyous event occurred during our ministry at Cassville. Our first baby was born! Our doctor was in my hometown of Lebanon, and I had taken Pat there to my folks' home a few days earlier. On a bright Sunday morning, November 19, 1950, Dr. Howard Carrington delivered Rebecca Jo Vernon at the hospital as I proudly but anxiously stood by in the delivery room. What a beautiful, blue-eyed, blonde little doll I soon held in my arms. And she is still so beautiful, inside and out.

Early in 1951, Dr. F.W. Strong, beloved founder of the college, became quite ill and eventually passed on to his reward. As a graduating senior, I was asked to join the faculty and take over his and President Edwin Strong's classes, which I was honored to do. And the extra pay helped us with our increased family expenses. After my graduation, we continued our full-time ministry at Cassville. But increasingly I was feeling a pull and calling to the evangelistic field. About that time, an influential member and prominent but rather prideful state senator came along with his wife to our home with a grievance. He said that I had failed to publicly recognize him on his monthly visit from Jefferson City (Missouri's state capitol) to our church service, and he came to set me straight! I apologized, of course, but a little stir was caused in the congregation, and that, plus my passion to get into full-time evangelism, led me to resign a little time later. But it was very hard to leave a lot of dear friends there, including Carl and Naomi, John and Penney, Max and Sue, Glendale and Helen, as well as many others we had grown to love.

Having made many friends across the country in our basketball playing and as a quartet, we were able to schedule for the last half of 1951 our evangelistic meetings, concerts, and special appearances. Bill, B.J., and I, together with Willis

Harrison, an excellent pianist and singer, had gotten together to lay out our plans, pray, make calls, and write lots of letters. And, of course, our wives played a very important part in our travels and meetings, forming their own girls' quartet. And, we had another traveler along, who was a hit everywhere, our baby girl, Becky!

CHAPTER 11

The Gospel Messengers

WE CALLED OUR team "The Gospel Messengers," which included our men's quartet, "The Gospel Harmonaires," and the women's quartet, "The Gospel Harmonettes." Fancy names, huh? It's amazing that we were so successful, and surely we had God's blessing since we were all just kids. But spiritually, even in the months before, I had been preparing myself, praying and humbly planning for those days. In my diary, as the year of 1951 was about to end, I had written:

> "I got up about 5:30 and memorized the 19th Psalm. Yesterday I preached both morning and evening services here in DeWitt on 'Faith' and 'What shall I give Thee?' I was paid $50.00, for which I am thankful because we were flat broke. I am in a state of turmoil and confusion at the group's future plans. Right now they are so uncertain. Oh Lord, please forgive me and guide my steps that I might do your will. As to the evangelistic party, I am anxious to get back and find out what correspondence has come in … I am definitely going to strive to put II Corinthians 5:17 into practice. What a wonderful thing! A new creature in Christ! This opportunity and challenge to put away 'old things' – sins; bad slothful habits; wrong desires; worldly ambitions. The attempt, with divine help, to be a true imitator of Christ."

Throughout 1951, I had been wonderfully blessed, along with my family and the team, in conducting eight revivals, most of them for two weeks, including DeWitt, where I did the preaching and Pat was the hometown heroine, doing her chalk artistry nightly!

From my diary, I note that Pat and I, along with our one-year-old cute baby doll – and what a doll she still is – spent the Christmas and New Year holidays with Pat's folks in DeWitt, Arkansas. Little Becky Jo had made a good and delightful traveler and was a "hit" during all our meetings in 1951. We three certainly needed a break and time of relaxation, and we got it at "Mamaw" and "Papaw" Anderson's.

On January 7, 1952, I started my first revival at Etterville, Missouri, with B.J. leading the singing. He also preached a night or two during those two weeks. The weather was frightful, and we only had about 58 present the first night. But by Friday evening, the attendance was 140. I wrote in my diary, "There is much growing enthusiasm and interest. Thank you Lord! We are praying for visible additions. Lord, keep me humble, like a little child." A week later, there were 250 packed into that little church building, and the responses to the invitation, including baptisms, grew to 13! On the closing Sunday night, January 29th, in describing the service I wrote:

"We again had a glorious service with approximately 300 present. The house was packed. Besides the adults seated, all the children were sitting around the platform. I barely had room to stand. I preached on 'Misconceptions of New Testament Christianity.' Fred Morgan, a Catholic and a fine man, his wife Melba, and their daughter Sonja, made the Good Confession, and we had the baptismal service that night. Also, Mr. Ozzie Jones, an immersed Methodist, placed his fellowship, thus uniting their family. There were 20 additions altogether. The meeting was greatly blessed by the Lord, and was a rich, spiritual feast."

The success of that meeting was typical of almost all our revivals, and even exceeded in some of them during 1952. The four of us plus our wives participated in most of our meetings that year. Space prevents me from describing these two-week campaigns for the most part, but here, in order, are the places where we appeared in our busy schedule of 1952: Etterville, Missouri; Tuscola, Illinois; St. Joseph, Illinois; Dewey, Oklahoma; Dallas, Texas; Barnett, Missouri; Rolla, Missouri; Kiamichi, Oklahoma; Rinehart Church, Missouri; Thayer, Kansas; Ulman, Missouri; Norfolk, Virginia; Olean, Missouri; Central Church, Oklahoma City, Oklahoma; Bucklin, Kansas; Stilwell, Oklahoma; and Forrest Hill, Oklahoma City, Oklahoma. I started out the year doing all the preaching, but eventually I shared this wondrous privilege with Bill and B.J., and it worked well. Of course, Willis Harrison played a very important role in the meetings as an excellent pianist and baritone in our a cappella men's quartet. And his wife, Lora, added her valuable presence as the alto voice in our women's quartette; with B.J.'s wife, Lodi, singing contralto; Bill's wife, Joy, first soprano; and my wife, Pat, second soprano. Each girl's voice in the treble range corresponded with her husband's: Bill, singing first tenor; me, Bob, second tenor; Willis, baritone; and B.J., with that deep bass voice! What a joy, but also what a challenge for the eight of us, along with our baby, to travel from place to place with no trailer but staying in the homes of members where we were conducting revivals. I must admit, by the end of the year we were all getting weary, and the girls, especially, were longing to settle down to a regular "home" life and located ministry. And by this time, B.J. and Lodi had welcomed baby Linda Gayle! After a "family pow-wow" and looking "unto Jesus, the author and finisher of our faith," we stuck it out and started mapping out a tour to the West Coast. But before proceeding with describing that series of meetings, let me say that our last revival at the Forest Hill Christian Church in December of 1952 was very eventful! Boyd Lammiman, the minister, had done a great job of advertising and preparing for the meeting, including arranging for us to make our very first appearance on television! On December 7, 1952, I wrote in my diary:

> "We made our debut on TV this afternoon at 5:00. We sang 'In the Garden,' and 'There is a Fountain' on WKY-TV, Oklahoma City, Oklahoma, hosted by R.T. Williams Jr. on his program called 'The Singing Pastor.' Next week, all 8 of us will appear … I hope that these appearances will lead to some profitable way of reaching people with the Gospel."

I guess I was prophetic, for two years later, on December 10, 1954, the four of us ministering Vernon Brothers – Bill, B.J., Don, and I – started our regular weekly program on television.

Another very important factor during the Forest Hill meetings was that Dr. Lester Ford, the president of Midwest Christian College, attended the meeting, was very impressed with our preaching and singing, and greatly encouraged us with many helpful suggestions. On December 9, 1952, in my diary I wrote:

> "He proposed the idea of changing the name to 'The Vernon Brothers.' I said we've thought of that, assuring the Association would be organized with the purpose of advancing New Testament Christianity in America and the world: reviving weak churches, establishing new congregations after the New Testament order, and breaking down denominational barriers and traditions … This to be done, not by browbeating, or by unduly offending, but

by teaching and instructing ... in the way of God more accurately. This message presented in the Spirit of Christ, is to be preceded by an attractive program of congregational singing and special music to be given by members of evangelistic party."

Dr. and Mrs. Ford hosted our whole team in their home for fellowship and a delicious dinner, had us present a program at the college, and were especially gracious and encouraging in every way.

On Christmas Day, December 25, 1952, all seven of us brothers and our families gathered with our dear parents at the Homestead, our childhood home. What a great and festive time we had! Mother fixed a fabulous breakfast, assisted by our wives, of ham and eggs, biscuits and gravy, hot oatmeal, orange juice, and coffee. Afterwards, Dad, with his Santa hat on, called us all into the living room, where he opened the Bible and had one of us read the Christmas story about the birth of Jesus. Then we had a joyous but noisy time of opening our gifts. I wrote in my diary: "I got a watch, shirt, jewel case, pair of trousers, and pajamas. My darling wife sure was good to me. Oh yes! I got a silver dollar, an apple, orange, and candy in a bright red Christmas sock from the folks. Just like old times!"

On a more serious and reflective note, I penned, concerning our ministry and future:

"To justify our remaining together as a team will require our accomplishing at least four times as much as what we could individually do in separate ministries. Without any spirit of pride, and as I write this, I have tears in my eyes, it is my deep feeling that God has endowed us, i.e. the members of our team, with talents and abilities that can and must be used in extending His Kingdom upon the earth. If we do remain together as a unit, MUCH is certainly going to be required of us."

After such soul-searching and a few more fun family days at the farm, Pat, Becky, and I headed to DeWitt, Arkansas, to spend the New Year holidays with Pat's folks before our team's tour to California.

CHAPTER 12

Revival Time!

ON JANUARY 10, 1953, I wrote a letter, excerpts from which I quote below, showing my deep conviction about our plans for the year and the future:

"This letter is of the greatest importance to me, because it concerns the future plans of our evangelistic group. We have been in this work for almost two years, striving to advance the cause of New Testament Christianity... Starting this year, we have decided to broaden the scope of our work, and to make an all-out effort in the field in which we are laboring. We are forming an evangelistic association in order that we might more effectively carry out our ministry. We have planned to work not only in our scheduled revival campaigns, but also in radio and television if the opportunity presents itself. Our two television programs in Oklahoma City proved to be very effective in publicizing our meetings there ... We are taking a tour to the West Coast starting January 11, in an effort to stir up interest ... We are striving to the best of our ability to present to people the pure Gospel as it was in the days of the Apostles, previous to the introduction of human traditions and alterations. We believe that division within the ranks of Christianity is contrary to the spirit and will of our Lord, and that it is hindering the cause of righteousness … Brethren, we must do something, and do it now! We must somehow, some way, reach the people with the saving, unifying message of Christ!"

On January 11, we all met at Clarendon, Texas, to start our scheduled appearances on the way to California. That morning, we sang and I spoke about our ministry and plans for the future. That afternoon we traveled to Hobbs, New Mexico, getting there in time to present our program. We were royally received, and the house was packed. The next night we were hosted by our friend and former classmate, Julian Whitworth, along with his congregation at Winslow, Arizona. The next morning, January 13, we got up very early and drove to awe-inspiring Grand Canyon and then on to Needles, California, for a program that night. The next day we spent a very hot but enjoyable time at Death Valley, then drove from the intense heat there to the bitter cold the next day, Thursday, through the deep snow and up, up, up the winding mountain to Sequoia National Park. We barely made it and arrived so late at the lodge that we had to wake up the receptionist. We were told there was no heat but that they could accommodate all eight of us. Shivering in the frigid darkness, we unpacked and bedded down with piles of comforters smothering our freezing bodies! The next morning, Friday, we saw what an exquisite winter wonderland it was. I wrote in my diary: "It was really a beautiful sight – the giant Redwood trees, snow three feet deep, the huge Pines!" We had gotten up at 5:30, eaten breakfast at the lodge, and bundled up in heavy coats to go outside just to view such a spectacular scene. We couldn't tarry, though, because we had to be in San Jose that evening for a program. The event scheduled that night was the annual San Jose Bible College Conference. It was a very full and moving program, featuring and honoring the aged and retiring minister, Ernest Beam. So it was indeed a privilege for us to be invited, and we were very warmly received and applauded after our presentation. I noted in my diary that we sang "Anchored in Jehovah," "Peace in the Valley," "In Tenderness He Called Me," and "God So Loved the World." It turned out that our choice of songs was very appropriate, for the message that followed was a heart-felt plea for unity and love in the Body of Christ. "Brother Ernest Beam delivered a very wonderful message on the matter of fellowship," I wrote. Frail and unsteady, he was led and helped to a chair from which he eloquently and lovingly spoke.

It was a nine-hour drive to Los Angeles the next day, and fortunately, we had no program that night, for we were "bone-weary!" The next morning, Sunday, we presented our program at the Inglewood Heights Church of Christ to about 200 people, Brother Francis Arant, minister. We sang "God So Loved the World," "The Old Book and the Old Faith," "In Tenderness," "I Shall Not Be Moved," and "I Want to Walk Where Jesus Walked." I then presented our plans for the future, speaking on the subject, "Is There a Place for Us in the Restoration Movement?" I put my whole heart into the message, and the congregation seemed visibly moved. That night we appeared at the Florence Avenue Christian Church, Harold Gallagher, minister. We sang "Anchored in Jehovah," "Just a Closer Walk," "Amen," "In Tenderness," "Let the Church March On," "Shall I Crucify My Savior?," "Thou Blessed Rock of Ages," and "Wonderful is He." I then took about fifteen minutes to deliver my "Challenge!" Fortunately, that was our last program, for we were all exceedingly weary and got to relax in visits with cousins Clyde and Francis Vernon, Ruth and Ace Ray, Lucille and Curly Gragg, and Pauline and Lee Street, along with their families. What a treat! I had taken the flu real bad by the time we got to Pauline's house in Oceanside. Bless her heart, when she saw that I was so sick and running a high fever, and not having room to sleep us all, she doctored me up and put me to bed in a motel right on the beach. I chilled all night and think I heard every wave that hit the shore! But that was the best thing for me, 'cause by morning my fever had gone down, and though weak, I was able to enjoy a delicious breakfast she prepared for the whole gang. All's well that ends well!

We soon headed in our two cars to Carlsbad Caverns for a quick "look-see" and then the long haul Missouri bound. Arriving after an arduous but successful mission tour, we all took a few days off before settling into our homes and business at hand. Our team held a revival at the Christian Church at Clarendon, Texas, in February 1953. Bill's father-in-law, Brother Leo Oliver, was the minister, so we had Bill do the preaching, and he did a great job. Shortly after that meeting, the eight of us were in charge of the music at the Mid-Winter Ozark Bible College Convention for three days, and at one of the sessions, I delivered a message on my assigned topic, "Working Under the Authority of Christ." Guy P. Leavitt, esteemed editor of the *Lookout,* was also present and one of the speakers. I wrote in my journal:

"He seemed very impressed by our music, and I particularly noticed his attentiveness during my sermon. I talked with him for about an hour and a half Thursday about our plans. He was overly enthusiastic about the possibilities. He gave me very helpful suggestions and advice, dictating a letter for us to send out, then advised as to the follow-up procedure."

The very next day, I got another encouraging surprise, and I wrote: "Professor Edwin Hayden pulled me aside and told me that Brother Leavitt had asked him to interview me and get a story for the STANDARD and LOOKOUT ... The Convention did more to inspire and unite us than anything has for a long time. We needed it!" The following Sunday evening, our team of eight was in charge of the entire service at the Westside Christian Church in Wichita.

In March of 1953, our team held two great, Heaven-blest evangelistic meetings! Here is a quote from our monthly publication:

"BULLETIN – Fifty responses were made to the Gospel invitation in our latest meeting at Tuscola, Illinois. Thirty-four of these were by baptism, fifteen by transfer, while one young lady rededicated her life to the Lord. There were overflow crowds in all but two services, and an all-time Bible School attendance record of 349 was set on the closing Lord's Day. E. Gean Davis is the minister of this fast growing congregation."

And continuing:

"TWENTY-ONE ARE BAPTIZED AT MT. PLEASANT, MISSOURI – The entire community around Mt. Pleasant, Missouri experienced a real revival of New Testament Christianity recently. People in that area were greatly stirred for Christ and came from miles around to attend the services. Many expressed themselves that this was the greatest meeting they had ever attended. Eleven days proved far too short, and it was regrettable that the meeting couldn't continue for two more weeks. There were many highlights in the meeting. Twenty-one people submitted their lives to Christ in primary obedience to the Gospel, while three were added by transfer. It was a glorious experience to go the same hour of the night, and baptize into Christ those who had publicly made their confession of Christ. One such service actually occurred at the midnight hour in a nearby stream, as penitent believers were buried with their Lord in baptism and raised to walk in newness of life."

The rest of our revivals for 1953 met with similar successes when it came to overflow crowds and responses to the Gospel invitation. Space prohibits details and comments about all of them, but I will try to mention some highlights. Before that, let me show you our busy schedule:

Hobbs, New Mexico	April 12-26
Kiamichi Clinic, Oklahoma	May 5, 6, 7
Lamar, Missouri	May 10-24
Eldon, Missouri	May 31 – June 28
Rylie, Texas	July 27 – Aug. 23
Bayard, Nebraska	Aug. 26 – Sept. 13
Council Grove, Kansas	Sept. 20 – Oct. 11
Kissimmee, Florida	Oct. 19 – Nov. 8
Oklahoma City, Oklahoma	Nov. 15 – Dec. 6

From the May issue of our monthly publication is this excerpt: "In Hobbs, New Mexico, the building was filled every night, and in many of the services, chairs had to be put down. In the first week of the meeting at Lamar, Missouri, crowds have averaged over the 200 mark." Both revivals resulted in baptisms and additions most nights. Our four-week tent revival in the city park at Eldon, Missouri, was highly successful. The team asked me to do almost all the preaching, which I was so honored to do, pouring my heart and Scriptures into every sermon. And, of course, there was special music from all of us every night, plus rousing congregational singing. On the opening night, I wrote this in my journal: "There were 331 present. I preached on 'God's Power for a Power Age.'" My heart was overflowing with praise to Almighty God for the interest and response at this great beginning, and by the end of the week I penned this: "Saturday night we had a wonderful service, great crowd, 652 were counted, every seat taken besides some 200 others around the tent ... I preached on 'Lukewarm Christianity.'" Crowds continued coming during the meeting, spirits were soaring, souls were being saved, rededications and confessions were being voiced, and people were being baptized. Toward the end, it was decided that there was sufficient response to start a new church. In my diary I wrote: "There were fifty-eight additions in the recent meeting concluded at Eldon." Thirty of them were rededications, twelve won from denominations to the New Testament position, and sixteen precious souls were baptized. From our paper, I quote: "Because of the hearts of many people in Eldon and surrounding area, a brand new congregation of 'Christians only' has come into being in that city, with 50 members. On the very first Lord's Day meeting of the congregation on June 28th, 89 persons were present."

Our next meeting was also a tent revival, hosted by James Earl Ladd, minister at Rylie, Texas, from July 27th to August 23rd. Man alive, was it ever hot! But the first week was preparatory with a lot of prayer and calling on prospects. We brothers took turns preaching during the next three weeks. From my journal, I quote:

"My task, and a colossal one it is, is to remain steadfast and point men to Christ in this increasingly complex, changing world. With all the powerful developments and amazing achievements in the world, man is still lost. He has no power to compare with God's power. Man has not invented anything to overcome sin. He has not discovered a way to fly to Heaven!"

So in the eleven services I preached, I sought with all my heart to present God's love and plan of salvation revealed so clearly in the New Testament. My brothers did the same. There were eighteen responses, seven baptisms, and eight rededications and transfers.

But on the lighter side, we all went golfing early one morning, and I was a casualty on the fourth hole. I noted this in my diary: "I hit the golf ball, it hit a tree and came flying back at me smashing my upper lip!" First aid at a nearby clinic and ice packs felt better than golf!

Our next two revivals were at Bayard, Nebraska, and Council Grove, Kansas. We brothers took turns preaching at the meeting hosted by Brother Roy A. Coop, and Bob Scott, our friend and classmate when we were at Ozark, ministered at Council Grove. We had nine additions to the church at Bayard, and though it was a very busy bean harvest time, the crowds were good and the church was greatly strengthened. At Council Grove, we had responses and baptisms at about every service during the twenty-one days, with a packed house nightly. Something very personal and special happened during this meeting. My wife, Pat, expecting our second child, was at her folks in DeWitt, Arkansas. But she was overdue three weeks in the expected time of birth. I got so concerned about her condition the third week of our meeting that I flew there and spent three days with her, walking those dusty roads trying to rush that child's "coming out" party, efforts to no avail! So I flew back to Council Grove for the last few days of the revival. Finally, on Friday October the 9th at 2:30 in the morning, I was awakened with the good news, and I recorded it this way in my diary: "It's a boy! Praise the Lord! Carolyn Eddy called while ago to tell me. I'm so excited! 10 pounds and 5 ounces, wow! A little giant! She said both were doing fine. I do so hope they are." Gregory Mark was born at 1:45 a.m. that morning. What a proud and overjoyed papa I was, receiving loads of congratulations the next two days as we closed the meeting with me preaching on "The Birth of the New Testament Church" and three more souls responding to the Gospel invitation.

Our next meeting was at Kissimmee, Florida, with a dear friend, Delmar Debault, the minister. What a great time of fellowship we had, plus a deeply spiritual and successful revival. It was a three-week period, and I was privileged to preach fourteen times, with Bill and B.J. at the pulpit the other services. There was a total of eighteen additions. Following that was our last revival of the year at a repeat meeting in Oklahoma City, Oklahoma, with the Forest Hill congregation. It was also a three-week time of fellowship and evangelism. Boyd Lammiman had prepared well, with the first week designated for prayer and home visitation. He also had arranged for us to present programs and music on several radio and television stations. Pat, Becky, Gregg, and I had it nice as a family to be able to stay in a motel which the church had arranged. Again, we brothers shared in preaching, and we rejoiced at the beginning morning service when three people responded to the invitation. In my diary, I wrote that they were:

"... Mr. and Mrs. Robinson and Brother A.B. Carpenter (a retired minister), who will be 90 the 7th of December. We had decided to visit him, as well as some ladies in a rest home, which we did last week. They really appreciated our visit and singing! I know some day I will be old and may have to spend my last lingering days in such a home."

(Comment: That day has come for my dear wife, since she has now been in a nursing home for six long years, and as I write this, I will soon be 89 and hope to put that day off for a while!)

I continued in my diary:

"We came by Brother Carpenter's little apartment and visited with and sang for him. Poor old man! But his mind is still keen and he's very spry. I couldn't help but feel sorry for him, what with the unkempt little apartment he lived in. Yet I have to admire him for his spunk! He had been fixing up a room and had overdone himself, and had just recently gotten out of the hospital. He showed us his 'art gallery' – pictures posted on the wall – the president, a baby, Einstein, and others."

The next day, we men in the team had a very cordial, lengthy, and important discussion, questioning the future of our work together. We were all getting quite weary of constantly being on the road, especially our wives. This honest and loving conversation took place on Monday, November 23, 1953. The church at Eldon had a great desire that I would come and be their first permanent minister, and the other men were also getting offers from churches. And, needless to say, the girls longed to have a normal "home life." I expressed my feeling, and it seemed to be the consensus of everyone, that we should at least take a hiatus of a couple years, keep our evangelistic spirit alive in serving individual churches, but come together as a team for special events and revivals quarterly. I then said I felt led of the Lord to pursue and explore the possibility of using TV in our ministry. That very evening, before our service at Forest Hill, we were on TV again for another program. I noted in my diary that we sang the following songs: "The Old Book and the Old Faith," "Everything Has Been Made Right," "Won't It Be Glory There," "You Must Open the Door," "Shall I Crucify My Savior," and "Let My People Go." I wrote further:

"Harry Abbot of KTVQ-TV is originally from Lebanon. He is very well pleased with our programs, and said if we lived here, there was no doubt but what we could get sponsors.

He said two had already inquired. He gave me the following information of TV personnel he knows. KTTS-TV in Springfield, Pearson Ward, General Manager; KYTV in Springfield, Gordon Wardell, General Manager; and KCMO-TV in Kansas City, Sid Tremble, Program Director."

On December 2, 1953, four days before closing our revival in Oklahoma City, I wrote in my journal:

"I forgot to mention that Jake Yearout from Hobbs, New Mexico called last week, and they want me to come and be their minister, at $90.00 per week plus parsonage. That's quite an offer. I would benefit personally, no doubt, by going there, but I told him I felt obligated to go to Eldon, for a while at least. Well, today I talked to President Ford in his office at Midwest Christian College, and he made another offer – full professorship here at Midwest. It certainly made me feel humble. He wanted me to set up an evangelism department to do research study in that field, and become an authority concerning that subject. I have to admit it is quite a temptation, but I told him I felt constrained to go to Eldon for a while. We talked for thirty minutes concerning problems in evangelism. He wanted to start January first. Just last year I received offers from Atlanta Christian College as well as Ozark, to come and teach. I just don't know what to do. May the Lord's will be done."

In further discussions before leaving Oklahoma City, we made the final decision to cease the full-time "Gospel Messengers" evangelistic ministry. Willis and Lora Harrison went to Wichita, Kansas, where they led the music in a pre-Christmas revival and spent the holidays visiting Lora's folks in that city. We Vernons traveled to our hometown of Lebanon, Missouri, and loved getting back to the farm and visiting our folks. They had moved back to the Homestead after living in town some ten years. On December 19, 1953, I penned this account:

"We are in our new home at 8 Cambridge Drive in Lebanon. We moved in a week ago tonight, a furnished house for $60.00 per month. We really like it. I have been working hard since arriving from Oklahoma City. Bill, B.J., Don and I bought and hauled thirty tons of hay out to the farm. Some of the bales weighed 150 to 175 pounds. Whew! We also castrated and vaccinated the calves, and hauled in and sawed wood. We also made and taped another radio program today with Don singing baritone. While we were at KLWT in Lebanon, we sang a song, 'Bound for the Kingdom' on the 'Birthday Club' program. I am traveling to Eldon each Sunday to preach, getting $40.00 per week before moving there. When that happens, they said they will pay me whatever I want. How we are loved by those wonderful people!"

Homestead USA Is Born

CHAPTER 13

Starting Churches And A Passion For Television

In early 1954, Pat and I moved to Eldon, Missouri, to minister at the 9th Street Christian Church, the congregation which we and our team had started. We stayed with them in a very enjoyable two-year period, leading them in continued growth, a successful building campaign, and expanding youth outreach. I had Joe Ellis, expert in utilizing and expanding the Bayne Driscoll "Decision Day" three-month program of evangelism, come to put it into action, and it succeeded so well. We set a goal of reaching fifty new baptisms and new additions through an intense "home visitation" program led by me and the elders, culminating in a great "Decision Day" service. What a blessing it was during that period, and what a glorious final day as we reached our goal! I'll never forget to my dying day two events, among many, that impacted our church so much. Two of us called one day in the home of an elderly couple out in the country west of Eldon. The gentleman was ravaged with cancer in the last stage and wasn't a Christian. But his mind was keen and open. For the next hour or so, I poured out my heart to him about the beauty of Heaven, the suffering Christ endured to save us from sin and Hell, and the Scriptures that tell us what to do to be saved. With tears in his eyes, in a weak voice he whispered, "I'd like to be baptized." We improvised and made use of a seven-foot cattle trough, brought it into the house, drew warm water to fill the trough, and gently carried him from his bed, setting him in the water. He made his confession, I baptized him, and being raised, it was as though he had the face of an angel! The second event, so uncanny, is indirectly related to the first. We learned that his son-in-law, who had come from St. Louis to help with the farm work, was out in the field at that hour. So we walked out and found him some distance away. He climbed down from the tractor, we told him what had happened, and urged him to also become a Christian. He was cordial, but wanted to get to work and finish before dark, so we didn't tarry. Three days later, this same man, an electrician in St. Louis, had touched a "hot" wire that caused him to be electrocuted and killed instantly! The news of it stunned me and the whole Eldon area. But the urgency of getting right with God and obeying the Gospel gripped the whole community.

While at Eldon, the thought and deep desire to somehow find a way to utilize television burned within my heart. About the Thanksgiving season, I made a journey to KOAM-TV, a powerful station reaching much of Kansas, Missouri, Arkansas, and Oklahoma. I introduced myself to the general manager and program director, showed them pictures of our family and ministry, told them about our musical background and history, and asked if we could possibly come each week to televise our own program. They were very receptive and asked if our quartet could start soon. I tried to conceal my excitement and sheer joy as I, of course, gave an affirmative answer. Lou Martin, the program director, said, "We have a 'live' program coming up in an hour. It's piano and organ music, so if you can stay a while, we'd love to have you sing a couple of songs." Delighted and ecstatic, I replied, "You bet I can!" The musicians showed up, the three of us rehearsed, hit it off real good, and I made my debut there with a Thanksgiving hymn and "White Christmas!" Afterward, I got to a telephone as soon as I could and called Bill, B.J., and Don. They were elated, and we agreed to start our program on December 10, 1954. I still have a picture of me singing on the air that first visit, accompanied by those excellent musicians. Since Bill was preaching at Quapaw, Oklahoma, B.J. at Cherryvale, Kansas, Don at the Washington church near Lebanon, and I at Eldon, Missouri, we met one day each week to rehearse and do our "live" TV show for the next three years, finally going nationwide beginning in 1958. At first, our show, called "The Vernon Brothers," was only fifteen minutes long, sponsored by the TV station. But we quickly built such a large viewing audience that we expanded to a half hour and occasionally included our whole families, our parents, and the Ozark Christian College choir.

About the middle of 1955, I received an offer from the Four-State Area Men's Fellowship in Joplin to serve as their evangelist. By this time, our Vernon Brothers TV program had become so popular that this meant by moving to Joplin I would be much closer, and the Fellowship organization agreed that I could continue with my brothers in that vital, expanding TV ministry. In fact, it would help and enhance the Fellowship's work of evangelism and new church planting. I accepted the offer, though it was hard to leave the wonderful folks and growing ministry at Eldon.

In Joplin, near Ozark Christian College, we found a spacious two-bedroom, full basement house at 606 North Pearl, owned by Brother R.E. Combs of Kansas. His son, who had been living in the house while a student at Ozark, was leaving, so the house was for sale. Brother Combs, a wonderful and generous Christian, sold it to us for $6,500.00 and loaned that amount to us at no interest with payments to him of $65.00 per month. Glory hallelujah! How good of him, and how great and caring our God was to lead us to that ideal and perfect house, our very first owned home for Pat, Becky, Gregg, and me!

We plunged immediately into our first project for the Fellowship, starting a new congregation in a nice vacant building that had housed a lumber yard. It was ideal, with a huge reception room that could accommodate 125 people, plus a half dozen rooms to be used for classes. We soon held a vacation Bible school with both Pat and me, along with others, teaching. We had about forty enrolled, including our two, Becky and Gregg, and our next-door neighbors' kids, Polly and Bobby Klein. They were Jewish, and we learned that their mother had grown up in DeWitt, Arkansas, Pat's hometown. Her father owned a rice mill there and occasionally came to Joplin for a visit. Seeds were planted in that Bible school, and years later we learned that Polly had become a Christian, and she and Becky had a great reunion! I have just now found a picture of kids and adult members in front of that lumber yard building. The caption reads: "This is the group present for services at Westside Christian Church one Sunday soon after the church was established. There are now 46 active members."

In the meantime, we had expanded our weekly television program to thirty minutes, with yours truly giving a conversational message on the Gospel and principles of the New Testament Church. Of course, we now had to pay for the TV time. I wrote in our new TV News: "We are greatly indebted to Ozark Bible College for giving us moral, financial, and promotional support." In our beginning weeks, President Don Earl Boatman was so impressed with our programs, seeing the great potential it represented for the Restoration Movement, that he encouraged the expansion and inclusion of a Gospel message. The college, together with dozens of faithful Christians and churches, undergirded us with prayerful and financial support, and it inspired us tremendously to press on in our quest to go nationwide with our telecast. So in addition to my work with the new congregation, I started giving more time as well to the TV ministry, speaking and promoting this outreach. In a new publication, "Vernon Brothers TV News," is this notation:

"On Monday and Tuesday, October 24 and 25, 1955, Bob Vernon attended the radio-television conference held at the Cincinnati Bible Seminary, Cincinnati, Ohio. The conference was held under the auspices of the National Association of Christian Broadcasters. Ministers and interested persons from ten states attended the meeting. On the morning of the 25th, Bob spoke to the group, representing the Vernon Brothers telecast and was also elected secretary of the Association. In his presentation there, as well as at other meetings, here are excerpts from his challenge: 'Brethren, by conviction, I feel that here is a tremendous mission field. If one does just a little thinking about it, it will stagger his imagination! If television is revolutionizing political campaigns, as I heard a national chairman point out, and is affecting the entire social and economic structure of America and the world, can we not see that in religion as well, a new era of unparalleled success could be ushered in, as far as the restoration of New Testament Christianity is concerned! Through the miracle of television, the preacher is invited into many thousands of homes at the same time to talk about the love of God and the Gospel of Christ and His Church. He is not just a voice or speaker appearing before a vast throng; he is a very real, live, personal guest, coming by invitation into the privacy and seclusion of just one home, as far as the viewer is concerned. As these 'visits' continue week after week, a close attachment is made, and it is not long until lives are deeply affected by the Gospel, which 'is the power of God unto salvation,' as we read in Romans 1:16. Multiply this one home by 500, 1,000, 10,000 or 1,000,000, depending upon how large an area is covered, and you get a true picture. You can see then why I believe the value of television in preaching and dramatizing the Gospel events is almost immeasurable and incomprehensible!'"

That fall, in a great campaign, I had my brothers come and participate with me in a revival at the Westside Christian Church. How thrilling it was to work together again for a whole week. We had four responses the first day. On the third night, I noted in my diary the following:

"139 present, I preached on 'Why the Christian Church is not a Denomination,' our quartet sang 'Settle in the Promised Land' and 'The Old Rugged Cross,' Becky, 4 years old, sang 'For God So Loved the World' and 'The B-I-B-L-E,' Floyd Jones sang 'It Took a Miracle,' his wife Ann played the piano."

We had several more additions during the meeting, and the church continued to flourish throughout the following months, as we bought property and constructed our own building.

But I was consumed more and more with our television plans and activities. On May 3, 1956, during the three days of the Kiamichi Mission Men's Clinic in Oklahoma, I asked a dozen men from different parts of the nation to meet with me, to discuss the actions we Vernon Brothers were taking for the formation of a new ministry we were calling "The Christian Television Mission." From the record of that meeting, I quote:

"After an opening prayer by Don Earl Boatman, Bob Vernon discussed with the group a plan to film a television program, and to launch out in an effort to distribute the telecast for nationwide coverage. The response on the part of all was highly enthusiastic. All the men pledged themselves to promoting the ministry. After the discussion, Delmar Debault dismissed the group with prayer."

A week later, during the North American Christian Convention, on May 10, 1956, I got to speak in a special session about our plans. In my diary that night, I wrote: "A group of men, about 100, met at the Kentucky Hotel to discuss the need for a national TV program. I spoke, and WOW! What a wonderful reception I got after my speech!" I noted that Pearl Willis, Tommy Overton, and James DeForest Murch were appointed as a committee to explore the possibility of starting a national TV program. Of course, nothing came of it. Another group called the "Christian Telefilm Commission," headed mostly by my ministerial friends G.B. Gordon and Gene Carter, organized and sought to get a program off the ground. Esteemed minister Ernest E. Laughlin of the Westside Church of Christ was appointed to contact a professional Christian survey organization as to whether our Independent Christian Church Movement could afford a national TV program. He came back at the next meeting with a report that it was not possible, so that effort ceased to exist. Since we as the Vernon Brothers had a two-year history of television production behind us with pending plans already to go national, plus the faith and will to succeed, we felt more than ever that we had the blessing and approval of God who had cleared the way for us!

To move ahead with our plans and to create more interest, I organized a TV Symposium-Forum, asked the Four-State Area Men's Fellowship group to be present, and invited fellow ministers to come and speak. This important event was held on June 11, 1956, at our Westside Christian Church in Joplin to a packed house. After a couple of opening songs and prayer, a short business session of the Fellowship was held. Then followed six fifteen-minute brief assigned topics. Frank Grubbs thrilled the crowd about the "Success and Growth of the New Woodlawn Christian Church in Wichita, Kansas." Dr. Lester Ford, president of Midwest Christian College in Oklahoma City, spoke on "Why We Should Televise the Plea." Edwin Hayden, professor at Ozark Bible College in Joplin, gave a report on "Religious Television Programs." "The Scope and Success of the Vernon Brothers Telecast" was presented by Don Earl Boatman, president of Ozark Bible College. Chairman C.L. Devore, minister of the First Christian Church of Sapulpa, Oklahoma, discussed "Plans for the Future," giving a report on TV meetings at the Kiamichis and the North American Christian Convention at Louisville, Kentucky. John Greenlee, minister of the Westside Christian Church in Wichita, Kansas, concluded the speaking with a rousing challenge, "What Are We Waiting For?" We four Vernon Brothers were so gratified by the intense interest and encouragement generated at this inspiring and successful meeting. To God be the glory, for His blessing on this helpful symposium!

CHAPTER 14

A National TV Ministry Is Formed

I REALLY BELIEVE the reason we gained favor with God and so many people was because our first love was preaching. All four of us brothers had dedicated ourselves to the preaching of the Gospel. Each one of us, including our youngest brother, Don, who came on later, had held student preaching ministries for at least three years in local churches while in Bible college. And those ministries extended on beyond graduation. Even during our Bible college years, each of us preached in many revivals. Yes, we loved to sing, and God had endowed us with diverse voice ranges, enabling us to sing four-part harmony as a quartet. But singing was always secondary and preparatory to enhance the message of the Gospel. Added to our background experience, while Don completed his Bible college studies at Ozark and preached each weekend, Bill, B.J., and I spent almost three years of preaching in revivals throughout the nation. The miracle is that all four of us brothers married girls whose voice range corresponded with her husband's! God surely must have had something to do with that, don't you think? Sometimes people asked us, "What kind of test did the girls have to pass before you agreed to marry them?" We always assured people by saying, "No test, just the love test!" I must say that our wives added a lot and deserve loads and loads of credit for what success we've had in our work. Their faith, their beauty, their talent, their temperament, and their love – all these qualities made them perfect partners in ministry as we labored for Christ.

Speaking of the importance of preaching, we kept busy in our own ministries, preaching at four separate churches, plus the TV work. I had held a revival at Nowata, Oklahoma, all four of us brothers had preached in great revivals at Sapulpa and Stillwell, Oklahoma, and I had just recently returned from preaching a successful meeting at Rogers, Arkansas -- all this in a very busy period.

Shortly afterward, I resigned from my position with the Four-State Area Men's Fellowship and the Westside Christian Church to devote full time to the television ministry. Christian Television Mission became the official name of our Vernon Brothers organization on June 20, 1956, and on that date, my wife Pat and I opened an office in the basement of our home at 606 North Pearl, Joplin, Missouri. Because we needed to have a board of directors, I, as the executive director, invited six men besides myself to serve in this capacity. Since we had no money to hire a lawyer, I drew up the articles of incorporation, and appeared before the Judge of the Circuit Court in Joplin to obtain our approval. Following is the statement of that document:

"In the Court of Jasper County Missouri at Joplin, in the matter of the application of Christian Television Mission of Joplin, Missouri for pro forma decree of incorporation. To the honorable Judge of the Circuit Court of Jasper County at Joplin: Your petitioners, Charles L. DeVore, 310 E. Oak, Sapulpa, Oklahoma; Walter Goodman, 307 W. 12th, Lamar, Missouri; Ralph Dornette, 402 S. 15th, Muskogee, Oklahoma; Bob J. Vernon, 606 N. Pearl, Joplin, Missouri; Frank Grubbs, 1930 Hillside, Wichita, Kansas; John Greenlee, 1906 W. Douglas, Wichita, Kansas; and Dallas Vernon Jr., Rt. #1, Lebanon, Missouri, the undersigned, represent and state that they, in connection with others have associated themselves together by articles of agreement, in writing, as an association for the purposes set out in the articles of incorporation hereto attached under the name of the Christian Television Mission of Joplin, Missouri. Your petitioners beg to submit herewith articles of agreement in writing, and pray this court that a PRO FORMA DECREE of incorporation may be granted thereon, by this court, constituting them a body corporate and politic by the name Christian Television Mission of Joplin, Missouri in pursuance of the statutes in such case made and provided, namely chapter 352 of the Revised Statutes of Missouri for 1949."

Following is an abbreviated form of the Articles of Agreement also signed by the same men as listed above:

"First: The name of this organization shall be Christian Television Mission, Inc. Second: Its location shall be 606 N. Pearl Street, Joplin, Missouri. Third: Its duration shall be perpetual. Fourth: Every member of the Board of Trustees, and every employ shall be a member of the Christian Church, and must believe without reservation, in the full and final inspiration of the Bible to the extent that it is to him the infallible Word of God, and therefore, the all-sufficient rule of faith and life; in the deity and supreme authority of Christ; obedience to the Gospel; the divinity of the Church and the restoration of its unity on the New Testament basis. Fifth: This organization shall be legally and ecclesiastically independent of the "Disciples of Christ" denomination, and any and all other denominations. Sixth: The objects, purposes, and powers of the organization shall be as follows: To foster and promote New Testament Christianity primarily through the medium of television, and secondarily through the use of other media as might be deemed advisable; to organize churches after the New Testament pattern, which churches shall be known as Christian Churches or Churches of Christ, and whose members shall be known as Christians only and which churches shall be congregational in form of government, and shall have no creed or articles of faith other than those contained in the New Testament, and which churches shall observe the ordinances of baptism and the Lord's Supper, the former by immersion only, and the latter each Lord's Day; to purchase, own, or rent real estate to be used in connection with carrying out the objects of this organization; to receive, hold, and administer gifts; to buy, sell, hold or lease real or personal property and to erect structures on real property; to hold services for Christ; to employ agents, and enter into contracts; to borrow money and incur indebtedness; and to have all powers granted which the laws of the State of Missouri dealing with such corporations and associations provide, and more specifically granted under Chapter 352 of the Missouri Revised Statutes, 1949, as now constituted or hereafter amended or changed."

After an examination of our Application for Incorporation and Articles of Agreement by the court, we received in due time the following acknowledgement that we had submitted:

"... to the Court the Articles of Agreement of said association, together with a petition praying for a pro forma decree thereon, in manner provided by law, and it appearing to the Court that said petition has remained on file in the Clerk's office of this Court for at least three (3) days, since the same was first presented to the Court, and the Court having examined said Articles of Agreement and being duly advised in the premises doth now consider, adjudge and determine that said Articles of Agreement, and the purpose of the association as therein expressed, come properly within the purview of Chapter 352, R. S. Mo., and are not inconsistent with the Constitution of Laws of the United States of America, or of the State of Missouri. Therefore, it is ordered, adjudged and decreed by the Court that the petitioners and their associates named in said Articles of Agreement be and are hereby created a body politic and corporate by and under the corporate name of Christian Television Mission of Joplin, Missouri."

This whole process consumed a good deal of my time, but it was very important from a legal and Biblical standpoint, not only to satisfy the law, but also to signify to people what we believe.

I wrote the following "OPEN LETTER TO THE BRETHREN" on June 20, 1956:

"On July 1, I am launching out to serve full-time in the missionary field of television evangelism. This is by far the greatest step of faith I have ever taken. From the human standpoint, it is foolish for me to sever all ties which supply present living, and to announce my intention of devoting full time to a work for which I have no guaranteed support. I can explain only that I have a strong feeling that I MUST GO AHEAD, and that not to do so would be going against the will of God. If the Restoration Movement ever does have a national TV program, somebody simply must step out in faith, offer a program and plan, rely on God, and say, 'Here it is, Brethren, will you share in it?' In spite of the fact that I honestly do not know where support for us will come from, I am proceeding with the utmost faith and confidence in God, that every need for my family and for the television mission will be supplied. We pray that those of you who have been regularly contributing to the Vernon Brothers' program will continue your gifts, and that many new friends will begin sharing with us in the Christian Television Mission. Address all correspondence and contributions to: Christian Television Mission, Box 707, Joplin, Missouri."

Besides our continuing weekly TV show on KOAM-TV, I had a promotional film made and started showing it locally. From our hometown newspaper of Lebanon, Missouri, appeared the following article:

"Bob Vernon, one of seven outstanding sons of Mr. and Mrs. Dallas Vernon, was in Lebanon recently, directing the production of a sound movie being used by the Vernon Brothers in the interest of their nationwide television program. And incidentally, Lebanon will receive some fine publicity through this medium. The Christian Television Mission, with Bob Vernon as Director, is promoting this project. Shots were taken at the Vernon homestead farm, showing Dallas and Beulah Vernon and crippled son Ward; the Lebanon High School; the sign on Highway 66 of 'Our town – Your town'; Commercial Street; Detroit Tool and Engineering plant, where Bill and Bob worked while in high school, along with older brother J.P., and where Dallas Jr. is now employed; the home and family of Dallas Jr. and Mabel on Bland Road; and various other places, to acquaint the public with the Vernon boys' background. This film was shown at the Washington Church of Christ near Lebanon, where Don Vernon and his wife, Mary Jo, minister, and was received with great interest. A generous offering was given in support of the work. Since that time, it has met with the same success in other places. Bob Vernon is giving his full time in the promotion of this ministry. While the film was being made, some of the equipment was set up in the Dallas Vernon home and a scene was taken, showing the parents reminiscing about the boys. Also some of the scenes in the film were taken in the KOAM-TV studios, where the live telecast is seen weekly, showing all eight of the young people, Bill, Bob, B.J., and Don, and their beautiful respective wives, Joy, Pat, Lodi, and Mary Jo, rehearsing and singing, with Bob bringing a message. Now a pilot 15-minute production is being completed in Joplin this week for promotion of the work, and about 100 men from 20 churches have signified their approval and will assist in publicizing and backing the nationwide efforts. The magazines HORIZONS and CHRISTIAN STANDARD have recently carried stories about the Vernons and their television outreach. The Vernon Brothers and their wives will be in charge of the music, singing, and showing this latest film at the National Christian Education Convention that will meet in Music Hall at Cincinnati, Ohio, August 28-31, 1956."

A terrible and tragic happening occurred shortly after we had finished that new 15-minute film that Mary Jo, Don's wife, had appeared in along with the rest of us. She was instantly killed in an automobile accident while driving alone. When topping a hill, a careless truck driver, without warning, turned right into her car causing a head-on collision. She had been on that gravel road just a few minutes to see her sister Loyce, our first cousin Roger Tribble's wife, to do some laundry. When our brother Don, working at the farm, got the horrifying news, he almost collapsed. The following days, our whole grieving Vernon family huddled together as a mother hen to console our dear loved one, and to help give Mary Jo a loving and fitting memorial service and tribute. I noticed in my diary that Mary Jo, on at least three occasions, had presented a Bible flannelgraph lesson as a segment on recent programs we had telecast on KOAM-TV. They were very effective and well done, and the subjects were the baptism of Jesus, his temptations in the wilderness, and his calling of the twelve disciples.

The news of her untimely death spread quickly across the nation stunning members of the brotherhood, and when we premiered the film at the convention in Cincinnati, as soon as Mary Jo so prominently appeared on the screen, the thousands there seemed deeply moved, with many weeping in sympathy, love, and heartfelt tribute to this devoted young woman of faith. Long and sustained applause filled the hall when the film reached its conclusion. Mary Jo's brief but full and faithful life, together with her tragic death, was used of God to bless our ministry, and to spur intense and widespread interest in, and support of, our efforts to be successful in attaining nationwide television coverage of "our Plea" for Unity and Restoration of the New Testament Church. Yours was a life well lived, Mary Jo, and you fulfilled and lived out the words of Paul in Philippians 1:21, "For to me, to live is Christ and to die is gain" (Phil. 1:21, NASB).

Don moved in with us at our home on North Pearl for the next semester at Ozark Bible College, since he was now a student there. Several months later, he spotted a beautiful brunette standing on the top row of Ozark's choir who was appearing on our TV program. He pulled me aside and asked me if I thought it was too soon to have a date with this gorgeous young woman. I replied, "No, not at all. That's Carol Sue Fielder from Dewey, Oklahoma. She's not only pretty, but very dedicated. Bill, B.J., and I found that out four years ago during our two-week revival at Dewey. It didn't take long to get acquainted with that cute, vivacious teenager who attended every service, and was a winner in the Bible drills we had for the kids!"

So a few nights later, Pat and I escorted Don and Carol on their first date, driving from Joplin to Springfield to see a basketball game. The romance budded, she fit right in as the alto voice in the Vernon Girls quartet, and they were married October 12, 1957.

I continued to write letters, speak at promotional rallies, and raise funds for our newly organized Mission. Also during the last half of 1956, with Pat doing her colorful chalk art drawings in the services and me doing the preaching, we held revivals at Phillipsburg, Missouri, and Washington, Indiana. I failed to mention that when we moved to Joplin, Pat was asked by President Boatman to join the faculty of Ozark in teaching a course in chalk art. She enjoyed it immensely, and her artistry proved to be a real blessing in our meetings, as it was very popular in that era.

Financial support for the Mission was so good that by August of 1956, my twin brother Bill came on board in a full-time way. Response grew, and B.J. and Don joined us in May 1957, resigning from their full-time churches. Now, with the four of us Vernon Brothers together as an evangelistic and TV team, we went "full-force" in rallies, revivals, and church planting. Besides the very successful establishment of a New Testament Church we had completed earlier in Eldon, Missouri, as well as doing the same in Joplin, the four of us preached a two-week revival starting a new congregation in our hometown of Lebanon, Missouri. We also held a great meeting for the congregation at Meadville, Pennsylvania, with our good minister friend, Bob Phillips, and another revival with devoted friend Delmar Debault, minister of the church in Kissimmee, Florida.

On May 1, 1957, I note in my diary that we held our TV board meeting and sang at the Kiamichi annual meeting, then jumped in our cars, making the long and fast trip to Pittsburgh, Pennsylvania, for the North American Christian Convention. We got to speak and sing during some of the sessions, and were very warmly received and applauded. I wrote: "Friday evening after the session, we presented a short concert and rally to a packed house in the huge banquet room. It was very successful, and we were received very enthusiastically." The next evening, Saturday May 4th, I recorded: "The youth banquet was at 5:30. We sang several numbers and I spoke on 'Working Under Christ's Authority,' receiving very warm response. I also spoke during the radio-TV workshop, where we sang several songs, and were applauded for an encore!"

CHAPTER 15

Decision To Film Homestead USA In Hollywood

To SHOW OUR determined commitment to see our TV program expand to the whole nation, we brothers were gone from our homes the entire month of May 1957. We traveled together, not only to the Kiamichis and the North American Christian Convention, as I have pointed out, but also continuing on in film showings and programs in Pennsylvania, Ohio, Indiana, Kentucky, and Illinois, all churches; and at Lincoln Bible Institute and Kentucky Christian College. One of us would speak, then a song by the quartet, followed by another brother's speech, etc., with the fourth brother introducing the film and closing by giving an enthusiastic challenge. That formula worked well, giving the audience a chance to hear each brother's conviction and commitment to the cause.

We had only one day at home before each of us started a promotional tour separately to different sections of the country. From an issue of our *Christian TV News* concerning the tour appears this article:

"The four Vernon Brothers will be going four different directions during the month of June. Bob will be going west through Oklahoma, Texas, New Mexico, Arizona, and into California. B.J. will be traveling north through Missouri, Iowa, Minnesota, Wisconsin, and Illinois. Don will go east through Missouri, Tennessee, Kentucky,

Virginia, and North Carolina. Bill is to go south and southeast through Oklahoma, Texas, Louisiana, and Florida."

Pat accompanied me on this tour, along with our 3-1/2-year-old little boy, Gregg. We left 6-year-old Becky with my parents at their Homestead farm, which thrilled her. Traveling and presenting programs on the way, we arrived in California on Saturday, June 8, 1957. I wrote in my journal that night: "President Kenneth Stewart of Pacific Christian College really went to bat for me to arrange some appearances, for which I am deeply grateful." One of them was at the college, where there were so many compliments after I spoke. In continuing with what I wrote that night was this prayer:

"Oh Father in Heaven, please make my life such that Thou canst bless me and use me to the glory of thy Son and the winning of great numbers to His precious Name. Bless Bill, B.J. and Don as they travel and present the Word. May thy divine Power be strong in the lives of all of us, so that Thou canst truly do 'exceeding abundantly above all that we ask or think.' Give us all courage, boldness, and grace as we present the work. Forgive all of us of our sins, Oh Lord, in Jesus Name, Amen."

Strengthened and encouraged, I spoke and made good contacts in several churches, then spent a few days gaining valuable information about film and TV production. I visited Desilu Studios, getting permission to watch "live" filming of the *I Love Lucy* show using three TV cameras. And quoting from the August issue of our newsletter, describing these contacts, I wrote: "I conferred with Sam Hersh of Family Films, the

Producer of the Lutherans' TV show *This is the Life*; Dick Ross of World Wide Pictures, Producer of the Billy Graham movies; Cliffie Stone Productions, handlers of the *Tennessee Ernie Ford Show* telecast which I witnessed ..." plus producers at ABC and NBC. Continuing the article: "Both World Wide Pictures and Family Films expressed great interest in our project, and the former company offered a proposal – to be under consideration by the Executive Committee of Christian TV Mission." This being completed after such a good but tiring trip, I put Pat and Gregg on a plane to return home. Leaving Southern California, I attended and spoke at a Christian youth camp in Central California, then drove on, rejoicing, and enjoying appearances at Ceres, Napa, and wonderful hospitality and reception at San Jose Bible College. I finally concluded this journey of faith, speaking at several churches in Oregon, plus an appearance at Puget Sound Bible College in Washington.

Returning home, we brothers and our board of advisors met, and, after much soul-searching, prayer, and consultation, decided to take a big "leap of faith" and accept World Wide Pictures' proposal to do our filming in Hollywood. Dick Ross, the producer, came to Joplin to meet with us and our board to go over plans. This meant going from $136.00 per program on KOAM-TV to $1,000.00 per film that we had originally planned for in going nationwide, to "first-class" productions at thousands of dollars per film!! Were we out of our minds? No, we just had to proceed on faith and do this right so TV stations would accept our product, but it was an exceedingly difficult decision to make!

I must admit, I waivered at times wondering if we really could pull off this giant step. One time, I had a long phone conversation with Dick Ross, almost calling everything off, but he assured me that he would work with us on the matter of financing the project.

And instead of trying to do all thirteen of the necessary films in the series, we would only do the first film of *Homestead USA*. We brothers would premiere it all over the country, raising funds, then make two more trips to Hollywood to complete the series. That was the plan we would pursue, beginning in February 1958.

The rest of the year 1957, we continued our rallies, fund raising, and special events. These included the National Christian Education Convention in Springfield, Illinois, the Milligan College Conference, a youth round-up in Lincoln, Illinois, an area-wide rally hosted by the East Tulsa Christian Church, the Southwest Christian Camp at Clovis, New Mexico, a two-week revival at the Westside Christian Church in Wichita, Kansas, and the Alumni Convention of Atlanta Christian College. Between all the appearances, we met often with our board members who were so supportive. We prepared scripts, rehearsed music with our wives, put out the TV News, wrote letters, and worked on budgets. And then on November 16th, Pat and I joyously welcomed the birth of our third child, Karen Elizabeth Vernon!

On a very cold, zero-temperature night, Dick Ross and Ralph Carmichael, our music arranger-director, flew in for a conference with us. That evening of December 2, 1957, at the Connor Hotel in Joplin, was a very momentous one. It saw us working far into the night, exploring many ideas for a film title and format, explaining our New Testament beliefs, choosing the theme, the songs, and the sermonic message, and familiarizing our producer and musical director with our family background in growing up on our beloved Homestead. The mention of that word "homestead" sparked an immediate response from our producer. "That's it!" he exclaimed. "You're a real family, you grew up on the Vernon Homestead and you love the Lord and want to share the Gospel with the whole world!" Excitement filled the air as we all agreed and explored this idea and this theme of the "Christian Home," using our whole family on the film, including our parents, our children, and featuring us four brothers and our wives. Mulling it all over, somebody said, "Since you want the telecast to cover the country, why not add 'USA' to the title and call the program *Homestead USA*?" No sooner than those words had been uttered, the rest of us in the room, almost in unison, shouted out, 'WOW!! YES, YES, YES!'" Now we were getting somewhere. Everything fell easily into place after that. All the details of our planning session were worked out, including the dates we would leave for the West Coast to do the filming. We ended the meeting about 1:00 a.m. with a season of prayer, praising God for blessing us with His guidance and inspiration in all the decisions we had reached.

We continued to rehearse and work on our filming plans, with a myriad of details to take care of since it would involve our parents and our families. The four of us brothers held a revival during this time with minister Claude Lorts and his congregation at Hugoton, Kansas. January of 1958 was a very busy period of continued preparation.

On January 27, I received the following telegram from Dick Ross in California:

"RECOMMEND HOMESTEAD INTRODUCTORY THEME FOR PILOT. SUGGEST PROGRESSION FROM DON'S WEDDING PICTURE TREATMENT TO STAGES OF FAMILY RELATIONSHIP FROM CHILDREN TO OLD AGE USING FAMILY PER-SONALITIES. BIBLICAL FLASHBACKS COULD PARALLEL EACH OF THE MAIN STAGES CLIMAX-ING WITH MESSAGE BY BOB ON 'THE HOME.' SUGGEST TUNES WE ALREADY CHOSE. SELECT PASTEL WARDROBES FOR GIRLS AVOIDING

WHITE. MEN BRING LIGHT COLORED SHIRTS AND AVOID BLACK SUITS. WILL DRAFT SCRIPT BETWEEN FEBRUARY FIFTH AND TENTH. COR-DIALLY, DICK ROSS WORLDWIDE PICTURES."

I replied quickly with the following telegram:

"PROCEED WITH HOMESTEAD THEME. SOME OF US WILL ARRIVE FEBRUARY SIXTH, REMAINDER ON ELEVENTH. GIRLS WORKING ON 'CLEANSE ME' AND 'LORD I WANT TO BE A CHRISTIAN.' OCTET REHEARSING 'BLESS THIS HOUSE.' MALE QUARTET SONGS AS SELECTED. AM WONDERING WHAT BIBLICAL FLASHBACKS YOU HAD IN MIND. STORY OF A CONVERSION AND BAPTISM IN ACTS EIGHT COULD BE DRAMATIZED. CONVERSION TO CHRIST IS PREREQUISITE TO HAVING A CHRISTIAN HOME."

CHAPTER 16

California Here We Come!
Filming At Universal Studios

ON FEBRUARY 6, 1958, B.J. and I, together with our families, boarded a plane for California to find housing and make last minute preparations for filming *Homestead USA*. Through a realty company, we were fortunate to locate and rent a huge residence that would nicely accommodate all four families, our parents, and the caretaker of our children. It would be available for the whole month we needed it, beginning on the 11th, the arrival date of Bill and Don, their families, the children's caretaker, and our parents. For the five days before that, we were able to stay with church friends. When the others arrived, we jumped into our two rental cars, picked up the keys to our new rental home, drove there, and moved in. It was perfect, with a nice and spacious gated yard the children loved. We slept well that night, had a good early breakfast, and were preparing to go to the studio. Well, wouldn't you know! We got a call from the realty lady, stating that the next-door neighbor had complained about our large entourage and had telephoned the owners of the house in Europe, who demanded that we immediately vacate the place! Oh my! What to do? We had legitimately signed the lease, paid the money, and moved in. Could we fight this terrible demand? Legally, yes. But it would take time and money. Besides, we were on a strict and tight schedule for rehearsals for filming, as well as appearances we were to make in the Los Angeles area. So reluctantly, we packed up and drove to the realtor to get our refund, then on to World Wide Pictures in the San Fernando Valley. We all agreed, "God will provide." Sure enough, when we got to the studio and were greeted warmly, Ann Thompson, the secretary to Dick Ross, had an answer to our housing problem. Since her folks were gone from their home in Burbank for a couple months, she volunteered their place for us to move into. It had two bedrooms, a door to a large, converted garage, an enclosed back porch, a big living room, two bathrooms, and a nice kitchen. It was quite a bit smaller than the mansion we had vacated, but we "made do" and were very comfortable.

We spent the first thirteen days rehearsing and recording music, working on the script, getting waivers for ourselves and the children from unions, and making some personal appearances in the area. These included programs at the Bell Gardens Church of Christ, South Gate Church of Christ, Victory Center Church of Christ, First Christian Church of Inglewood, a one-week revival at the South Broadway Church of Christ, an area-wide youth rally at the University Christian Church, and speaking and singing in chapel services at Pacific Bible Seminary. You can see how busy we were!

On February 24 and 25, 1958, we found ourselves unbelievably treated as film stars by the crew of some fifty movie technicians on the historic *Phantom of the Opera* sound stage at Universal Studios! Wow! What a dream come true for four Missouri farm boys who had dedicated their lives to the Lord. We almost had to pinch ourselves that it was real! Just before starting the filming early that first morning, I asked for quiet on the set, introduced ourselves to the crew, thanked them for their valuable part in the production of the film, and requested everyone to join me as I prayed for the Lord's blessing on our efforts together. I still have a picture of that very moving and spiritual moment.

As I am sure you know, movie-making calls for each segment of the film to be shot separately, usually requiring one, two, or more "takes." It is a tedious and painstaking but necessary process. But it is a fool-proof and effective procedure used by all studios, and when edited carefully with all the scenes composed into a unit, the result is a finished, first-class product of the highest order. This is what we brothers and our board of advisors authorized and needed for our TV series, and put more bluntly, the television stations required it. This is why it would take two days to do this first professional and deeply spiritual film.

My twin brother, Bill, did a superb job in hosting the show, introducing Mother and Dad and all four of our families, with the camera first on him, and then slowly panning family members. The next scene shows a bit of banter between us brothers, followed by our singing "Mansion Over the Hilltop." Next shows our pretty wives talking while setting the table, interspersed with Mother in the kitchen at the oven roasting a chicken, as the girls sing "Cleanse Me Oh God." Following that is a tender scene of Mother and Dad turning pages of a photo album, with camera close-ups of Don and Carol's recent wedding and ancient pictures of our parents' "horse and buggy" courting days as they reminisced about that time, and later showing photos of us boys as we grew and eventually dedicated our lives to the Lord's service. Next were exterior scenes of some of our small children and others having fun out in the barnyard, followed by B.J.'s solo with the kids on his lap and huddled all around him. With his deep bass resounding, he sang "Down Deep in the Sea." After this, Bill comes on camera, inviting the viewers to join our extended Vernon family in a time of inspiration and devotion. Don gets up and goes to a lectern on which rests the big family Bible. He reads from Ephesians, the third chapter, verses fourteen through twenty-one. Then I, Bob, seated and relaxed with all the loving family members, begin a conversational ten-minute devotional on the importance of having a "Christian Home." I started out by saying that some folks have a plaque hanging on a wall in their home that reads, "Christ is the Head of this house, the unseen guest at every meal, and the silent listener to every conversation." We didn't have that plaque as we were growing up. "But we had something much better, Mom and Dad," I went on. "We had you!" I lavished praise on them for being such loving parents to us seven sons, teaching us to revere God and love His Word. I elaborated some on the Scripture that Don had read and said that every parent should live out, as our folks did, this prayer of Paul:

> "For this cause I bow my knees unto the Father, from whom every family in heaven and on earth is named, that he would grant you, according to the riches of his glory, that ye may be strengthened with power through his Spirit in the inward man; that Christ may dwell in your hearts through faith; to the end that ye, being rooted and grounded in love, may be strong to apprehend with all the saints what is the breadth and length and height and depth, and to know the love of Christ which passeth knowledge, that ye may be filled unto all the fulness of God" (Ephesians 3:14-19, ASV).

I also quoted the Scripture in Ephesians 6:1-3 (NASB): "Children, obey your parents in the Lord, for this is right. HONOR YOUR FATHER AND MOTHER (which is the first commandment with a promise), SO THAT IT MAY BE WELL WITH YOU, AND THAT YOU MAY LIVE LONG ON THE EARTH." I pointed out that we boys certainly didn't live up to our folks' or the Bible's teachings all the time, and that we had our shortcomings and sins. One by one, we all became convicted of our need for the Savior and His great love in dying for our sins and being resurrected from the grave, to give us what neither our parents nor we ourselves could give, that is, forgiveness of sins, newness of life, and a home in Heaven when we die! So in faith and repentance, each of us confessed Christ as the Son of God and were buried with Him in baptism and raised out of the water in a new beginning. The secret of happiness is truly found in the Bible. I quoted Whittier's profound poem, "The Book Our Mothers Read," when he penned this:

We search the world for truth; we cull the good, the pure, the beautiful,
From graven stone and written scroll, from all old flower-fields of the soul;
And, weary seekers of the best, we come back laden from the quest,
To find that all the sages said is in the Book our mothers read.

I then said, "I like the motto of our undenominational Church Movement that says, 'No creed but Christ, no book but the Bible, no name but the divine.' Sometimes we say, 'We are Christians only,' meaning we don't wear any distinctive, denominational name. In seeking to promote love and harmony in the whole world, and especially in Christendom, and doing it on the basis of Biblical teaching and Christ's fervent prayer for unity, we should all abide by the slogan, 'In faith, unity; in opinions, liberty; and in all things, charity!'" Nearing the end of sharing my devotional thoughts with the family, as well as with the TV viewers when it would be telecast, I quoted the pertinent and moving words of Edgar A. Guest's poem, "I'd Rather See A Sermon":

> I'd rather see a sermon than hear one any day,
> I'd rather one would walk with me than merely tell the way.
> The eye's a better pupil and more willing than the ear,
> Fine counsel is confusing, but example's always clear,
> The best of all the Christians are the ones who live their creed,
> And to see good put in action is this world's greatest need.
>
> I soon can learn to do it if you'll let me see it done,
> I can watch your hands in action, but your tongue too fast may run.
> The lectures you deliver may be wise and true,
> But I'd rather get my lessons by observing what you do.
> I may not understand the high advice you give,
> But there's no misunderstanding how you act and how you live.

Finally, I spoke these words: "In closing, let me say then, it's not enough to have a plaque that reads, 'Christ is the head of this house, the unseen guest at every meal, and the silent listener to every conversation.' It must be a reality in our homes and in our lives."

I had spoken from my heart there on the set without notes or a teleprompter, doing the whole scene in one "take." I was stunned and deeply moved when the entire crew stood as one, applauding long and wildly at what I had accomplished. I guess they weren't used to seeing actors do such a long scene in one "take." But I wasn't acting. To me, this was real. In my mind, I was speaking the saving Gospel to untold viewers who would later see and hear this telecasted message. Of course, I felt pleased, humbled, and relieved, but I had nothing to glory in. My applause was and is to my God!

The next scene after mine shows our quartet together with our wives singing Ralph Carmichael's great arrangement of "Home Sweet Home," after which Bill as the host thanks the audience for viewing and bids them goodbye 'til next week's program. The closing scene catches our four families departing from our visit to the Homestead, as the theme song "Homestead USA" is played, a family booklet is offered, and the credits appear.

It had been a very hectic but successful time of planning, rehearsing, and finally filming these two momentous days of February 24th and 25th in the year of our Lord, 1958. To God be the glory!

CHAPTER 17

Gratitude, Hometown Premiere, A Deep Heartache

IN WRITING THIS book and looking back on what had been accomplished in that first year and a half since the inception of our TV Mission, I am simply amazed at how God blessed us! But we had worked hard and traveled thousands of miles in promotional rallies, fund raising, and evangelizing. In scrutinizing our certified public accountant's audit for that period, I find that we had total receipts of $94,095.53!! And we had advanced from very inexpensive local production and programming to just having completed a first-class, professionally produced, color film with the best movie cameramen and technical crew at the world-famed Universal International Studios in Hollywood! No wonder we lavished praise on our Heavenly Father and His only begotten Son, our Savior and Lord! But I want to give credit to our dear parents; to my dedicated brothers Bill, B.J., and Don; to my darling wife Pat, and the other three wives, Joy, Lodi, and Carol, for their standing with us and keeping the home fires burning while we were on the road so much; to my oldest brother J.P., with whom I first sang on the radio as a kid, who mentored me in New Testament doctrine as a teenager, and who taught me to play chords on the piano; to Dallas Jr., the brother who was always the great bud and leader of us four younger ones, and who gave of his time and money in supporting us, serving on the very first executive board of our TV Mission; and finally, to the dearest, most kind, and best Vernon brother of all, our cerebral palsied brother, Ward, our greatest inspiration.

But I also must give credit to all our board members and fellow ministers across the country who helped us launch this endeavor and gave us their backing. The first one I need to mention is Charles L. "Chuck" Devore, our chairman. Right from the beginning he wrote, "The four Vernon Brothers do a magnificent job in blending their lives and voices to present the music and messages on film, for the cause of the Restoration Movement. It is tops in every way." John Greenlee wrote the following in a letter to the Brethren:

"During my term of service on the executive board of Christian TV Mission and in working with the Vernon Brothers, one thing has become increasingly obvious – television costs money! The tragedy is that our people have not yet caught the vision. The producers of the new film in Hollywood rate the ability of the brothers and the potential of the listening audience of the show extremely high. Now we have before us the opportunity to put this top program on a national network basis. Are you willing to give sacrificially to do it?"

Harold Davis, then minister of the historic First Christian Church of Canton, Ohio, said, "I am one hundred percent behind you in this and urge everyone else to have a similar faith in this great undertaking for God." Following his ministry there, Richard Crabtree encouraged us greatly and we held two different revival campaigns there. Ernest E. Laughlin wrote, "I believe Christian Television Mission offers the greatest opportunity to spread the Gospel of Christ in our time, and I urge everyone to do his share." Neil Kuns said, "The Maplewood Church is solidly behind the

Christian Television Mission. I regard it an honor to be associated with the campaign." Myron Taylor, who ministered at Toledo, Ohio, Mays, Indiana, and later at the Westwood Hills Christian Church in Los Angeles where he had the eight of us present a program, gave this statement, "We should unite in order that Christian Television may be a mighty force for New Testament Christianity." Russell Martin, famous across the nation for his ministry in building a great church in Miami, Oklahoma, wrote this:

"Our Christian people throughout the nation have evidenced a very tremendous interest in a weekly television program sponsored by New Testament churches. I shall never forget the huge crowd remaining until 10:00 p.m. at the Portland, Oregon North American Christian Convention, in order to see an after session showing of HOMESTEAD U.S.A.! It was quite a testimony to the real interest our people have in the presentation of the Gospel of Jesus Christ via television. We have in the Vernon Brothers and their wives perhaps the most unique combination of talents within one family to be found anywhere in the country. Best of all, they have the drive, determination, and devotion to carry on this magnificent ministry in the Name of Christ as our people and churches provide the financial backing."

Just a personal note here of remembrance and appreciation to Brother Martin for all these kind words, and the fact that he had us sing several times at his Sunday night services, then on his radio sports show, way back when we were in Bible college.

Right from our beginning, Don Earl Boatman, president of Ozark Christian College, our alma mater, befriended and encouraged us constantly. Even before we were able to produce our first *Homestead USA* film, when we were traveling all over the country holding conferences and rallies, so many ministers and churches came to our aid. On Saturday, May 18, 1957, I wrote in my journal, "At noon we had a very successful luncheon-conference at the Broadway Christian Church in Lexington, Kentucky, with 22 men present. The spirit was excellent! All seemed to be very optimistic." Ard Hoven, famous minister of the church and speaker on *The Christian's Hour* radio program said, "I'm sorry I have to leave shortly, but before I do, I want to say that I am heartily in favor of this ministry. You fellows make a fine, creditable presentation. I wish you success in your conferences across the nation, and this may well be the one thing on which our Brethren will unite." This meeting and the spirit manifested there was typical of the dozens we held during the whole year of 1957. And we got endorsements and expressions of support from all the college presidents where we appeared. One such president, Bill Jessup of San Jose Bible College, wrote us this note of appreciation after seeing one of our telecasts on KGO-TV in San Francisco:

"Last Sunday was the first opportunity that I had to see your program over KGO-TV. It was such a soul-stirring program! My wife and I thrilled as we realized the potential power of such programs. This is something that will grow and bear fruit for years to come. Our prayers are with you."

Among our other benefactors who gave generously of their time and money were Leroy Trulock; Alex Grossnickel; Richard Becker; Floyd Collins; and especially, Mildred Welshimer Phillips of the B.D. Phillips Trust Foundation. We had met her years before at the basketball game where Bill, B.J., and I on the Ozark team defeated Milligan College. She was the dean of women at that time and never forgot us or that occasion!

Though we had reached the successful milestone of producing our first *Homestead USA* episode, we now faced the very hard task of raising funds to produce twelve more for the series of thirteen that TV stations required! It seemed like an impossible undertaking, and from a human standpoint, it was. Only faith, hope, and long months of hard work ahead could make it happen. We plunged into premiering this one introductory film all over the country in individual church showings, with special production offerings being taken.

Our very first premiere was a resounding success in our hometown of Lebanon, Missouri, at the high school field house with 1,000 people present. The *Lebanon Daily News* described the celebrated event in a front-page article on May 8, 1958:

"The premiere showing of 'Homestead U.S.A.' at the Lebanon High School Field House last Saturday was seen and enjoyed by more than 1000 residents of Lebanon and the surrounding territory. The Vernons, including 'The Vernon Brothers,' Bill, Bob, B.J. and Don, together with their wives and Mr. and Mrs. Dallas Vernon, Sr., were introduced by Dr. Frank Heagerty, Superintendent of Schools, who spoke of the interest the Lebanon Schools have always had in the Vernons. Mayor J.C. Benage welcomed the crowd in his usual gracious way, expressing his pleasure that Lebanon was chosen for the first premiere showing. Mrs. Vernon in a few brief remarks previous to reading a speech she wrote about the 'History of the Vernon Homestead,' spoke of the part the Lebanon School had in the training of her sons, six of the seven having graduated here, and the palsied son, Ward, with limited learning ability, having attended the local country school in the Blackfoot community, near their Homestead home."

Before continuing with that article in the Lebanon paper, I think it would be interesting to you, the reader, for me to include in full that good and pertinent background speech Mother gave that night, so here it is:

"The cry 'Westward Ho!' echoed through the hills of Kentucky and Tennessee during the early part of the 1800's, and a young giant of a man, Obadiah Vernon, his wife, Sarah, called Sally, with their young son, Josiah, and Sally's mother, Patsy, who was a widow, joined the wagon train leaving Tennessee for Missouri in 1844. There were other of the Vernons but our story concerns only Obadiah and his progeny. They journeyed over hills and vales to a place about 50 miles north of Springfield, Missouri. A small town called Lebanon had sprung up on the well-traveled road between St. Louis and Springfield, known as the 'Old Wire Road,' now cross-country Highway 66, and it was in this area that Obadiah pitched his tent. He must have chosen the high plateau with a creek and some hollow land because it reminded him of his native Tennessee. The Blackfoot Indians had roamed this particular area in Southwest Missouri, and the settlement was called 'Blackfoot.' A 'dry' cave and 'wet' one are nearby and are filled with ashes from Indian camp fires. Also Indian 'arrow heads' are still found in plowed fields. The wooded hills and the plentiful water supply made it an ideal place for the Indian to pursue his natural habitat, with fowl and game all over.

"Obadiah Vernon built a log cabin in which to house his family and went to work to clear some land. In 1857 he was given a patent to 160 acres of land under the Homestead Act signed by President James Buchanan, and two years later he patented another 80 acres further south called 'Horn Hollow.' By this time, seven more children had been added to the family circle. But hard work, death and disease took their toll among the early pioneers, and in the year 1860 at the age of 39, the valiant young father was claimed by death. Young Sally was left with eight children to fend for herself in feeding and clothing her brood. Her mother, Patsy, had by this time married Col. Miles Vernon, who with his Vernon clan had come to Missouri in the same wagon train and settled north of Lebanon.

"The second eldest son of Obadiah, James Polk Vernon, was 13 at the time of his father's death, and he loved the Homestead and had boyhood dreams of someday owning it. But as a young man, our country was in the throes of the Civil War and Missouri being a border state, was full of 'bush-whackers.' Young Jim was tall and lanky and his looks belied his age. He had to hide out to escape them. At one time his mother pried a board from the floor and hid him under there until they were gone. His brother, Joe, was already serving with the Union Army, so in desperation, and to escape the 'bush-whackers,' he at the age of 16 (though his discharge shows his enlistment age as 17), enlisted and was assigned to patrol duty with the Cavalry. They patrolled the old 'Wire Road' over which supplies were moved from St. Louis to Springfield, and their patrol duty was carried out on foot and horseback. After the war he returned to the Homestead to help his mother with the young children and the farm work. Later, one by one, he 'bought out' his brothers and sisters and became owner of the Homestead, although his mother continued to live there until her death in 1901. After her death,

James, now married and with children, moved his family from his place in 'Horn Hollow' to the Homestead, and in 1908 replaced the log cabin, which had been added to with a big room and breeze-way, with a large two-storied, six-room plus hallway, farm house. But James was more than a farmer. He owned and operated a threshing machine in the summer and fall, and a saw mill during the winter. Both were lucrative businesses as there was much grain grown and the native forests provided the trees for lumber. He was a part of the transition period from oxen to power machinery. His four-yoke of oxen were a part of his early threshing equipment. These were replaced later with a modern steam engine. These old oxen yokes are treasured relics of the Vernons, along with the old log granary which still stands proudly in the corner of the yard, by an old cedar tree set out years and years ago by young Jim, a monument to the early pioneers.

"James Polk Vernon was the father of three sons and three daughters, and one of these sons, Dallas, had the same burning ambition that possessed his father – the desire to own the old Homestead. After a period of working on the railroad as a telegrapher, he settled down to farming and teaching school, and in 1918 he persuaded a young teacher, Beulah Ida Tribble, that the Vernon Homestead would be an ideal place to make a home and rear a family. And what a family! Seven boys to whoop and holler and go galloping over the pasture on their ponies – 'Hi yo Silver' echoing loud and wild over the country-side! After our first three boys, J.P., Ward, and Dallas Jr. were born, came these four youngest sons who are being welcomed and honored in the High School from which they graduated by their home-town friends, citizens, and Lebanon area neighbors. We are indebted to this outstanding school, and prior to the training they received here, let me say that an acre from the Homestead was given, furnishing the ground for the two-room Blackfoot school – a stone's throw away – where all our boys attended elementary school. And lumber from the tall trees in the 40-acre 'Sink Woods' of the Homestead built the Church House where they worshipped as youngsters, as well as providing the building material for the Homestead home in which they were loved and cherished! What greater heritage could one ask for? Ladies and gentlemen, we now present to you four of these young men raised on our Homestead, Bill, Bob, B.J., and Don, nationally known as the Vernon Brothers of 'Homestead U.S.A.'"

After Mother's inspiring background speech and introduction of us brothers, the Lebanon newspaper continues the article's description of the evening's celebrated film event, as follows:

"Bill Vernon, as Master of Ceremonies, presented the speakers and members of the Vernon family who were present, and B.J. introduced the film. Following the showing, Bob Vernon, Bill's twin, spoke on 'The Challenge of Television' and outlined the work of Christian Television Mission, Inc., and the future plans. Don gave the closing remarks and Roger Tribble, their cousin well known in these parts, pronounced the benediction. The film, which is the first of a series of 13, will be shown in 100 places over the United States by the Vernon Brothers during the next month, and production of the remaining 12 programs will be in July and August, and released for Nation Wide Telecasting in the fall. Those who were present for the premiere showing of the first film predict that the entire series of films will enjoy a great success across the Nation and will be a valuable contribution to Christian education."

But unknown to the receptive audience of that successful and celebrated evening, my darling wife and I disguised a deep heartache inside our souls that had come crashing down on us just two weeks prior. There was a gathering of our four families at Bill and Joy's home where we were rehearsing, enjoying a meal, and welcoming an old Drury College classmate from ten years back in his visit from Connecticut. He was a Jewish friend from those days that we hadn't seen in a long time, named Bernard Bleich. He was holding our beautiful 6-month old baby, Karen Elizabeth, adoring her. But suddenly he said, "Bob, I hate to say this, but I'm afraid Karen isn't able to move her arms and legs like I think she should." I was inclined to think it was just because of her young age. But the next day I drove Pat and the baby to our pediatrician to get her checked out, and because of pressing and urgent matters relating to our premiere scheduling, I dropped them off and hurried to our office. At my desk for only a few minutes, the telephone rang and the call was for me. It was the doctor on the line, and she softly said, "Mr. Vernon, I need you to come to the office, please, as soon as you can." Very alarmed and almost under my breath, I replied, "I'll be right there." As I opened the door to walk the three blocks to her office, the sun was shining brightly on that beautiful spring day; but to me, feeling limp as I hurried along, it was the blackest of any midnights. When I arrived, there was Dr. Kiehl sweetly holding our little one, and Pat weeping softly. Slowly and with deep sympathy, as I held my darling wife, the good doctor started explaining to us what was our worst fear, that there was something deficient and terribly lacking in the baby's development of muscle strength. As she went on carefully discussing her observation and analysis of such cases, she said:

"My preliminary judgment and diagnosis is that Karen has a very rare disease called 'Amyatonia Congenita,' which means that she has a deficiency of muscle tone. But I'm making an appointment, if it's all right with you, to go to the University of Kansas Medical Center in Kansas City for three days of thorough tests by a team of the best physicians and specialists in this field."

Early the very next day, we left Joplin at 4:30 in the morning because we had a first appointment at the Medical Center in Kansas City at 10:30. After checking in at a nearby motel for our three-day stay, we went for our introductory consultation and Karen's admittance to the hospital. Over the next scheduled 72 hours, she underwent every kind of neurological, physical, and experimental examination known to medical science at that time. We saw our baby and the specialists every day to be briefed about the tests and what progress they were making. At the conclusion of all the extensive exams, the kindly doctor in charge ushered us into his office, and in a soft-spoken but clear voice, explained the nature of the disease and why it was incurable. Like a caring father, it was as if Pat and I were his children, as he cautioned and advised us not to seek promising or false cures. It would drain us emotionally and financially. He said:

"Your baby is bright intellectually and functions well with her involuntary muscles, but not the voluntary ones. The great danger for ones with this malady is pneumonia, and life expectancy is two years. Your pediatrician was correct, the diagnosis is Amyatonia Congenita."

I told the doctor about our family's filming activities, including our children, and wondered if we should halt our plans for returning to California, asking if our baby could stand the trip. Emphatically he replied, "Don't change your plans! Try to live a normal life with your other two children and your baby. She appears happy, she laughs, she responds. Whatever happens to her can happen anywhere." Deeply saddened that nothing could really be done for our baby, and grateful for the sound counsel we had received from the doctor, we thanked him profusely and left for home.

The next day, our four families huddled together in deep prayer and supplication, kneeling and asking our Heavenly Father and our Savior, the Great Physician, to intervene in Karen's behalf. We carried out the instructions written in James 5:14 and 15. But above all, though we had no doubt whatsoever that God could provide a miracle, we trusted Him completely to bless and carry out His perfect will for our child. Thousands upon thousands of people, as soon as the news got out, were lifting Karen up to the Throne of Grace. Knowing that Pat needed me at her side during this period of grief and trial, my brothers relieved me of going out that month on the premieres, so they and my parents took over all the full schedule, showing the film and raising needed funds for the next five productions. Dad and Mother, at the ages of 68 and 67, became missionaries, speaking in Illinois, Ohio, Indiana, Tennessee, Kentucky, Pennsylvania, Virginia, and West Virginia! While the premieres were being held in May and June of 1958, I attended to duties in the Mission office as well as in my study at home, preparing for the next set of productions.

CHAPTER 18

More Rehearsal For Films, More Tears

JULY WAS SPENT with us brothers in premieres, in rehearsing music, and preparing scripts and messages. It was a very busy time. In addition, I asked for our executive committee to meet, which we did at the Mickey Mantle Motel on July 24, 1958. Here are some excerpts from that meeting:

"Meeting called to order by Chairman C.L. DeVore. Frank Grubbs led in the opening prayer. Those present were the Vernon Brothers, John Greenlee, Frank Grubbs, Floyd Collins, Glenn Wheeler, Lester Pifer, C.L. DeVore, Bob Scott, and Ragon Flannery ... Bob gave a report of present standing on finances and prospective filming. He states the possibility of doing the films for $8,500.00 each. Bob mentioned a suggestion by Walter Bennett, our distribution agent, who distributes all the Billy Graham telecasts, that we produce only five more films now, besides the pilot film we already have, making a total of six to begin national televising in October ... Motion made by Lester Pifer that the Vernon Brothers have the 'go ahead' to make five new films in Hollywood, then seven more in September as finances are raised. Second by Floyd Collins. Carried unanimously ... Roy Blackmore and Olin Hay were added as members of the Executive Committee, after which the meeting was adjourned."

All our families went to California late in July, though weary, and were there for five weeks rehearsing and again filming at Universal International Studios under the direction of Dick Ross. This time, to make our living conditions more suitable and easier on the families for such an extended period, we stayed in apartments. God had blessed us in the premieres greatly, and we all, kneeling in fervent prayer every day, praised Him in providing generously for all our needs. But while filming, a terrible tragedy and trial swept us up in deep sorrow. Our baby Karen became very ill and had to be hospitalized. Pat and I had to do our scenes as scheduled during the day, then rush over to the hospital across town to be with our baby two or three hours every night. Our God, our family, and the whole film crew at the studio gave us support and incredible strength during this trying time. We all successfully completed the five films, and everyone took flights back to Missouri, for by now school was starting. That is, everyone but me. Karen had improved some but was still very ill in the hospital, so I stayed to be with her. Not being able to cough, mucous had filled her lungs and would collect in her mouth and nasal passages, making it hard to breathe. She was enclosed in her bed by an oxygen 'tent,' had all kinds of tubes and an IV line inserted in her little body, and had to be suctioned often. Still, she had periods of relief where she would smile, and those beautiful blue eyes would sparkle! On one such occasion, in my journal I wrote:

"I started singing lullabies to the baby, and reached into the tent and stroked her little hand again and again. She seemed to be in complete ease by this time. It was so good to see her breathing normally and not having to frantically gasp for air. As I continued softly singing to her, she soon was lulled to sleep. Before long, a particular melody that I thought up came out of my heart and lips. With tears in my eyes, the melody I was singing to my little 'baby boo' took on the following words:

"My little baby, my little baby boo,
You are an angel, with eyes so twinkling blue.
You are so weak and tired, you've suffered so,
But on your face there stays a sweet and heavenly glow.

"I do not understand, and deep pain fills my heart,
To hear that you must go and from this world depart.
But I rejoice to know my Lord will keep you in His love,
For it's to such as you, belongs that land above.

"My little baby, my little baby boo,
You've taught me lessons, you've helped me through and through.
A better person, I'll always be,
Because God let you come and dwell awhile with me.

"Oh how grieved and pierced my heart feels to know how many times Karen has struggled to stave off the 'grim reaper!' Oh how she wills to live! May my insistence in keeping my spirit and soul alive be as great as Karen's strong desire to keep her body alive!"

In the file Pat and I have kept about Karen, I found this letter I had written to my wife from the apartment at 6633 Elmer Avenue in North Hollywood on September 10, 1958, as follows:

"Darling Pat, it was so good to talk with you again on the phone tonight. I do miss you terribly … It is 3:15 a.m. I am getting a lot done tonight, and am meditating and praying. We have so many crucial items at hand that there truly needs to be a lot of deep, fervent prayer, more than just a few passing words. I definitely feel that God is answering my agonizing prayers. Oh, I do need you so much to help me, and I do love you, Pat darling. And I love our children. When I realize that one of them is in grave danger, I hurt all inside, as I know you do. If only we tell God these things, He is willing to share with us in our need, and supply more than enough power for any situation. I will be so glad to see you again and hold you so tight in my arms, and feel the warmth of your response to my outpourings of love. Darling, I love you, I love you!"

A few hours later, Karen was relieved of her suffering, and God gave her the ultimate healing, a glorious entrance into the eternal Kingdom of our Lord and Savior Jesus Christ. By the mercy and blessing of God, it was Marian Shaeffer, a devoted missionary nurse, who had served faithfully in India, who called me at 6:30 the morning of September 11th to break the sad news of Karen's death.

In the obituary section of the *Lebanon Daily News* of September 23, 1958, is found a tribute to Karen, which reads in part:

"Karen Elizabeth Vernon, 10 month old daughter of Bob J. and Patricia Vernon of Joplin, passed away in General Hospital of Los Angeles, California, September 11, where she had been critically ill for the past month. Funeral services were held in the Phillipsburg Christian Church Sunday afternoon, September 14th, at 2:00 p.m., with the Steve Parker Mortuary of Joplin in charge. Roger Tribble conducted the funeral service. The Vernon Brothers,

J.P., Dallas Jr., Bill, B.J., and Don, sang 'Home Sweet Home' and Bill, twin brother of Bob sang 'Jesus Loves Me,' accompanied by Miss Donna Graves, cousin of the Vernon brothers. At the beginning of the service, Bob sang 'Lullaby to You,' a song of which the lyrics and music had been composed by him while sitting with his very sick baby in the hospital. Karen was a victim of Amyatonia Congenita, a rare incurable disease, and during the last of July her condition became much worse. The Vernons had gone to Hollywood to produce more films of their 'Homestead U.S.A.' TV series. Under the strain of this crisis, Bob and Pat, the other three brothers and their wives and the children, plus the brothers' parents, all went before the cameras to complete the planned five films. All of them returned to Missouri, while Bob remained with Karen until her death. She was brought eventually to the home of Dallas Vernon Jr. to lie in state until the funeral. She was laid to rest in Mt. Rose Memorial Park. Pall bearers were five Vernon brothers."

CHAPTER 19

More Films Completed And On National TV

AFTER THE FUNERAL, I hardly had any time to grieve, for the next day we had a very important executive committee meeting in St. Louis. Following are excerpts from that meeting:

"The meeting was called to order by C.L. DeVore at 8:20 p.m., and in addition to him as Chairman and the Vernon Brothers, those present were Glenn Wheeler, Roger Tribble, Al Karges, Roy Blackmore, Joe Eggebrecht, Gene Wilson, Robert Scott, John Greenlee, and Ragon Flannery. Bill Vernon gave a general report on filming. The families were in Hollywood 5 weeks and completed 5 films. Plans call for a return to California for rehearsal and shooting the remaining 7 films, departing shortly, in just 4 days, on Friday, September 19. The question of film distribution by Walter Bennett, our agent, was discussed. Mr. Bennett has promised that he would be able to place the films on approximately 100 stations, starting October 5. Roy Blackmore made a motion that our Chairman and Bob Vernon go to Chicago to talk about and confirm this very certainty with Mr. Bennett. Second by Glenn Wheeler. Carried unanimously. B.J. Vernon read a letter from Frank Grubbs stating his interest as a representative in fund raising. Al Karges moved that we go on record commending the boys for the present format used in the films, realizing that we are operating under sustaining time, and that we continue this same format. Second by Glenn Wheeler. Carried unanimously. Ragon Flannery made the motion that the Mission pay the balance of hospital, doctor, and funeral bills of Karen Vernon. Second by John Greenlee. Carried unanimously. Dismissed with prayer by C.L. DeVore. Ragon Flannery, Secretary."

The next day, our General Board met in formal session, confirming all the action taken by the Executive Committee as presented and passed in their session. Then other action came:

"... with Bob Cox leading in prayer. Chairman C.L. DeVore made some opening comments concerning the magnitude of Christian TV Mission. He exclaimed, 'The accomplishment already made through faith is tremendous!' Glenn Wheeler moved that we as a General Board extend our deepest sympathy to Bob and Pat Vernon in the loss of their baby daughter. Second by Lester Pifer. Carried unanimously. Mr. DeVore suggested a letter to this effect be sent to them. Carl Matthews made the motion that we raise the salary of the Vernon Brothers to $150.00 per week, plus $500.00 per family for filming wardrobe, and that we give Mom and Pop Vernon a $500.00 honorarium. Second by Bob Bradley, and carried by the Board. Frank Grubbs gave a report about his grueling schedule. He was very optimistic in his observations about the future of Christian TV Mission. Looks great! Meeting was adjourned with prayer by Carl Matthews."

We brothers returned to Joplin and in just a few days left for California with our wives for rehearsals, memorizing music, preparing scripts and messages, and pre-recording songs at Capitol Records and Whitney Studio – all this prior to going before the cameras in filming seven more episodes! Our children stayed with relatives and caretakers to come out later when we would start the actual filming. It took almost three weeks before we needed them because of all the preparatory work. On October 13, 1958, I wrote in my journal at 10:55 p.m.:

"We just returned from the Los Angeles Airport where we picked up Mrs. Garnett Mauller, her son Larry, Betty Weaver – all caretakers – plus Becky, Gregg, Linda, Mike, and Jamie. Richard and Diane had come out earlier with their parents. I am sitting on the edge of the bed. Gregg is hugging me and jostling around. It was so good to see the children again!"

Simply on faith, on the morning of Tuesday the 8th, we had signed the contract with Dick Ross and World Wide Pictures to do the filming at Universal Studios for the seven new episodes. I had written to Dick much earlier the following letter:

"I am taking this means of informing you of our decision to exercise the option mentioned in article six (6) of our contract with you, dated August 15, 1958, which states: 6. It is mutually understood and agreed that an option is hereby granted by World Wide Pictures to Christian Television Mission for seven (7) more films in addition to the five, at the same price of $8,500.00 per unit."

At that time, 30-minute films at the studios were costing at a minimum, $30,000.00. So we were getting a real bargain! The only problem was we needed $59,500.00 to pay for the seven new films, $15,000.00 at the time of signing (which we had on hand and paid), $15,000.00 a week later on the 15th, $15,000.00 on the 22nd, and $14,500.00 on the 29th of October. We desperately needed another $45,000.00 besides the $15,000.00 we had just paid! What in the world could we do? We knew the world wouldn't help us, but Heaven could. So the eight of us gathered together in one room, knelt down, and with "all prayer and supplication," as the Apostle Paul points out in Ephesians 6:18, cried out plea after plea, asking God to give us wisdom and an answer as to what to do. There were lots of tears shed in that prayer meeting. For a few moments after arising, we mulled things over and finally someone (I don't remember who) said, "Why don't we send out telegrams to our supporting churches and individuals telling them that we're about to start filming, but have a very urgent need before proceeding, suggesting that if possible, they wire us $1,000.00 by Western Union over the weekend?" "That's God's answer," we all chimed! So we got out our donor files, picked out the likeliest responders, compiled our list, and on the Saturday night before the following Monday's start date for filming, we four brothers found the closest Western Union establishment and sent out the night letters. We knew that they would arrive in time for the Sunday morning church services, where they could be read. Oh! How the Lord blessed! On that Monday at 11:30 p.m., October 20, 1958, the miracle was happening! In my journal at that late hour, I wrote:

"Praise God from whom all blessings flow!! This is what my heart is singing tonight. It looks as though $13,000.00 has already come in as a result of the telegrams. Today was the first day of filming, and I thought it went off in excellent fashion! Everyone at Universal International Studios' set was delighted and glad to see us back. Dick

Ross was his usual superb self in directing, and everyone in our family knew their lines and did well before the cameras, I thought. How I pray that God will take what we are doing to bring glory and honor to Christ. I must quit now and look at my scripts."

The next day I wrote: "Another good day. We completed shows 7 and 8. Gave Dick another check for $15,000.00 this morning!" More responding telegrams of support and money kept arriving, and by the end of the week, we had received, praise God, $30,000.00! We all were so encouraged by seeing the power of strong faith working!

With this astounding experience behind us, through long hours and days of rehearsing and appearing before the cameras, we were able, with God's blessing and strength, to complete the final seven films of the first *Homestead USA* television series. To add to the joy of this accomplishment, before leaving Hollywood, we got word from the Walter Bennett Agency that they had cleared for televising the first three TV stations in San Francisco, Chicago, and Charlotte, North Carolina! Oh, how we praised our Lord that after all these nineteen months of travel, hard work, and faith since we began, our prayers and dreams were finally coming true!

By the end of 1958, as we continued to hold rallies, evangelize, and pray, the number of stations cleared was 100 and climbing!

CHAPTER 20

Movie Stars Get Involved! Our Network Expands

I MUST GIVE credit, before continuing on in writing my book, to Ruth Noble who served faithfully and effectively as our secretary since the first day of this Mission. And right from the beginning, when we started in the basement of our home before we were able to rent offices, she had been on the job. Then as we grew, Roberta Miller, Jodi Gardner, Janis Stenzinger, Jill English, and our capable and dear cousins Donna and Sheron Graves were added as needed.

I also want to say how much I appreciated the letter of encouragement from my high school principal, Ellis C. Rainy, soon after the premiere of our first film. He wrote:

"Dear Bob, I want to tell you how much I enjoyed the program you boys presented last Saturday night. I believe everyone was of the same opinion. If you can, and I know you will, keep the level of the program up to that point. I believe you really have something. Certainly our best wishes go with each one of you individually and the collective group. If we can be of any service to you at any time, just let us know. Sincere personal regards to each one of you and to your families. Very truly yours, Ellis C. Rainy."

1959 was a very busy and fruitful year for us Vernons. We were invited by Gale Storm and her husband, who had been contacted by Frank Grubbs, to fly to California at their expense. What a great time we enjoyed with them, rehearsing songs around their grand piano, and within a few days, again at no cost to us, recording songs for our first album, which we titled, *Homestead USA*. Gale's husband, Lee Bonnell, had been raised in a Christian church at South Bend, Indiana, and was such a Christian gentleman and successful executive in the insurance field. He was on hand every day in the control booth as we were recording and got in touch with Randy Wood, president of Dot Records, who agreed to put our recording on that famous label. This was the label that Pat Boone was an artist with at the time, and through that influence, I was able later to be with Pat on several occasions and get him to appear on some of our shows. Lee and Dot Records picked up the tab of all the recording expenses. Lee and Gale were so very hospitable to us in every way, including in their home. Gale had the girls go through her room-sized wardrobe closet to pick out a fashionable evening gown which each of them chose, and they took all eight of us to a ritzy, charitable banquet for Goodwill Industries, where, as I recall, we sang our theme song, "Homestead USA."

We brothers loved our hometown of Lebanon, Missouri, but ever since we had dedicated our lives to the Lord's service, our souls were burdened to see a New Testament Church come into existence there. There was a Disciples congregation, where, in his day, the famous novelist, Harold Bell Wright, had preached and written several popular books; however, the congregation over the years had embraced a very liberal position on some of the most foundational and basic teachings concerning Jesus and the inspiration of the Scriptures. So we cleaned up the grease and leftover debris and rubbish of a huge, abandoned garage on Main Street, and from April 26th through May 10th, the four of us and our cousin, Roger Tribble, took our turns preaching, and as a result, the Southern Heights

Christian Church was born. There were 500 people present at that crusade on the very first night, with tremendous support, attendance, and response from the town citizens. Our brother, Dallas Vernon Jr., a respected leader and elder, who eventually became president of the local tool and die engineering firm, was also very instrumental in establishing the church. He and his wife, together with our father and mother, and crippled brother, Ward, became charter members, and the congregation under the ministry of Roger grew to be one of the largest in Lebanon.

All eight of us and our children, plus Willis and Lora Harrison, who worked with us as the Gospel Messengers from 1951 through 1953 in full-time evangelism, held a crusade in Southern Illinois. From an article in the August issue of *Christian TV News*, I quote:

> "More than 3,000 people attended the Southern Illinois Evangelistic Crusade held at the Oil Belt Christian Service Campgrounds near Flora, Illinois from July 12 to 24, 1958. Approximately 80 congregations demonstrated a great unity in working together. During the daytime, our team taught in two weeks of Youth Camp."

But this same issue records that in spite of the fact that we were on the air with *Homestead USA* all over the country, and the success of all the premieres of the previous year, our offerings had dropped and we were in a financial crisis. So to alleviate the situation, without panic or thinking it was hopeless, we all went off salary for two months, and each of us brothers raised our families' needs by taking a speaking tour, letting all the offerings coming directly to the Mission be used for operational expenses, TV production, and debt liquidation. We had put all our hearts, souls, and minds into this endeavor, and we were not about to quit! I quote again from the August issue of our *Christian TV News*:

> "We have tried to formulate plans that would assure the making of at least one series (of 13 films) each year, and yet jeopardize neither Christian Television Mission nor the cause of New Testament Christianity on a worldwide missionary basis. Our basic plan was, and is, this: to get at least 500 churches to give $10.00 per week to make possible a national television program with continuous production, and every one of these congregations, besides others who would help some, would have the accomplishment and satisfaction of carrying out the Great Commission to the whole world! It sounds so simple. But at this writing less than 100 congregations are continuous supporters of this Mission. The next 60 days will determine the fate of this effort and possibly the success or failure of any large missionary endeavor attempted by congregations devoted to the Cause of restoring New Testament Christianity."

We wondered why in the world more of our Brethren and churches wouldn't join in supporting this successful mission outreach, now that after so much "blood, sweat, and tears" we were getting such great response in letters from viewers watching on TV stations in Hawaii, Alaska, and the states all over the country! Following are excerpts from lots of letters that had poured into our office from viewers:

- Oaktown, Indiana – "I have told lots of people about you. They tune in to the shows, and tell me they watch and are so inspired weekly."

- Atlanta, Georgia – "We really enjoy the program which is on WSB-TV."
- Castle Rock, Washington – "I've been watching your program and love it!"
- Salem, Ohio – "I would like a copy of yesterday's message and prayer. We need men like you!"
- Grand Junction, Colorado – "Would appreciate the booklet. You're great!"
- Little Rock, Arkansas – "I watch every week, and enjoy it so much!"
- Terre Haute, Indiana – "I work, but my husband watches. Says it's the best program on TV, and tells me what it's about."
- Minnesota – "We need more high-caliber programs like this!"
- Washington – "Enjoy you! Excellent music and messages."
- Florida – "Thrilled my heart to see and hear your songs and speech."
- Manchester, New Hampshire – "Your programs help, here where we're not known!"
- Tennessee – "What a blessing listening to you! Keep it up!"
- Nebraska – "It's the best program on KSTF-TV, Scottsbluff!"
- Virginia – "Would be great if you'd be on also in Canada and Mexico!"
- Florida – "We thrill to the message and the beauty in your music!"

I could go on and on with stations cleared and glowing comments from viewers. We got mail from viewers who watched from stations all over! Space prohibits me from listing every one of them, but here's a few more cities that had a TV station televising our series: Honolulu, Hawaii; Danville, Illinois; Columbus, Ohio; Indianapolis, Indiana; Miami, Florida; Jamestown, North

Dakota; Hoffman, Minnesota; Ft. Wayne, Indiana; Kansas City, Missouri; Atchison, Kansas; Valley City, North Dakota; Bismarck, North Dakota; Minot, North Dakota; Peoria, Illinois; Tucson, Arizona; Sioux Falls, South Dakota; Salem, Oregon; Petersburg, Virginia; Austin, Texas; Thermopolis, Wyoming; Springfield, Missouri; Dayton, Ohio; Cedar Rapids, Iowa; Medford, Oregon; Charleston, West Virginia; Decatur, Illinois; and Los Angeles, California. As time went on, we had built a network of 150 and more. The point I'm trying to make is this: how shortsighted could members and ministers of our many Restoration Churches be not to realize how far-reaching and valuable a tool television is in spreading the Gospel, proclaiming "our Plea," and winning souls to Christ? And the amazing thing is we were being given thousands upon thousands of dollars' worth of free television time, not having to pay a cent in almost all cases to be on the air! For our programs were of such high quality production wise, that we qualified for what the industry calls "sustaining time," written in the rules that every TV station must abide by in order to obtain a license to go on the air. They have no choice. They are required to give a certain amount of free time!

Another reason we qualified for "sustaining" time was because it was a family program with four real, honest-to-goodness ministering brothers and their wives, children, and parents, engaged in normal, enjoyable activities, singing and sharing inspirational AS WELL AS DOCTRINAL TEACHINGS FROM THE SCRIPTURES! In the messages, we were sharing with the family members, but more importantly and in reality, viewers at home were the listeners who were getting the message of the Gospel! We had no limitations whatsoever in this kind of an informal home setting on what we could say or teach. It was not only acceptable to program directors or managers, they clamored for our TV series. Here is an example of the many such praises and requests we and our distributing agent received:

> "I see that the 'Homestead USA' series number 2 shooting schedule is set for January. Please do not fail to notify me the moment this series is ready for release, as our success with it in the past is indication enough that it is an asset to our religious programming schedule."

The extraordinary fact that we were a true-to-life, blood-related family had a distinct appeal to program directors as well as to the viewers. At first, many people thought that surely we must be actors. Here is a very nice letter and inquiry we received from Frank Ritchie, president of Orange County Aviation Corporation in Fullerton, California:

> "Gentlemen: We would like to congratulate you for the high quality of your television program on Channel 5. We feel that 'Homestead U.S.A.' is one of the finest offerings on the video screen. Recently on one of your programs you had an older couple that you referred to as your parents. Is it true that these people were actually your parents and that the entire family is so talented as to participate as a unit? We would like to hear from you regarding this question."

The answer, of course, was that yes, these were our real parents, and we were blessed by God, as a real family, with such talents that could be used to glorify Him and inspire people. There is no doubt our variety of music, beautifully arranged by the famed Ralph Carmichael, had an appeal to viewers as well as to program directors, and helped us qualify for free, sustaining time on the television stations. And not only was our singing an advantage, but also our dramatization of Biblical events and use of special guests. We were so thankful that we had succeeded after so much planning, praying, traveling, and fund raising, in producing films that affected people so deeply! To illustrate this fact, let me quote again a few commendations from viewers:

> From California: "We hope you folks never find it impossible to carry on your work in His name. Thanks again for bringing us God's Word in such a marvelously entertaining manner. Many folks in our town now know about you and 'Homestead U.S.A.'"

And this comment from Canada: "We so enjoy your broadcast on mornings up here in Canada."

> From Washington: "Since Christmas, when I acquired a TV, I have been delighted with your program. Its simplicity, naturalness, but tone of encouragement to worship, has always enchanted me. And the program of February 21 has crowned them all. Congratulations on a splendid, timely performance. All the world should see that one."

And finally, just as a sample of the many letters that flooded into our office, here's this one from Florida:

> "After watching you on television for several weeks, we feel that we really know each and every one of you, as though we're invited right into your living room as members of the family. Your meditation time with the whole family around the Bible is such a friendly and informal and wonderful way to bring the Gospel of Christ to TV viewers. And we thrill to the message and the beauty in your music. Please

continue to present your programs in the very same way. They cannot be improved."

Knowing that myriads of viewers were being blessed, and deeply grateful for those who were encouraging and supporting us, we pressed on! Since videotaping programs was now being utilized and was more economical, I made a trip to New York to see about making our next series there. Following is the report in late 1959 which I wrote in the November issue of *Christian TV News*:

"It was rough, I tell you. Not to know a soul among so many teeming millions! Dwarfed by the immensity of towering skyscrapers, somehow I had to meet people, important people in the communications field. I had to learn for myself from them the answers to very vital questions. Where would I find them, the first floor or on the fiftieth? Who were they? How could I interest them? What would be the best approach? It took all the faith and courage I could muster, and praying for wisdom, I 'waded in.' I knew with God's help, I would succeed. Only three short years before, I faced the same situation in Hollywood. Visiting studios, observing production, getting prices, meeting people. Hoping and praying for a 'break-through.' On the very last day, I was able to talk with Dick Ross, and out of that situation there ultimately developed the present series of 'Homestead U.S.A.' films.

"In New York, I found out in visiting all three TV network headquarters that they were not interested in carrying our programs at the network level. Next I tried the public service departments. After introducing myself, and showing one of our films at local network stations, I asked if on a sustaining basis they might be able to authorize or help us get on the network instead of clearing individual stations. Everyone I talked to was very cordial, but I was told that councils were set up for all public servicing. I continued my search, visiting various productions, including the 'Pat Boone' show and personally getting to talk to him again. He was very warm and friendly, expressing pleasure when he heard of our new 'Dot' album."

CHAPTER 21

I've Got A Secret

"Not giving up in my quest at New York, I found a public relations agency which showed interest in our project. We went over our whole history and they kept pictures, materials, etc., and were quite sure they could get us some guest appearances, singing hymns and having an interview. Most hopeful was the Garry Moore show, 'I've Got a Secret,' but don't count on it until we know for sure. Make it a matter of prayer. We want to leave it in the hands of the Lord. All in all, the trip was very worthwhile, not only in gaining information about production and distribution, but also in making some excellent contacts for the Mission."

1960 WAS AN extremely busy, successful, but trying year for me, my brothers, and our families. But it was an exciting year of great accomplishments, three in number primarily: (1) returning to Hollywood to produce in color the dramatization of the conversion and baptism of the Philippian Jailer; (2) a three-month professional fund raising campaign; and (3) our four families' trip to New York to appear on *I've Got a Secret!* The "Philippian Jailer" film was made at Lucille Ball's Desilu Studios with William Beaudine of the *Lassie* shows as our director. Our first choice to direct was Dick Ross, but he was in Africa on a mission for Billy Graham. Our film met with high acclaim from the TV industry as well as with our own Brethren. The story line was that upon the arrival of our four families at our parents' home, our 9-year-old daughter, Becky, was mischievously taunting our 6-year-old little boy, Gregg, and keeping it up, had to be punished by banning her to a bedroom. Her cousin, 8-year-old Linda, slips into the room and tempts her to leave and go outside with her to play, which she declines. After a while, Gregg goes into the room and they apologize to each other, as I watch. Proud of Becky for turning down the temptation to leave the room, I pick up the Bible and start reading the account of Paul and Silas who, after being arrested and beaten, were singing praise songs in prison, but didn't leave when a sudden earthquake flung the prison doors open. During all of this reading, the camera segued into a "flashback" recreating the dramatization of the entire account, including the earthquake, the witness to the jailer, his conversion, and baptism by immersion. Then Pat and I, proud of Becky for not leaving when Linda had tempted her by leaving the door open, congratulated both our kids for settling their differences, and went on with family activities.

Our "Million-a-Year" fund raising campaign was carried out by us four brothers, directed and assisted with a professional firm. It involved three months of travel, rallies, and hard work, primarily in Illinois, Indiana, Ohio, and Kentucky. It proved to be extremely difficult and almost "back-breaking," and we and all who sacrificially worked with us were only partially successful, raising almost half a million in gifts and pledges to cover the next three years. Although exceedingly weary and exhausted after it was over, we were indeed grateful for the amount raised and those who helped and participated.

I was elated when the agency I had contacted in New York informed us that they had arranged for our four families, plus Mother and Dad, to come to New York to appear and sing on the CBS network's show, *I've Got a Secret*. We were all so excited! B.J.'s wife, Lodi, was pregnant, so the network flew them and their children to New York, while the rest of us drove. They put us up in a very nice hotel, and on August 17, 1960, our guest appearance took place. It couldn't have gone better! The host, Garry Moore, was so friendly and genial, introducing first our parents, while the rest of us waited backstage. He asked them to whisper in his ear what their secret was. Our mother said, "But Garry, we have our four sons who share our secret." The four of us brothers walked out in single file, he introduced us, and again asked us to whisper our secret. We said, "But Garry, our wives are here, and they share our secret." The audience roared with laughter! Then our beautiful spouses gracefully ambled out in single file. The panel of Johnny Carson, Bess Myerson, Betsy Palmer, and Bill Cullen seemed delighted and amused. "All right, now that we have you all out here, let's have your secret," Garry stated. Pat, Lodi, and Carol had agreed to have Joy speak, so she answered, "But Garry, our children are backstage, and they share our secret." The crowd exploded with applause and hilarity as the seven little ones sauntered out one after the other. The bench in front of Garry's desk seemed a bit short, and as he started to introduce them, handsome little Jamie tried to squeeze in to be seated, and in only partially succeeding, stole the show! The crowd loved it! So Garry reached over with his mike in hand to interview Jamie. But Jamie was just dead silent. The audience roared with laughter at this spontaneous, unplanned scene! Garry finally succeeded in introducing all the kids, asked us to whisper our secret, and proceeded to quiz the panel members to see if they could guess our secret. They got close, but never quite got the answer. He then revealed the secret that the Vernon family were "stars in their own TV program." The panel and people in the studio audience applauded their approval, and Garry announced that we had a nationwide show called *Homestead USA*, sponsored by the Christian Churches and Churches of Christ. But he said, "They have traveled to raise the funds themselves in order to produce the films in the series, singing and starring in the Christian family shows." He then turned to me to be the spokesman in explaining further our work and our family. I said, "Garry, we have no pretentious boasts about ourselves or who we are. But with our God-given talents and such as we are, we're trying to inspire people with the good news of the Gospel, especially as it relates to the needs and problems of the modern day world. We do it through songs, dramatization of Biblical events, and inspirational messages." We all agreed and laughed when he said, "With such a big family, you surely must encounter some problems yourselves!" The panel and on-lookers enjoyed the banter and burst out in laughter with us! We closed by singing a spirited song entitled, "I'm a Trampin'," with the kids chiming in loudly on "Hallelujah!" There was thunderous applause at the finish as Garry bade us "goodbye," and we walked offstage thrilled that our appearance had gone off so well! Surely God had opened the door for us to have had such an opportunity to explain our efforts to millions throughout the country!

I still have a copy of a letter, dated August 24, 1960, from Deanne Stern, the executive in charge of programming for *I've Got a Secret*, and I quote:

"Dear Bob, I am sending you under separate cover the letters and postcards which we received in response to your appearance on I'VE GOT A SECRET. I thought you would like to have them and also to know that this is the greatest mail response that we have received on any spot in over three years. When I realized the volume of mail, I called Bob Troup over at CBS and told him about it. He was delighted to hear about it and said it confirmed his opinion that yours is quite a talented family. In case you don't get around to reading all the letters, let me tell you that a great many of them want to know where they can see your program. So I should think that if the question of continuing or discontinuing 'Homestead USA' ever comes up, this mail should be taken into account. Thank you again for being our guest on I'VE GOT A SECRET. I wish you continued success with your program. Sincerely yours, Deanne Stern."

Among all the productions we made at studios, we produced one on location at the actual Homestead, nine miles west of Lebanon, Missouri. All seven of us brothers, our families, and our parents appeared and sang on the program. We used the videotape method in the production of this episode of *Homestead USA*, utilizing the facilities of KYTV, Springfield, Missouri, and their crew. I regret that this episode, along with several of our original films, were destroyed by water damage from leakage in the roof of a building where they were stored.

With all the extensive travel, fund raising, rallies, and production we had completed by the fall of 1960, we four brothers and our families were quite weary and exhausted. But with the need of fulfilling a scheduled six-week promotional and fund raising tour of Oregon and Washington, I braced myself with the Lord's strength and took off in my car for a distant Northwest. I spoke night after night in mission and financial rallies for that period, concluding with speaking on "The Great Commission" the final night at a gigantic two-state missionary conference in Eugene, Oregon.

I was so worn and homesick that after greeting people and receiving warm response to my message, I foolishly left for home in a blinding snowstorm. After a few miles, the highway was getting slick and hazardous, and I was in a winding, mountainous area that went on and on. Slowly and cautiously, I crawled along in my car, tense and praying that surely I would come to a motel. Nervously, I had to pick up enough speed going down one mountainous slope to be able to get up the next steep one. This went on for many, many miles with me fearing that I would slide and careen off the road down a mountainside. Finally, thank God, the terrain plateaued, my terror-filled heart calmed, and the welcome sight of a motel came into view! This certainly was the most harrowing and dangerous experience I have ever had on the road in all my life. Totally spent, I slept 'til noon in that motel before resuming my trip for home sweet home.

Home and family never looked so good as I was lovingly welcomed with wide open arms after such a long absence. Though the Mission was helped greatly with such a successful year up to this point, it had taken a toll on my health. I developed a serious case with my digestive system, including stomach cramps and colitis. In spite of this, I knew we had to proceed with our plans for continued production. I recommended to my brothers and to our board that with constant filming ahead, our four families should move to the West Coast to be close to the studios. This would save the expense and burden of making trip after trip with our families. Everyone agreed, especially since our production and operating income had increased considerably from the fund raising campaign. But with a full schedule already certain in the Midwest, we put off the move until the summer of 1961.

One of the original log cabins on the Homestead from 1844

Young Dallas Vernon, the Vernon Brothers' father (top right), with his father James Polk Vernon and his family on the Homestead, 1898

The Homestead home as it looked when Bob and his brothers were growing up

Bob (Bobby Jean) and twin brother Bill (Billy Dean)

All seven young Vernon boys with parents Dallas and Beulah on the Homestead

Bob with brother B.J. and twin brother Bill, cousin Roger Tribble, and others from OBC basketball team. An occasional opponent was the baseball legend Mickey Mantle!

Bob and twin brother Bill at Drury College

Bob in the Navy
Submarine Service
during World War II

Patricia at around the
time she and Bob first
met

Bob and Patricia's Wedding

THE LEBANON DAILY RECORD | JULY 31, 1948

Singing Vernon Boys Are Active In Church Work, Heard Weekly On Radio

One of the first newspaper articles with the early version of the Vernon Brothers-J.P., Bob, Bill, B.J, and Dallas Jr. and their first radio broadcast!

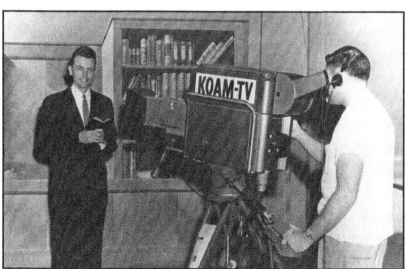

Pioneering early religious broadcasting on June 21, 1954 at station in Pittsburg, Kansas

All the Vernons gathered at the Homestead for Thanksgiving 1959

The Vernon Brothers Quartet

Section B ★

LARGEST EVENING CIRCULATION IN THE WEST'S LARGEST CITY

LOS ANGELES EVENING

2nd FRONT PAGE

HERALD EXPRESS

VOL. LXXXVIII   WEDNESDAY, NOV. 26, 1958   NO. 210

Vernon Tribe Click in Hollywood

17 in One Family on TV

THE VERNON BROTHERS—BOB, BILL, DON AND B. J.
As a Gospel Singing Quartet, They Launched Their TV Career in 1954—Now
They Are Stars of 13 Half-Hour Religious TV Shows

'ONE MAN'S FAMILY'—THE WHOLE VERNON CLAN
Mr. and Mrs. Dallas Vernon, Their Four Sons and Daughters-in-Law, and
Seven Grandchildren Give Thanks at the Dinner Table

Well, that's exactly what happened when the Vernon family of Missouri "went Hollywood"—but big—and came to the Universal Studios to make a pilot TV film for World Wide Pictures.

Today, as they sit around a mammoth-sized table munching their Thanksgiving meal, each and every member is grateful, though still somewhat startled by their good fortune.

REAL FAMILY

Similar in format to the fictitious "One Man's Family" of long-standing radio and TV fame, the Vernons differ in fact because they form a real, honest-to-goodness, blood-related family.

By name and number (at the last official count) they include Mr. and Mrs. Dallas Vernon of Lebanon, Mo.; their four sons, Bob, Bill, Don and B. J.; their respective wives, Pat, Joy, Carol, and Lody; and thence, their seven offspring.

The talented Vernons are more than the stars of 13 half-hour religious TV shows called "Homestead, U.S.A." Almost unheard of in the modern scheme of sponsored TV programs, they even went so far as to put up the all-important payola for the series.

EVANGELIST CLAN

Each personable, photogenic, and musically inclined, the Vernons are actually a clan of traveling evangelists, who have turned to TV, to raise money for the Christian Church.

The idea for the program originated with the four brothers, all ordained clergymen of the Christian Church and graduates of the four-year Ozark Bible College of Joplin, Mo., where the hearquarters of their venture, the Christian Television Mission, is still located.

As a gospel singing quartet, the brothers launched their TV career in the fall of 1954 over KOAM-TV at Balesburg, Kansas.

Popularity of the program kept expanding until four

(Continued on Page B-9, Col. 7)

Vernon Family TV program
featured in Los Angeles newspaper

VERNONS APPEAR ON "I'VE GOT A SECRET"

I'VE GOT A SECRET
375 PARK AVENUE
NEW YORK 22, N. Y.

August 24, 1960

Dear Bob:

I am sending you under separate cover the letters and postcards which we received in responses to your appearance on I'VE GOT A SECRET. I thought you would like to have them and also to know that this is the greatest mail response that we have received on any spot in over three years.

When I realized the volume of mail, I called Bob Troup over at CBS and told him about it. He was delighted to hear about it and said it confirmed his opinion that yours is quite a talented family, or words to that effect.

In case you don't get around to reading all the letters, let me tell you that a great many of them want to know where they can see your program. So I should think that if the question of continuing or discontinuing "HOMESTEAD, USA" ever comes up, this mail should be taken into account.

Thank you again for being our guests on I'VE GOT A SECRET. I wish you continued success with your program.

Sincerely yours,

Deanne Stern

Deanne Stern

The Vernons were invited to New York to appear with Gary Moore on the "I've Got a Secret" Show.

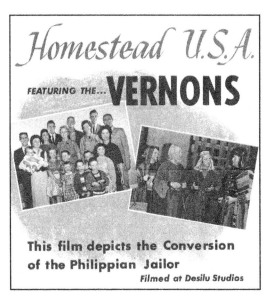

Poster of the Vernons and their new television program seen each week across the nation and overseas

"Homestead U.S.A." promotional flyer

Pat and Bob taking a break in filming
television series at Universal Studios

The Vernons rehearse for their
TV show - Bob holding newborn
daughter Debbie

Bob from "Homestead
U.S.A." television series
on set with Bible

Filmed in 1964 and 1965, Bob gained access to areas in the former Soviet Union not open to anyone from America or the West at the time. Film culminates in Africa with mission work and revival on the continent.

Bob and Pat traveled to Israel to film "Back to Jerusalem" which depicts the birth of the Church and New Testament Christianity. "Back to Jerusalem" was shown nationwide on the CBS television network.

Bob & Pat filming
"Back to Jerusalem"
in Caesarea

Bob, Pat and
crew filming
"Back to
Jerusalem" on a
rooftop in
Jerusalem

Bob being
interviewed
immediately
following the
nationwide
premier
showing of
"Back to
Jerusalem" on
CBS TV
network

Bob and
daughter Becky
on Viet Nam
USO tour
in 1967

Bob and daughter
Debbie at the
Grammy Awards in
New York City. Bob
became a member
of the National
Academy of
Recording Arts &
Sciences soon after
his first record
albums were
produced.

Bob and son
Gregg in
Australia on the
Great
Barrier Reef

Bob signing with
Capitol Records
in 1966

Family preparing for
their 1967
"Tell America" Tour

Family in
the 1980's

Bob and family with guest star Pat Boone on the "Inspiration of Bob Vernon" television special

Bob and son Gregg in studio preparing post production of TV programs they produced in Thailand. Religious programming is not usually allowed, but they were given the opportunity to produce four programs for national broadcasting.

Bob with actor portraying Benjamin Franklin and director Don Buccola discussing scene in one of four Bicentennial Specials produced by the Vernons

The Big California Earthquake
January, 1994

Unsafe sign posted on front of our place

Pat stares at cracks

Bob at weak foundation

Vernon
Family
Reunion
at the
Homestead
in 1993

Bob Vernon
Family at
beach
celebrating
Bob's 75th
Birthday

The combined
families at the
beach,
Paradise Cove

Daughter Becky, son-in-law Stephen Walker, and
the Walker grandchildren Jeremy and Jessica

Bob with grandson Jeremy and granddaughter Jessica on Christmas

Bob's daughter Debbie, son-in-law Randy Ballas, and the Ballas
grandchildren Emma, Beau, Drake and Colton

Grandchildren Emma, Beau, Drake and Colton with Bob at
the cemetery on the day Patricia was laid to rest

Bob and son Gregg at The Refuge
Church where they ministered
each week for over twenty years

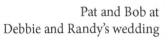

Pat and Bob at
Debbie and Randy's wedding

Bob on his 90th birthday
celebration!

SECTION V

Triumphs, Tears, And Tours

CHAPTER 22

Another New Church And Promotional Tours

THE NEW YEAR of 1961 began with our preaching a crusade in the early stage of starting a new congregation, the Park Plaza Christian Church, January 8-15, in Joplin, Missouri. The church closed its charter with 76 members. Then on January 29, we held an area-wide 5th Sunday Christian TV Mission Rally in Dallas, Texas, with all the New Testament churches in the region. Afterwards, we received this letter from our minister friend, Ronnie Hanna:

> "This rally was one of the best attended and most successful endeavors ever attempted by the Christian churches of the Dallas-Fort Worth area. Not only did the rally help to get the work of CTM before the people and challenge them, but more than that, it brought the area churches closer together in spirit, fellowship, and cooperation – something that has been needed for a long time. I want to thank you again from the bottom of my heart for giving of your time to come and be with us."

The auditorium was packed, with the cooperation of Ronnie, President William Nash of Dallas Christian College, thirteen area ministers, and members of their congregations.

February was busy with an important board meeting in Indianapolis on February 4th, and our attendance and

185

participation at the Ozark Bible College Convention, February 21-23. A thrilling and very successful Tri-State Revival Crusade was conducted by us and our wives in the City Auditorium of Ft. Wayne, Indiana, April 2-7. The cooperative effort of all our churches in the corners of Indiana, Ohio, and Michigan made the meeting possible. In the prior calling campaign culminating with the crusade, there were 133 baptisms into Christ and 30 transfers of membership, as reported by leading ministers Joe Ellis and Bill Lauer. Opening night attendance was 2,000 and averaged 1,300 the entire week. It was my great privilege to preach the messages during the meeting. The first night was videotaped through the facilities of WPTA-TV and was shown on their station from 9:30 to 10:30 that evening. We used this videotaped program in edited form in our next film series later in the year. We had two more dates on our schedule before the task of packing and moving to California. The first, participating on the program of the North American Christian Convention in Wichita, Kansas, April 19-23, and second, the "Greatest Gathering This Side of Heaven," the annual meeting of thousands of men in the Kiamichi Mountains at Talihina, Oklahoma, May 2-4. It's a meeting, the first of which I was privileged to attend in 1948 when there were only about 40 or 50 present, but which grew in attendance to 10,000 or more! Brother A.B. McReynolds had started a mission in those mountains, and later organized from scratch this event with the theme, "How can I make my life count more for Christ?" He advertised it as a meeting for men with this description, "No shaving, no women, and no neckties." He was a very colorful, "one-of-a-kind" man, but a giant of a servant of God with his missionary work, MX3 (referring to Malachi 3:10) brand and proponent of tithing, and influence in leading thousands to make their lives count more in the service of Christ.

June of 1961 saw us four brothers and our families saying goodbye to friends in Joplin and starting the task of packing, loading our furniture and belongings into moving vans, and heading for California. Upon arriving, our move took a disappointing turn for me personally, as in a search for housing, we all finally landed up sixty miles from the studios in a new tract of homes in the city of Orange. But we settled in there, finding four homes close to each other, and plunged into preparations for making another series of thirteen programs. We hired William Beaudine Jr., who had worked with us in producing the "Philippian Jailer" film as our director, paying him $300.00 per episode. We worked the whole month of July in preparing the scripts and rehearsing new music we would use. From the July-August issue of *Christian TV News*, I quote:

"Again the familiar sound is being echoed, 'Lights! Camera! Action!' HOMESTEAD USA is now back in production. The scripts for the new series are now completed. The contract with Paramount Pictures, parent company of KTLA-TV where we are doing the programs, has been signed. The week of August 13, 1961 was the time of filming the first episode of the new series. Thereafter, one program is being made each week for 13 weeks, with the option to continue for another 13 weeks. Each episode contains the dramatization of a Biblical event, similar to the dramatic sequence of the earthquake and baptism of the 'Philippian Jailer.' The first episode has guests Eugene and Helen Morse telling of their missionary labors and their harrowing escape from Communist China's aggression and infiltration of their work. Eugene, who along with his famous parents J. Russell and Gertrude Morse, and his brothers, had been a missionary to China, Burma, and Thailand for the last forty years. The Biblical drama in this program depicts the conversion and baptism of the Centurion Cornelius, as related in Acts, the 10th chapter."

I would add how moved and inspired I was way back when I was a student at Ozark Bible College, Eugene's elderly parents came and spoke in chapel. Mother Morse was able to leave China on the very last airplane as the Chinese communists were approaching, but her husband was arrested, tortured, and imprisoned for almost three years, with the last fifteen months being spent in a tiny isolated cell before finally being released.

As part of our contract with Paramount and KTLA-TV, it was agreed that with no extra charge to us, they would televise our series on Sunday nights from 9:30 to 10:00 beginning on August 27th. What a great viewing audience we had, covering all of Southern California, and the mail started pouring in. Sunday, August 27, was set by most of the churches in this huge area as *Homestead USA* day with special offerings being taken for Christian TV Mission. We continued the series, including dramatization of Peter and Pentecost, Judas' betrayal, the rich man and Lazarus, all of these following the first one depicting the conversion of Cornelius.

Pat and I had been quite concerned and doubtful about having any more children after discovering in 1958 that our Karen had a congenital disease called "amyatonia congenita," soon becoming so critical during our filming, and then passing away. We had read a news article that one family had experienced the death of three of their children afflicted with this dreaded malady. Though we both had great faith, still some fear gripped our souls, especially Pat's. But after three years, we both longed to have another child and prayed fervently that we would have a healthy, beautiful baby. Sure enough, God answered our prayers, and we were blessed by a beautiful, disease-free angel coming to us from Heaven, and we named her Deborah Elaine Vernon. Her birth took place in Long Beach, California on July 25, 1961.

Besides successfully producing the new series and happily having a sweet, new face in our family, as well as in B.J.'s and Don's families, we pressed on in our work, holding rallies and appearing at special events. One such appearance was with J. Wycliffe Busch and the small but visionary Mar Vista Church in Los Angeles, giving us a sacrificial gift of $300.00! In addition to this appearance, here is the heavy schedule we carried out in the first five months of 1962: First Christian Church in Anaheim; city-wide rally in Tucson, Arizona; rally at Hobbs, New Mexico; Central Christian Church rally in Oklahoma City; CTM Executive Committee meeting in St. Louis; First Christian Church rally in Dodge City, Kansas; revival with Lomita, California Christian Church; revival with Bell Gardens, California First Christian Church; revival with First Christian Church of Anaheim, California; and revival with First Christian Church in Downey, California.

It almost makes your head swim to think of all these appointments and appearances we made, and more travel, promotional rallies, fund raising, and evangelistic meetings facing us if we continued as a team. Besides, members of our group were getting weary and worn down, especially our wives, not having a "normal" home life as new little ones were coming along. And since the four of us brothers had dedicated our lives to the preaching of the Gospel, and this was our first love, not singing, and we had all preached in located ministries for some five years prior to this work, talk began about transitioning back to the Midwest. But I had put my heart and soul into our TV ministry, and though I always considered us brothers as equals and still do, I felt bad that I was the one who recommended our move to California. The feeling was strong in Bill, B.J., and Don and their wives that they really desired to move back into preaching ministries, and I couldn't fault them for that. Those who know me know that I too am passionate about preaching. From my Navy days and on through Bible college and ministry, I have memorized and used a great deal of the Scriptures in pouring my heart out in preaching. But what should I do? Should I stay in California, set up a production office, and oversee a yearly series of television films that would have the other families coming out one week each year to be involved in the films? I was in a real dilemma. Fearful that the TV ministry might end, I prayed hard for wisdom, and concluded that the best course would be for us to move back with the group, and for me to continue on as the Executive Director of the TV Mission. The other three brothers said they would continue a part-time relationship with Christian TV Mission but take full-time ministries. So we moved the Mission's offices to Springfield, Missouri. Don and his family moved there also and started the Glendale Christian Church in the Mission's building. Bill and his family moved to Shreveport, Louisiana, where he took the ministry of the Fairpark Christian Church. B.J. and his family moved to Dewey, Oklahoma, where he had a church ministry for the next several years. Pat and I with our family also moved to Springfield where I continued carrying the load of the TV Mission on a full-time basis as the Executive Director.

In the July-August 1962 issue of *Christian TV News*, I wrote after our move:

"We dedicate ourselves anew. Gratefully and humbly, we submit this issue of CHRISTIAN TV NEWS to our readers. It contains important news about the brand new, far-reaching production and distribution program we have launched. This is not an outlandish plan incapable of attainment. It will not cost a half or a quarter million dollars. It does call for a budget of $140,000.00. Gifts and earned income during our last fiscal year, as our audit showed, amounted to $137,256.00. Our present indebtedness stands at $5,900.00 as opposed to the almost $100,000.00 two years ago. All four of us brothers will appear at occasional gatherings such as we did at the National Missionary convention in Denver. We also will sing and preach for an evangelistic crusade at the First Christian Church in Lincoln, Illinois, December 2-10, 1962. We commit ourselves and the Mission to God and to you whom we are trying to serve. Do with us as you will. As long as you want us and support us, we are yours to serve. We dedicate ourselves anew to evangelizing and televising."

After living in a small rented home in Springfield for a short period, Pat and I were able to purchase a nice six-room split-level house in a new tract of homes. The price was $22,500.00, but with a small down payment, we were able to finance the remainder on a 20-year loan. It was close to a new high school and elementary school, and eventually, with Don as the minister, the growing Glendale Christian Church erected a beautiful building nearby. So our family settled in nicely at 2256 Mayfair Drive. We had sold our home at 4205 Kentucky in Joplin for a good profit over the $14,000.00 it had cost. God had blessed us in a great way and continued to do so in this transitional period!

Making the best of our newly-developed Mission operation with me full time and the other three brothers part time, I busily "put my shoulder to the wheel" mapping out plans to carry on the work. The four of us did come together the last half of 1962 for the North American Christian Convention in Lexington, Kentucky, the National Missionary Convention in Denver, Colorado, and a revival with Leon Appel and the Christian Church in Lincoln, Illinois, December 2-9. But people were anxious about the future of the Mission during this period. This was expressed in a letter from Frank Lillie and the good supporting church of Columbiana, Ohio. Here are excerpts of my answering letter to their questions:

"(1) What are your future plans and intentions with the Mission? –Our plans for the year include the production of 13 new films and distribution to 100 TV stations. (2) Do you personally feel that the great outlay of funds for your films has been worthwhile for the Church of Christ? –This is a very difficult question to answer. Only eternity will reveal the true worth and value of such a ministry. I will say that I am still thrilled and excited beyond measure about this work and its value to the Kingdom, and the vast potential yet untouched. We are not some new heroic messiah-like movement New Testament people are looking for to cause denominationalism to crumble overnight! (3) When will your 2nd series be shown on stations here? –I am reasonably certain that Pittsburgh will come through. We're in an arrangement now with Frank Block Associates to distribute our films and think they'll be successful."

CHAPTER 23

Off To Israel And Europe To
Film Back To Jerusalem

THE YEAR 1963 saw me traveling a lot in meetings, rallies, and in promoting our work. Bill and I have always been very close as twins, except a period during World War II when I was on a submarine and he an aircraft carrier. So I called him and asked if he and Joy would like to move up to Springfield and resume the work with me on a full-time basis. They thought and prayed about it and decided to do so, which pleased me to no end! It helped so much with him taking over the editing of our TV News, making appearances, and just assisting with the work load.

For a long time, I had held a very deep desire for a documentary movie made in color to be produced on the history of the Church, leading up to the Restoration Movement. I asked a group of trusted leaders to serve on a script committee, including Neil Kuns, Harvey Bream, Seth Wilson, Lewis Foster, Edwin Hayden, Carl Ketcherside, John Greenlee, Harold Davis, and J.D. Murch, a historian in our Movement. We met twice in developing the script, and following is a valued letter from Lewis Foster of Cincinnati Bible Seminary, written by hand in Prince Edward Island, Canada:

"Dear Bob, my apologies for not sending the manuscript back to you weeks ago. I have been on the road for over a month now, and I have read over the script again and have written down some notes that convey my suggestions. Best wishes in the fulfillment of your plans in the Lord's work. Sincerely, Lewis Foster." Letter dated 8/13/1964.

The whole first half or more of 1964 was taken up with planning for this production, meeting with the advisory committee, choosing a film producer, and finally preparing for and holding a Television Mission board meeting in St. Louis during our attendance at the North American Christian Convention. The men enthusiastically authorized the making of this special film, with cost of the project to be $30,000.00. As the executive director, after interviewing others, I selected Irwin S. Yeaworth to be our director. From Chester Springs, Pennsylvania, he had an excellent reputation as a filmmaker of documentaries, as well as having made a full-length movie for theatrical showing. He had appeared before our board giving his background and credentials as a filmmaker, as well as his belief in the Bible as the Word of God and his commitment to Jesus as the Son of God and Savior of the world. He had used award-winning cameraman Fritz Maeder from Switzerland in previous projects, and said he would be available for our job. Saying that there would be the need for a script continuity person to keep a running record of the continuous filmed scenes, and having met my wife in his visits with us, he said Pat could do that if she could go for the three weeks. Of course she quickly accepted the offer, and our kids were thrilled with the idea of having a three-week vacation on the "Homestead" farm with my parents! So we started preparing and packing for this exciting, adventurous trip to produce *Back to Jerusalem*, a dream I had held in my heart for so long!

On August 11, 1964, a hot and very busy Monday, I wrote:

"Hey, look! You're being caught up in the dizzy whirl of life! Take time! The furious pace of modern life should be avoided by Christians. Don't rush! Yet here I am, specializing in television and film production, in the midst of a project which has 'go..go..go' as its motto. There has hardly been any time for eating or sleeping during the past three days. I have caught myself literally gasping!

"But I feel a strength and serenity even in the midst of all this frenzied activity. You see, I have been preparing to leave on a filming mission to Europe and the Holy Land, and one cannot go on such a two-month foreign trip without finding himself tending to seemingly endless details. Getting shots (ooh, my arms), obtaining international drivers licenses, purchasing drip-dry clothes, having endless phone conversations with our producer about filming details, arranging schedules for countries to be visited, having photos made, getting passports, and solving a serious problem with Pat's lack of a birth certificate! We learned that she had none, and further that she hadn't been born in DeWitt, Arkansas. So after a mystery search, we discovered her birth place was Vicksburg, Mississippi. So we hurriedly called the Bureau of Statistics in Jackson, sent them the fee, got the birth certificate, and to Pat's astonishment, learned that her real father was Melvin Weakley. Probing further, we discovered that when Pat (Patricia) was about two years old, as best as we could determine, her father left her mother and the home, and simply disappeared. Her mother in time was married to Gus Anderson, a successful rice farmer west of DeWitt, Arkansas, who became her stepfather."

Getting that settled, I turned to some important last-minute details, including an immediate need for funding the film project. Fortunately, Gene Cantrell, who had been our banker in Joplin, had moved to an executive position with Empire

Bank in Springfield where we banked. He took my request and supporting documents to Keith Davis, the bank president, and after a tense day or two, my faith paid off. Without having to put up any collateral, by departure time I had $15,000.00 and more to come as needed! God is so good!

On Tuesday, August 12, 1964, I had prayer and read one of the Psalms with my family, and we shed a few tears as I kissed them goodbye, then headed to the airport. Pat would join me in New York in three days. I needed a few days there to get visas at Consulates, buy some cameras and lots of film, and meet our film director. Quoting from my journal, "I left Springfield at 2:15 p.m. on Ozark's flight 252, and connected in St. Louis on TWA's 62, a jet star-stream. I'm staying tonight at the Statler Hilton for $10.00 a day, and will stay at that rate while here."

I met Pat at LaGuardia Airport at 12:15 p.m. on Saturday the 15th, and we went directly to the hotel. I noted, "She looked so sweet, but was a little nervous from the plane trip. She's really got a lot of flying ahead of her! We spent the rest of the day getting things ready for the schedule ahead of us, mainly trying to eliminate some items." We ended up sending a whole suitcase of things and clothes back home because of the baggage limitations. On Sunday, we attended services at the Manhattan Church of Christ, took a stroll through Central Park, and went over our travel plans. On Monday, it seemed I was in and out of taxicabs all day, going to Consulates for more visas, buying more raw film, getting more shots, making phone calls, and conferring with our film director. Finally, at 5:15 p.m., we checked out of the hotel and headed for JFK Airport, where we joined our director Irwin Yeaworth (called "Shorty" because he was so tall!) and checked our luggage. Before boarding the plane, we gathered together, bowed our heads, and asked God's guidance and blessing to be upon us as we went forth, and that the film we were to produce would be a useful, effective tool for the advancement of His Kingdom. I further penned:

> "The breathtaking thrill of making our first transoceanic flight, and that in a modern, sleek jet Starstream, gripped the hearts of all three of us as we boarded the plane. Our conversation centered around our excitement about it, our gratitude and our amazement that we too were in the picture of this modern era of technology. Little funny quips punctuated and relieved the more serious thoughts about our mission."

We made stopovers in London, Belfast, Glasgow, and Paris, where with my own movie camera, I filmed strategic and important scenes, especially as they had relevance to our Movement or general church history. In Belfast, Pat and I overnighted with a lovely aged minister and his wife. He was a minister of the Church of Christ, and in County Down, he took us to various locations where Thomas Campbell and his young son, Alexander, had been. Included was an ancient church building where Thomas had preached before coming to America in 1807. I found there this brief, prized record of his life, which I quote:

> "Born in County Down, Ireland February 1, 1763 and died at the residence of his son, Alexander January 4, 1854, aged 90 years, 11 months, and 5 days. He was for many years a minister of the Secession Presbyterian Church in Ireland. Upon arrival in America, he soon withdrew from the Presbyterian conference and advocated a platform of primitive Christianity."

Let me insert here that in 1809, he wrote a famous and scholarly document with a plea for Christian unity, called "The Declaration and Address." It contained thirteen proposals, the first of which includes this declaration that the Church of Christ on earth is "essentially, intentionally, and constitutionally one."

Now back to the written tribute to Thomas Campbell I was referring to:

"In conjunction with his son, Alexander, he labored in this work with much success more than 40 years. In Christian learning and piety, he had few equals, and as a Christian minister, husband, and father, he had few superiors. Strong in faith and hope, he triumphed over death and reposes in Jesus without any sorrow or fear. Happy are the dead who die in the Lord, for they rest from their labour."

After the enjoyment and hospitality of the Hendrens in our short stay at Belfast, Pat and I went to Edinburg, then Glasgow, where Thomas Campbell had studied at the University there. We had the knowledge that his wife and seven children had been shipwrecked in September of 1808 just off the coast trying to rejoin Thomas in America. Having been rescued, they were taken to Glasgow where Alexander enrolled in the University. So we drove the few miles from old Edinburg to the University of Glasgow, and doing some research, found the record of Alexander's matriculation and an award for his excellence in the study of Logic, as well as his proficiency in other subjects. I did some filming there, then we hastened on to Edinburg, flying from there to Paris, France. There we spent the next day filming at various locations including, of course, the Eiffel Tower and the architectural beauty of the famed Notre Dame Cathedral. During all this time, our film director had left us, going from London to Beirut, Lebanon, to make arrangements for a guide and crew, plus the Swiss cameraman he needed to schedule for the time he would come for the start of the filming.

So it was quite a huge task and responsibility our director had in those few days to round up and select a capable team. But soon, he wisely got quite a combination of people from different cultures and backgrounds. Our guide was an urbane, suave, and well-educated Lebanese man whom we called "Shane." The sound engineer was a Jordanian, a very nice, skilled person, whose name I unfortunately can't remember. Our driver and overall helper, Ernest Layman, was originally a Hoosier, but lived in Jericho doing mission and charitable work for the Mennonites, assisting the Arab refugees. Our cameraman, Fritz Maeder, so nice, was from Switzerland. Directing all the shots and scenes was Irwin Yeaworth Jr. or "Shorty" as he was called, an American of Norwegian ancestry, who picked this crew. The script-continuity overseer was my wife, Pat, born in Mississippi but raised in the flat rice country of Southeastern Arkansas, and I, a native Ozarkian, was born and raised on our Homestead farm west of Lebanon, Missouri, and I would be overseeing the whole project and narrating the film.

But before Pat and I arrived in Beirut to meet the other members of the crew now chosen, leaving Paris, we had a quick stopover in Athens, then flew on to Cairo for a two-day stay. We got there on Saturday evening, August 22, 1964, and it had been arranged for an Egyptian motion picture producer, named Anise, to meet us, and he drove us to the Hilton Hotel on the banks of the Nile River. He was a Coptic Christian, very courteous and accommodating, and on Sunday morning led us out to Giza to see the pyramids and the Sphinx. Three Egyptians met us with their camels, helped Pat and me mount separate camels, and laughed hilariously as we rode around for a while. They called Pat "Queen of Sheba." I took movies there at this scene of the pyramids and Sphinx. We ascended the Great Pyramid of

Cheops, which is around 455 feet high. Then inside, we reached the granite tomb of King Cheops. I wrote in my journal:

> "It was really exciting to stand there in the cloistered, sacred burial place of the king, and to touch some of the two million blocks of stone averaging 2-1/2 tons each, and well over 3,000 years of age! This pyramid is 740 feet long on each side of the base, and covers 12 acres. It is huge! We realized how big as we climbed, bent over, the small passageway to the top, and descended backwards, also in a stooped position."

I continued writing my account of the Cairo visit this way:

> "We had arranged with Anise to be able to attend church and take Communion at his Coptic congregation that afternoon. The church was packed with worshippers, and though we didn't understand the language nor some of the ritual, we felt we were in a praise service with congregants who loved Christ. They seemed to be chanting the songs with deep reverence. The segregated seating caused Pat to be forced to sit with the women on the right side of the church, while Anise and I sat on the male side. When it came time for the Communion, Anise and I walked forward, and I motioned for Pat to also go with the other women up to the altar. As I was about to be served the bread and cup by the minister, he hesitated, and in a moment of somewhat strained, hushed conversation, he asked in perfect English, 'What is your religious affiliation?' I answered 'A Christian.' 'Yes, but what kind?' he wanted to know. I said, 'Just a Christian, a non-denominational Christian.' As long as I live, I'll never forget his firm answer, 'It is not enough!'

Anise was very upset and embarrassed. Poor Pat, on the other side, saw what was going on and returned to her seat, as did Anise and I to ours. After the service, at the door, I asked the minister if it were not a man-made regulation to refuse Communion to another Christian? Slowly and smilingly, he agreed, and hoped for the day when the Coptic Church would correct this prohibition. In Anise's car on the way back to the hotel, we had a good long talk about the teachings of Jesus, His Apostles, and His Church that is revealed in the New Testament Scriptures."

Pat and I left our hotel in Cairo the late afternoon of August 23, 1964, to catch a plane for Beirut. On the way to the airport, we drove through the old part of the city, and I don't think I've ever seen such a mass of humanity, milling around in extremely narrow, crowded streets. So many mouths to feed, and so much evidence of poverty and hunger, not only for food, but also for the Gospel. Then mile after mile of another sight I shall never forget, the Necropolis, city of the dead! The cemeteries abound with beautifully designed and ornamented tombs, monuments, and vaults. "For the living, poverty; for the dead, beauty and prosperity," I wrote in my journal. Continuing my writing, I recorded: "These tombs were the burial place of many of the ancient, well-to-do Egyptians, who felt that above all, the body in death is the glory of existence, and adequate adornment must be observed to prepare for the gods."

Ernest Layman of the Mennonite Refugee Service, who served as our guide, interpreter, and helper, met us at the airport in Beirut, and drove us in his big Chevrolet Carry-all to our hotel, the Riviera, overlooking the Mediterranean. The next morning, we woke up to the splendor, at that period of time, of a great metropolis. That evening, I wrote:

"Beirut is a beautiful city, with a lot of Western culture and Christian influence, with 50 percent of the population being Christians. Big Dodge and Buick taxies are seen everywhere. There are modern business buildings and hotels all over, and Beirut is called the 'Paris of the Middle East.'"

But of course, as I write this in 2015, Beirut, Lebanon, Syria, and the whole geographical area are torn apart with bombings and terror attacks by Islamic evil extremists. And just now, I am watching all the television reports of the barbaric and cowardly terrorist attacks by the Islamic revolutionaries in the city of Paris!

Pat and I enjoyed getting acquainted with our new crew members, and we all spent time outlining our trip through the "Holy Land" countries, and last-minute errands in purchasing for our filming needs. This all took a couple of days, during which I also secured visas for Poland, Russia, Kenya, North and South Rhodesia, South Africa, and Australia, for my extended travel after we would finish filming *Back to Jerusalem*.

Before leaving Beirut, I penned this:

"We did get to relax and get some sun for a couple of hours at the beach. In fact, I water-skied for the very first time in my life on the Mediterranean Sea! The first two tries up on the skis were unsuccessful. But a couple of minutes later I was breezing along on top of the waves like I was an old hand at skiing! We made a couple of big sweeps in the sea far from the shore, and I never did fall."

On August 28th at about 10:00 that morning, we left Beirut, headed for Syria. With all our equipment, luggage, and personnel, the Chevrolet Carry-all lived up to its name! We soon started winding our way upward and over the mountainous heights, about 5,000 feet in elevation, past the famous Cedars of Lebanon, from which lumber had been used to build the Temple of Solomon in Jerusalem as a gesture of friendship from Hiram, King of Tyre. Descending on the eastern side of the Lebanon mountain range into the rich, fertile Bakaa Valley, we saw majestic Mt. Hermon and her heights with fleecy clouds around her queenly summit. Some scholars think the transfiguration of Christ may have taken place on Mt. Hermon.

In writing about this trip, I recorded:

"Crossing the border from Lebanon into Syria proved to be quite a challenge. Very suspicious, they examined our luggage, equipment, passports, visas, Pat's purse, and wallets, besides having to make a declaration of how much money we possessed! It's a good thing we had Shane and Ernest, both of whom spoke their language and explained our mission. With great relief, we finally were motioned through. In about an hour, we came to the ruins of the ancient temples of Baalbeck, where we did some filming and picture taking. Started by Nero in A.D. 57, by the time of Constantine and Theodosius, the temples were converted into churches. But through the centuries, pagans, earthquakes, and wars have taken their toll on the temples, and as we know, there has been much fighting in that area during the Syrian civil war.

"Going on, we drove through the hot Syrian desert, and came to the little primitive village of Malulah, set in a valley under high cliffs. Our purpose here was 'to film a local person who would be filmed speaking the words of Jesus, in Aramaic, 'By this shall all men know that ye are my disciples, if ye have love one to another' (John 13:35, ASV). We made quite an enormous hit and attracted a large crowd to view the filming. The local barber, who seemed to be the mayor of the town, was told by Shane what we wanted to do. He agreed to our wishes, and we soon had a willing 'actor' to say the lines, after which there was loud applause from the on-lookers."

We finished there about sundown, and drove on to the city of Damascus. This of course was a major stop for us, as it plays such an important, big role in the historic saga of Christianity, with Saul of Tarsus' dramatic repentance on the road to Damascus, and his baptism by Ananias three days later in the city. We filmed at various places mentioned in the New Testament account, including at "the street called Straight," and the wall over which he escaped persecution and possible death later in his ministry.

CHAPTER 24

Back To Jerusalem Completed And Shown To The Nation On CBS Television

ON THE ROAD to Jerusalem, we saw the primitive way that lots of Bedouin tribes live, out in the desert sands with their flocks. Then it got quite mountainous much of the way before we got to the Jordan Valley, where we crossed over the bridge of the famed Jordan River. A bit further, it became desolate and rugged in the topography of the craggy mountains before passing Bethany and finally arriving in Jerusalem on Thursday, August 27th.

At that time, the city was divided, and the section that we were in was Jordan. I wrote in my journal, "So this is the Holy Land! The holy city! It doesn't seem holy, only historic. Perhaps it is because we can look out our hotel window and see no-man's land, a strip of territory with vacant buildings, and soldiers standing guard at the border line, right directly under us." In the hotel restaurant that first evening, the Jordanian waiters were nice but seemed to be so morose. I asked one of them the reason, and he sadly replied, "Because our land is taken from us." He pointed to my bowl of soup and said, "This is yours. If I take, you kill me." I answered, "No, this is not the way to settle things." He firmly replied, "Yes it is. They take, we kill!"

The next day we started the process of shooting scenes all over the old walled city and at the Via Dolorosa, the way of the Cross which Jesus was so cruelly forced to walk, bearing that heavy, wooden instrument of torture on which he would be crucified.

The next day was filled with filming at Bethany, the traditional tomb of Lazarus from which he was raised, and the place where Mary and Martha's house had stood. Then down we traveled on the curved, dangerous road to the deserted, mountainous area where Jesus was tempted. Further was the Jordan River where Jesus was baptized, and not too far but descending even more, we came to the Dead Sea, 1279 feet below sea level, and hot! Surprisingly, it had sharp, jagged little rocks on the shore, and we had to walk extremely carefully into the very warm, salty water to take a dip, just for the novelty of it. And novel it was! The water literally buoyed me up so that it was almost impossible to sink. But after only a few minutes in the hot, grimy, salty feel of the swim, I was glad to get out. I was never so happy to take a shower as I was on that day!

We drove back to Jerusalem, and later went to film at the Garden Tomb, where so long ago, Jesus lay wrapped in death linens after he was crucified. Whether this is the authentic place of his burial or not certainly known, many scholars believe it is. If so, it's where Jesus' body lay for three days and nights. Then suddenly, the impossible happened! He arose from the dead, this greatest event in history, believed with certainty by untold multitudes because of the accurate evidence and eyewitness accounts, but doubted or ignored by so many. But man's doubts cannot destroy God's deeds!

On Monday, August 31, I wrote:

"Today was quite a busy, important day, for we shot my opening lines of the script for BACK TO JERUSALEM, the film we had come to do. The making of this production had been a vision and dream of mine for a long time, and now it was coming true! The film is an attempt to recapture the spirit and pristine beauty and relevance of original, non-sectarian Christianity, with its emphasis on unity, love, and spirituality. The Church began in Jerusalem, and that's why I wanted to come here for the beginning of our documentary movie."

I continued my record of the filming:

"The day started at 6:30 in the morning. Immediately after breakfast, we went by truck with all the equipment to a spot near to the old 'Wailing Wall.' This is very close to the place where the Church began on the first Pentecost after the resurrection of Jesus. Our actual filming took place on a roof-top four stories up, overlooking almost all the old city. We lugged all our film equipment up many, many flights of stairs, to the top of a residence right next to the minaret of a very big mosque. It was a spectacular, breathtaking view, and a cool breeze helped relieve the hot rays of the sun. The flat area of this spacious, open-air veranda so high up was about thirty feet square, and even with our crew plus all of our cameras and film paraphernalia, we still had ample room. The house belonged to Rashid Massoud, a very courteous Moslem who gave us Christians permission to be here."

What a feeling came over me as I stood in the area where the supernatural events of Pentecost took place. The boisterous crowd from all over the Middle East seeing and hearing the miraculous tongues and mighty wind that the ascended and exalted Christ had emitted from Heaven! The filling of the Holy Spirit. The Apostles speaking in languages other than their own, and the crowd hearing and understanding in their different languages. The forceful sermon by Peter declaring that those who had cried for the crucifixion of the Son of God at the hand of the Romans were guilty of a great crime, and showing by Scripture and eyewitness proof that God had raised Him from the dead! Their heartfelt admission of this, their deep conviction, and their cry to be forgiven and saved. Peter's reply, in the New American Standard Bible account in Acts 2:38 through verse 42 is this: "Repent, and each of you be baptized in the name of Jesus Christ for the forgiveness of your sins; and you will receive the gift of the Holy Spirit. For the promise is for you and your children and for all who are far off, as many as the Lord our God will call to Himself." The account reads on, as recorded by Luke, a devout Christian and physician in the first century: "And with many other words he solemnly testified and kept on exhorting them, saying, 'Be saved from this perverse generation!' So then, those who had received his word were baptized; and that day there were added about three thousand souls. They were continually devoting themselves to the apostles' teaching and to fellowship, to the breaking of bread and to prayer." The Church was born that day! The King James translation of the last verse of the second chapter of Acts says the converts were "praising God, and having favor with all the people. And the Lord added to the church daily such as should be saved."

I penned these words late that August 31ˢᵗ night after a full day:

"How thrilling to know that near here, all this happened! It is not fiction. It is not hearsay. It is fact, full of excitement, drama, and mystery. Facts do not cease to exist because they are ignored. God moved, and men marveled! God offered, and men accepted.

"We were up on the roof from 8:00 till 12:00, and again from 3:00 to 4:00 p.m. The breeze stopped and the extremely hot, dazzling rays of the sun made it exceedingly difficult to keep from squinting my eyes as I spoke the lines of the narration. Thankfully, much of it was off camera. But when looking into the lens before me, and speaking, the sun was so bright that we had a problem of adjusting the lighting, getting sunburned, and trying to look fresh in my suit, tie, and makeup, under such non-ideal conditions."

But we succeeded in getting the job done, and everyone who viewed the film in premieres and on television after it was edited and completed applauded it and said it was a classic. On September 1, 1964, I wrote: "Today we crossed over into the 'Promised Land.' I am referring of course to the State of Israel, which has become a land of hope, of life, and of joy to multitudes of Jews." Because of the bitter enmity between the Arabs and the Israelis, I scribbled:

"Thus one can better understand the almost secretive way we were ushered out the 'back door' of Jordan to the crossing in a little alley at the Mandelbaum Gate. We had to walk and carry our luggage, as well as all our film equipment, out the back way from the YMCA hotel, about a hundred feet up the alley in 'no-man's-land.' There at the crossing were soldiers of both sides with their guns 'at ready,' with us in the middle. We presented our credentials on the Jordan side, the pole was raised, and we walked across. Going a few yards, we showed our passports and visas to the Jewish officers who stamped them, and we were in Israel!"

We deeply appreciated the courtesy we received in Jordan, but I wrote:

"It was like stepping from the first century to the twentieth when we crossed into Israel. Modern buildings, wide streets, dashing young executives, and citizens who love America. It is truly amazing what has been accomplished. A desolate wilderness has been transformed into a fresh, flowering oasis. And the Jews are very proud of it. Everywhere there are young trees that have been planted, symbolizing the young life and growing vitality of the new nation. But we need to pray for the peace of Jerusalem, and that the 'chosen people' sooner rather than later, might come to receive with honor, their greatest native-born son, none other than the SON OF GOD, their Messiah unrecognized!"

But we were not finished yet, for we had lots of places in Israel to film, scenes that would be included in our production. Our first stop was Mount Zion, in the "new" Jerusalem, where we shot various scenes, including King David's tomb. Next, by climbing a long steep flight of stairs, we entered the Hall of the Last Supper, where Jesus ate the Passover meal with His disciples and instituted the Lord's Supper. From Mt. Zion, we drove to Bethlehem, the little town where Jesus was born in a manger. Then by taxi, we went to Tel Aviv where an Israeli government press man, Isaac Austrian, accompanied us on a four hour drive to Tiberius, on the Sea of Galilee. It was midnight by the time we arrived.

On Wednesday, September 2, I wrote:

"Today was such a beautiful day. We arose at 6:00 a.m. and breathed in the breathtaking view of the Sea of Galilee from our hotel window. After dressing, we went down to the spacious balcony restaurant and enjoyed a hearty breakfast. Then it was off to a full day of filming. It included Capernaum and the ruins of the second century synagogue, built on the location where Jesus worshipped and taught; the sloping shore above the sea where our Lord gave the Sermon on the Mount, and later where he provided a miraculous feeding of the five thousand. And of course, at the beginning of his ministry, it was at the Sea of Galilee that Jesus called his first disciples, Simon Peter, Andrew, James and John. So we shot a scene at the shore where those fishermen became 'fishers of men.'"

We wanted a "boat scene" in the film, so we hired a boat from one of the fishermen nearby, and Shorty, our director, was in the water trying to position the boat just off the shoreline. This was to depict the account where Jesus was in a boat near the shore, teaching the people. Shorty was struggling somewhat in the deep water attempting to get the boat just right for the scene. It was an extremely hot day there at 600 feet below normal sea level, and I was perspiring profusely several yards up the slope getting the equipment ready for the filming. I looked down and saw that our conscientious but sometimes mischievous director had disappeared. "Oh my! Maybe he's drowned," I thought to myself. So I ran flying down the steep shore through the thick, stalky weeds and thorns intending to rescue him. Suddenly, the prankster's head appeared, and laughing hysterically yelled out, "I fooled you, didn't I? You thought I was drowning!" I stopped in my tracks, sweat pouring down my face, and cried out, "You rascal!"

I wrote in my journal:

"After we finished filming here, we drove on to Nazareth, the boyhood home of Jesus. We also saw the precipice where the people tried to push Jesus over its edge for claiming to be the Messiah. After shooting these scenes, we went on to the beautiful valley of Megiddo, stretching for miles in the distance. This is the plain where many Bible scholars believe the final Battle of Armageddon will be fought. It is such a peaceful landscape with well-tended, rich fields. It is heartrending to imagine armies clashing here, cluttering up this serene expanse of territory with dead and wounded bodies scattered everywhere in such horrifying blood-letting! But what man does, cannot be figured out. He is unpredictable, and as the New Testament says, 'Destruction and misery are in their ways'" (Romans 3:16, ASV).

We went on to Haifa and Mt. Carmel, where Elijah called down heavenly fire to triumph over the priests of Baal. Then on to Caesarea where we filmed ruins of some of the Crusaders' buildings, situated right on the side of the Mediterranean Sea. But in thinking about these crumbling structures, I wrote that night these words:

"In building for the Lord, ruin and decay, time and wear can never affect souls that are redeemed and sturdily built in the image and strength of Christ. Oh Father in Heaven, help me not to forget this! Please help me to build faith, character, and solidity into the lives of people! And may these qualities be always found in my life."

Still at Caesarea, we saw remains of Herod's 2,000-year-old walls, and a replica of an original and authentic plaque with the inscription of Pontius Pilate who condemned Christ to death.

After the long day of September the 3rd, we returned to Tel Aviv, overnighted there, and the next morning very early, drove to the airport. Saying our goodbyes, our cameraman, Fritz Maeder, boarded a plane bound for Switzerland, and Shorty, Pat, and I took a flight to Athens, flying over Turkey and the island of Rhodes. As soon as we got checked in at the Amalia Hotel, we secured a car and Greek guide and drove a spectacularly, scenic route along the beautiful, blue Aegean Sea to the old city of Corinth.

In my journal I wrote:

"Strategically located on the isthmus west of Athens, Corinth was the locale for Paul's preaching for a year and a half on his second missionary journey. He lived with Aquila and Priscilla, since these two were Christians and also tent makers, and he spent much time teaching and preaching in the Synagogue. Crispus, the ruler of the Synagogue, became a believer through Paul's efforts, '... and many of the Corinthians hearing believed, and were baptized' (Acts 18:8 ASV). We spent a couple of hours examining the remains of ancient Greek, Roman, and Byzantine periods, particularly of the temple of Apollo, which is partially still quite intact. We shot scenes at these places as well as at the Agora (marketplace), Odeum (roofed assembly hall), and the Bema (speaking area and pedestal), from which Paul probably preached. Shorty filmed me standing and speaking in this very spot."

I drove the car back to Athens, where we spent the night. The next morning the three of us drove up as far as was possible, on the hill where the Acropolis is located. Our eyes took in all the relics and ruins of twenty-five centuries, including temples, statues, and the most famous structure, damaged but still standing, the Parthenon. Constructed from 448 to 437 B.C., it stands proudly like a crown on the high, rocky hill of the Acropolis, dominating and overlooking the entire city. Built of pure, snow white marble, 208 feet long, 100 feet wide, and 66 feet high, it is an imposing structure, in spite of the toll of years, wars, and thieves. Had it not been for the shellings, the structure might be in almost perfect shape today. Also on the summit is the famed Erechtheum, with pillars sculptured in the form of beautiful, draped female figures, carved life-sized out of pure white marble, supporting the roofed porch. I managed to position Pat alongside the lovely lasses and snap her picture. I also climbed the steps to the top of Mars Hill, just west of the Acropolis, where the Apostle Paul preached to the philosophers on the subject of the "Unknown God." Standing there, I quoted from memory this sermon which I had memorized some fifteen years previously. And how thrilling to be here where Demosthenes orated, Socrates taught, and Paul preached! I wrote, "I could almost imagine I could hear voices come alive from silent centuries. It was really quite a spine-tingling experience to me to be able to walk around on such historical ground."

But we had more filming, the last for our production abroad of *Back to Jerusalem* ahead of us in Rome, so we had to hasten on. We left Athens at 6:45 p.m., had a smooth four-hour flight to the "Eternal City," and checked in at the Excelsior Hotel at midnight. On the plane going to Rome, we met and made friends with Jay Miller, a cameraman for NBC. We learned that he and Al Rosenfeld, an NBC correspondent, had undergone heavy fire while on an assignment in Cypress not too long before. Al had been seriously wounded when their jeep was shot out from under them, and Jay had jeopardized his life while getting Al to safety. He was with us a lot in filming the next two days.

The next morning, Sunday, September 6th, Pat and I caught a taxi and went miles and miles to a church where we were served

Communion. The name of the place was Instituto Betanin, an evangelical group, and the service was in the Italian language. But we enjoyed worshipping there, and the people were very nice. In the afternoon, we spent a lot of time at the incredible Colosseum, enjoying and filming there. Vespian and Titus, father and son emperors, were responsible for the construction of this magnificent arena, started in A.D. 72, and completed in 80. It took its name from the colossal statue of Nero, seven feet taller than the Statue of Liberty. Titus reportedly pressed thousands of Jewish captives into service to speed up construction, and on dedication day, he delighted the 50,000 spectators by ordering 10,000 gladiators and 5,000 wild animals to be engaged in a gory fight to the death.

The next two days we spent shooting scenes at various interesting places, including at St. Peter's Square, the Vatican, and the amazingly beautiful Sistine Chapel, where on the high, vaulted ceiling are the timeless and priceless paintings of Michelangelo. It was also the experience of a lifetime to go down into the Catacombs, deep underground caverns that run miles on end! They served, among other things, as burial places for the Christians, where also they no doubt held worship services.

On the evening of our last day in Rome, Jay Miller joined us for a delicious Italian dinner at the Hotel Del Orso Restaurant. Guitarists came over to our table to play and serenade Pat and me while we enjoyed our tasty Roman meal. It was very special and pleasurable for our last evening together, and the next day Pat would fly home, and I would head for Russia. We said goodbye to our new friend, Jay Miller, as we had earlier that day to our director, Irwin Shorty Yeaworth, who flew on to Venice for filming there.

So the next day, September 9, 1964, Pat and I took a taxi to the airport, having completed our filming mission to make

Back to Jerusalem on an exceedingly successful tour together that we would never forget! We embraced and kissed goodbye, she boarded her plane bound for New York and connection on home, and I embarked for a flight to Warsaw and Moscow.

CHAPTER 25

Filming In Moscow And Mashoko Africa

I ARRIVED IN Moscow on a chilly and rainy afternoon, September 11th, after a day-and-a-half stop in Warsaw. The airport was way out in the country, a few miles from the city. That night I penned these words about my arrival:

"As I entered the terminal, I noticed two women in baggy overalls painting and cleaning. They appeared to be peasants. Feeling a bit lost inside, I finally located an English-speaking Intourist official who advised and helped me with my disembarkation card, my visa, and passport. I went through customs and baggage inspection fairly easily and was told that a car was waiting for me outside at the curb. I had purchased a package deal when buying my ticket earlier on the trip that included a hotel, three meals a day, a guide who would be my interpreter, and a car with driver. I knew that being in a strange and oppressive country, and hoping I could get around and do a lot of filming, this would simplify things for me, and it certainly did! That is, to an extent. The car was very old, and the driver was a mustached, poorly dressed peasant with a cap pulled down almost over his ears. But leaving the airport, my spirits were brightened by the gorgeous birch trees, the leaves of which had turned into their brilliant yellow color. My mood, however, wasn't helped any as we soon passed a little village of run-down, dilapidated shacks and old unpainted board houses. I was totally surprised! As we approached the city, almost all the apartments and business buildings were a drab brown color, but the streets were clean and very wide. The driver had to stop three times to ask directions to the hotel. When we got there and he let me out, he failed to get me my bags, and sped away. The poor man sheepishly walked in soon, much to my relief, but with only one bag! I told him through an Intourist clerk who was checking me in that there was another bag. He ran out to the car and quickly came back with the bag that had my two cameras and a dozen rolls of movie film! I really breathed a sigh of relief! By this time, I wondered what in the world I had gotten myself into!"

I was shown to my room in a rather run-down hotel, the Peking, but it was adequate, with a tiny desk in the corner and a twin-size bed. The meals in the restaurant were all right, but not served with any grace, charm, or favor! The best thing I found to order was a soup called "borsch" and a poultry dish "kievski."

The Intourist Service assigned me a guide who spoke perfect English and was very accommodating in taking me wherever I wanted to go. I was a little bit surprised since, in those years, it was a time of a tightly-controlled, sealed-off, and secretive communist society. I was stopped and challenged a few times as I was filming, but my guide always barked strong orders to the hostile and armed guards to "lay off," cease and desist, and they did every time.

The day after arriving, my guide came and escorted me to a place I had no idea I would be allowed to go – behind the walls of the Kremlin! Sure enough, a uniformed guard said, "Nyet" right at the entrance. With a stern look, my guide flashed a shiny and superior badge of authority, and the poor fellow meekly let us enter. Prince Yuri Dolgorukiy built the fortifications here on the banks of the Moscow River in the middle of the twelfth century and encircled them with a wooden wall. The present walls, above which nineteen towers rise, appeared by 1500. The cathedrals are in the center of the Kremlin. The largest of them is the Assumption Cathedral, crowned by five golden domes. It was built in the fifteenth century by Russian master workmen under the direction of Aristotele Fioravanti. Close by are the Annunciation and Archangel Cathedrals. Inside these ancient official houses of worship are beautiful icon paintings of religious events, some of them as early as the twelfth century. Russia does have a rich religious history in its background of times past, but atheism, brought in by revolution and communism, became its religion. Back in my hotel room, I wrote:

> "It really seems to me that evolution and atheism haven't done too good a job. Millions and millions of years for a few short breaths and years of life on planet earth? Man is glorious, and his brain is the ultimate for a little while, then death, and it's all over? Man, proud man, dies and it's kaput? My, oh my! Christ offers so much more!"

In the week and a half I was in Russia, I really got a view of what life was like. I visited and filmed in their Museum of Revolution, which traces the fiery history – the conditions under the czars, the uprisings, the defeats, the banishments, the retreats, and then the victory. Soviets flash a gleam in their eyes when they mention the word "revolution." In that noted building were proudly displayed many charts, artifacts, and pictures showing the excesses and "evils" of capitalism and Christianity, including a ridiculous cartoon of drunken Christians feasting on the bones and blood of the body of Christ in a church Communion service. What a false and sacrilegious depiction of this holy act of worship! A long line of young school children were there viewing all of this when I was visiting and filming in the museum.

One day I got in the three-block line of citizens from all over the soviet empire to go through the ornate mausoleum to view the well-preserved, waxened body of Lenin. To those people, it was a glorious experience; to me, it was eerie.

I was taken out into the countryside, including a young pioneers' camp, where bright-eyed, red and white uniformed boys and girls were present. They gathered around me and seemed elated to see an American, asking me many questions in almost perfect English about my life and family, about New York and Hollywood, and about the life of kids in our country. They were so very friendly!

But both at the university and the elementary school, where I was welcomed by a professor, I had to listen to a speech by a student spouting the glories of the communistic system, as opposed to our rights and individual freedoms. However, I think this was a necessary exercise and routine the officials of the government required, because afterwards, students were very friendly, asking for my address and anxious to hear about my life.

Before my trip, I learned about a 2,000-member church in Moscow, so on my first of two Sundays there, I asked my guide and driver to take me there. I couldn't get them to go inside with me. Let me quote now how I described that experience in my journal:

"Never in my life have I witnessed such a moving scene as I did this morning. The people were seated and standing in every available place, in the aisles and at the doorway, up in the crowded and cramped balconies circling the auditorium, as well as being pressed tightly together in the pews. There were some men, many peasant-looking women, all with scarves on, a number of middle-aged people, perhaps a couple hundred adolescents, and at least one soldier. Many in the congregation were dressed poorly, but there appeared to be quite a few 'cultured' worshippers, and the choir particularly impressed me, singing four exquisite anthems, led by a master conductor."

I continued my description of the service in these words:

"The congregational singing was so heartfelt, and the outpouring of worship by these dear souls was something to behold. I felt so sorry, though, for the old women who stood for the entire two-hour service. I was seated by a very courteous usher in the balcony, and was told that I could use my movie camera while seated, which I did unobtrusively for a couple of minutes. But I hastened to resume my worshipping with everyone else.… I was seated next to a nice looking couple, Ann and Antony Hippsillie, she from New York and He from England. They were students at the University, and having met there, were married. But they were devout Christians. Ann was quietly whispering to me the content of the minister's message. It was a comforting sermon about the raising of Lazarus, and the hope that we as Christians have because of the death, burial, and resurrection of Christ. A couple in Moscow had lost their 17-year old son in death, and the mother, in deep agony and distress, had disappeared over the last five days. The whole congregation was sharing in hers and the family's grief. The elderly presiding minister was 70, but he delivered his message with vigor and a serene kindness on his face. After church, I met with all the ministers and elders back in the study, where we had a good, long visit, and I was asked to preach the following Sunday evening."

I had picked up a newspaper, printed in English, called "The Moscow News," so I decided to go there to have an interview with the editor. He was cordial, but to no surprise, he made it plain that his paper and the governmental position was that "atheism is one of the planks of the Communist platform." He continued:

"Although we believe in the separation of church and state, and a man's religion is his own private affair, our official position is that there is no god. Ask any of our young people! They will quickly tell you this. We are using the educational processes, ever since the Revolution, to eliminate this out-moded, childish concept. Science will give us all the answers we need about our existence and life on earth as civilization progresses."

Of course, I witnessed to him about my faith in Christ, and the answers it provided me for happiness and fulfillment here on the planet, as well as for eternity. I asked him, "Is it not true that communism suppresses religion?" He laughed and replied, "Not really. We license churches as officially authorized and recognized organizations, and people are free to worship. But it's the elderly and unlearned peasants that do so, not the young and educated." But I knew that the officials had put many, many restrictions on churches. Churches cannot display prominent signs. They cannot have Bible schools for children or adults. Great numbers of them were closed and converted to become museums. Ministers cannot use radio, television, or newspapers to advertise or preach the Gospel.

Tuesday night, September 15, 1964, I wrote in my journal: "Tonight I had a very emotional experience." I simply couldn't contain my feelings as I thought of the atheism that abounds everywhere in this godless society, and as I reflected on the faith and freedom we enjoy in our country. Tears filled my eyes as I sat at the little crude desk and wrote a rather lengthy poem about the blessing of having been born in such a free and great nation. The words poured out of my heart and onto the page in this writing that I titled, *America – Land I Love*:

Why did the fortunes of life shine on our land
So bountifully, so beautifully, so freely?
Such a good and great land, a prosperous nation—
Like a dream world, one asks, "Did it happen really?"
Or is it all like a fairy tale
Of a land beyond the Sea,
With princes and castles and golden thrones,
And wonderfully beautiful things to see.

No, 'tis true, 'tis true! America is very real!
As tho' God Himself bent o'er Heaven's walls,
And looking o'er the entire world,
Chose her in His infinite zeal,
To fashion, to tenderly form in His own image,
And bless with His own seal
A country free, and bold, and good,
That would hold high freedom's great ideal!

But easy it did not come,
Nor without toil and sacrifice,
No miracle this, the building of our great land,
But slow, painstaking effort was all that could suffice.
Life and death in the Ocean crossings,

Hardship and disease in pioneer tossings,
Lives given in family-defending,
Blood spilled in freedom-tending.

Every man in America is a king,
And every woman, a queen,
Because we are free!
And the mind unbound rules o'er a kingdom unseen,
To set its course, to choose its way,
To climb the upward path
To knowledge and faith and the love of God,
And away from hatred and wrath.

No matter how poor, we all are rich
In the things that really count!
We are free to speak, to write, to worship.
Our freedom is a huge account.
Our government doesn't dictate how we must live,
Or what we must believe.
We can look and read, and choose, ourselves,
And the truth we can receive.

But what of the future of this land of ours?
What course will we pursue?
Greatness? Neighborliness? Belief in God?
Or greed, ugliness, and selfishness too?
The choice is ours, we each must decide
What is to be our destiny.
May all of us, with grateful hearts,
Choose the path of God and stay free!

Through all of my deep and fast-flowing thoughts as I wrote,
I found myself weeping in appreciation and thankfulness for

my faith and American heritage, and prayerfully hoping that somehow, some way, the barriers of communism would be broken.

Before leaving Russia, I was so blessed, perhaps as the first, or maybe one of the few, from America, to have the incredible opportunity of preaching to a receptive crowd of worshippers in Russia during the "Cold War." The evening service found me getting to church a half-hour early. I had allowed myself plenty of time, and sure enough, my driver, a different one this time, had difficulty in locating the address of the church. Following is a description in a report I wrote about this preaching experience, during which I spoke from my heart, using no notes:

"Moscow, USSR, Sunday, September 20, 1964 – Tonight I had the opportunity of speaking a half hour to approximately 1,200 Russians in church. It was quite a challenge and I must admit I was a little anxious about what to say. I gave greetings from the American Christians who are dedicated to the restoration of New Testament Christianity. I also spoke greetings in behalf of the American people. I told them that I was one of seven brothers, four of us being ministers of the Christian Church, working in film and television production, as well as in preaching the Gospel. I spoke of our dedication to unite based on Christ's own words in His great intercessory prayer. I quoted Jesus as He had been praying for the Apostles, when He said, 'Neither for these only do I pray, but for them also that believe on me through their word; that they may all be one; even as thou, Father, *art* in me, and I in thee, that they also may be in us: that the world may believe that thou didst send me' (John 17:20-21, ASV). I pointed out that all who are truly Christians, whether Russians or Americans, are one in Christ. I then quoted Ephesians 4:1-6, these words of the Apostle Paul, 'I therefore, the prisoner in the Lord, beseech you to walk worthily of the calling wherewith ye were called, with all lowliness and meekness, with longsuffering, forbearing one another in love; giving diligence to keep the unity of the Spirit in the bond of peace. *There is* one body, and one Spirit, even as also ye were called in one hope of your calling; one Lord, one faith, one baptism, one God and Father of all, who is over all, and through all, and in all' (Eph. 4:1-6, ASV). I elaborated on this Scripture to some extent.

"Then since the previous Sunday morning service had dwelt so much about suffering and the death of the 17-year-old lad, I thought it would make a deep and loving connection with these suffering saints to mention the sad death of our child while we were making a Christian film in Hollywood. I said that nothing, if we belong to Christ, can destroy the hope that we cling to because of our Lord's suffering and triumphant resurrection. I then quoted the little lullaby I had composed and sung to Karen right before she was taken to Heaven. The audience was deeply stirred as I could tell from the expressions on their faces. [The words of my lullaby appear earlier in my book.] I was able to speak with power and clarity, and the necessity of using an interpreter proved to be no handicap. The people seemed to receive what I had to say with deep and sincere appreciation. Through their worn, hard-working appearance radiated the glow of faith. Weeping, smiling, nodding agreement, they at times would softly and reverently utter what must have been the equivalent of our 'Amen.'

"I urged those in the congregation to be of good courage and of strong heart, and to keep the faith regardless of the circumstances of life. I said 'no peril, no anguish, no persecution that we might be called upon to endure could remove Christ's love from us.' As Michael, my interpreter, repeated the words I spoke, and as I listened and watched, I could see those who were seated and standing, straining to catch every word, every phrase, and every sentence. Smiles of appreciation, tears of joy, radiant countenances hungering for every utterance ... that is what I saw.

"I closed with these comforting words that I had memorized years ago, 'Who shall separate us from the love of Christ? shall tribulation, or anguish, or persecution, or famine, or nakedness, or peril, or sword? Even as it is written,

For thy sake we are killed all the day long;

We were accounted as sheep for the slaughter.

Nay, in all these things we are more than conquerors through him that loved us. For I am persuaded, that neither death, nor life, nor angels, nor principalities, nor things present, nor things to come, nor powers, nor height, nor depth, nor any other creature, shall be able to separate us from the love of God, which is in Christ Jesus our Lord' (Romans 8:35-39, ASV).

"At the conclusion, after the benediction, the congregation sang a stirring rendition of 'God Be With You 'Til We Meet Again,' as the presiding minister led me back to the pulpit. The whole building was a sea of white handkerchiefs being waved to me, together with the prolonged sound of 'Amens' reverberating all over. It was a scene I'll never forget!"

From Moscow, I flew to Africa, with stopovers in Nairobi, Kenya, breathtaking Victoria Falls, and on to Southern Rhodesia, where I spent several days. How blessed I was to be received so royally by the missionaries at Mashoko Hospital, the Teacher Training School near there, and going out in the "bush" to minister. I also went out to help comfort, assist with medical treatment, and witness to, the villagers standing in long lines with their needs. From the filming footage I shot there and previously in Russia, I later on edited and narrated a documentary film called, "As I Go, Moscow to Mashoko." I also composed and later recorded the song, "As I Go," one line of which reads, "I cannot help but feel pain and anguish so real, for humanity downtrod, without hope and without God." I also produced a good film about my experiences in Russia, titled "Eyewitness Behind the Iron Curtain." At Mashoko, it was hard to say goodbye to Dr. and Mrs. Jerry Smith; Madonna Burgett; Lester and Marjorie Van-Dyke; Don Stoll; young Darel Pruett; the Doug Johnsons; and nurses and workers. Dr. Dennis Pruett, who started this great work, and John Pemberton, were both in the States.

With a stopover connection in Johannesburg, South Africa, I made the longest and most tiring flight by a propeller plane I've ever been on to Perth, Australia. From there I flew to Melbourne, where Brother Arnold Caldicott met me, and I had the privilege of preaching and having fellowship at the Geelong Church where he ministered. He and his wife had been to America visiting churches, where we had met them. Our good friend, Doug Willis, had also been welcomed by us and many more on his lengthy tour in our country. He was holding a crusade nearby at Ballarat, so I joined him there for a rich time of ministry and fellowship for a few days, before at long last, heading for home!

In the meantime, prior to making *Back to Jerusalem*, we cleared more television stations and were in need of a new series. So in 1963, using the new videotape method, the four of us brothers and our wives went to Chicago, and at the NBC studios made thirteen new *Homestead USA* programs. The cost was only $1,000.00 per show, a great deal less than filming in Hollywood.

1965 was a very eventful year for me. Early in that period, I had to go to Chester Springs, Pennsylvania, where the studio of the *Back to Jerusalem* producer-director was located, to do some more shooting and narration on the film. It was completed in the spring, and successfully premiered in churches all over the country.

CHAPTER 26

New Album On Capitol Records

THE FILM RECEIVED rave reviews from ministers and people in the pew, as well as from television industry executives and program managers. Joe Ellis, minister and later a Christian College professor, said, "Back to Jerusalem is a superb documentary, a most significant expression of the ideal of restoring the Church to the New Testament level as a basis of Christian unity. The film is top quality, totally unlike anything yet produced and long overdue." Ernest H. Chamberlain, minister of the West Seattle Christian Church and a past president of the North American Christian Convention, wrote:

> "The camera work is of professional quality, the narration is positive, clearly enunciated, and convincing. At no time does the narration seem to become 'preaching' and yet the message of the restoration of simple New Testament Christianity is forcefully presented. This film should be in every church library, on every television network, and viewed by every class of Church history on every college campus in the nation."

And when I was invited and flown to New York by the CBS Television Network to show the film and be personally interviewed on the "Lamp Unto My Feet" program, I knew without a doubt, that my dream and vision to make this film was a dream come true! After I got home, I received a letter from Pamela Ilott, in charge of all CBS religious telecasting, and she wrote:

"This film is the finest of its nature that I have ever screened. It presents in such good taste what the world needs, and is the answer, ecumenically speaking, to what modern religionists are searching. Many who rejected credal authoritarianism would welcome this type of message, if only they knew about it. You owe it to yourselves and to the world to get the widest possible exposure of this production."

Because we Vernon Brothers were now only a part-time team, with B.J. preaching in a successful ministry at Dewey, Oklahoma, and Don, who had established a fast-growing new Glendale Christian Church in Springfield, Missouri, Bill and I carried on in the ministry of Christian Television Mission. But in reality, we just couldn't do what our united efforts had formerly accomplished in the past eight or nine years, as far as the Mission was concerned. And my success in film production, my longing to fulfill a hope of doing a solo album, plus a new passion for foreign missions, led me to form my own non-profit organization called Christell, Inc. So in essence, I then went part time also, launched out in faith, borrowed the money, and recorded my first album in 1965, titled *As I Go*. The famed Ralph Carmichael did the orchestrations, and I recorded it with the orchestra "live" in a Hollywood studio, and Word Records listened to it, liked it, and put it on their label! The album contained the "Lullaby To Such As You" melody I had written and sung to our very ill baby Karen before she died while we were filming in Hollywood in 1958. Other favorites on the album were "Stranger of Galilee," "Sweet Hour of Prayer," "Suddenly There's a Valley," "Tenderly He Watches," and the new song I had written after being on the go in filming, "As I Go." But we brothers remained very close in spirit, keeping the Mission intact and alive, while respecting one another's ministries and separate activities. At periodic times during the next few years, we would be together to produce more TV programs, hold occasional revivals, and appear at rallies, special events, and conventions.

WFAA-TV in Dallas, Texas, now had excellent production facilities to videotape color first-class programs, so as the executive director of the TV Mission, I contacted them, and got a good quote to do our next series there. On June 9, 1966, I wrote a letter to our supporters telling them about this, as follows:

"A new color television series is now in the planning stages, to be completed this summer! The entire cost for the 13 productions will only be $10,000.00, so much less than the film sequence procedure! More great news! 50 major cities across the nation will be telecasting this new series this fall and winter at an hour you can see. Isn't that wonderful!!"

I went on to thank them for their past support, and asked them to remember us with a special gift. So we went to work preparing the scripts and music, and on August 3, 1966, I got a letter from Bob Turner, manager of WFAA-TV:

"Dear Bob, this confirms your booking of Studio A, 9:00 am to 5:30 pm on Wednesday, August 31; Thursday, September 1; and Friday, September 2. I have in hand your check for $500.00 as a down payment on the production in accordance with our contract. I have booked Danny Franks, who has done all the lighting on the Billy Graham programs, as lighting director for those 3 days."

So we four brothers and our wives, plus mine and Pat's 15-year old daughter, Becky, enjoyed our time together, making these thirteen programs. Though so young, Becky was an accomplished pianist, known also as being a talented singer.

It was a very unsettled and volatile time in the 60's, what with the culture changing and America involved so deeply in the controversial Vietnam War. The wartime era, the civil rights marches, the assassinations of President John Kennedy, his brother Bobby, and that of Martin Luther King Jr., shook the nation. I was so moved by events in this critical time that I wrote in 1966 my third and fourth songs, "Tell America" and "Freedom Prayer." Feeling they needed to be recorded, I also selected other patriotic classics such as "God Bless America," "Battle Hymn of the Republic," "This Is My Country," "Born Free," and others, and got Ralph Carmichael to write arrangements for an orchestra and background choir. Mind you, this was all on faith and borrowed money! Then I took off for Hollywood, where Ralph as conductor, the orchestra plus choir, and I went into the studio and recorded the ten songs in a three-hour session. Then, in prayer, with all the faith, bravado, gusto, and courage I could muster, I walked into the prominent, tall, and circular tower of Capitol Records with my tape in hand. I was shuffled around to different people, in this and following days, but finally I was signed, and I got my album on the Capitol label!

1967 was a fruitful and important year for my family and me. It included a two-month musical tour for Pat, Becky, Gregg, Debbie, and me; a month-long Vietnam tour for Becky and me; and my ministry and film showings in South Africa.

From a picture poster publicizing our family tour, it reads, "Christell Inc. presents TELL AMERICA, a Concert and Rally by the Bob Vernon Family." At that time, Becky was 16, Gregg 13, and Debbie 6 years old. Our whole family sang four songs; Pat and I sang a duet; Becky played and sang a medley of songs; and Gregg on the guitar I had bought him played "Joshua Fit the Battle of Jericho." Pat had taught Debbie the cute song, and she belted out, "I don't have to wait until I'm grown up to be loving and true, there are many little deeds of kindness that each day I can do. I can read my Bible and pray, be a loving helper always. I don't have to wait until I'm grown up, to be what Jesus wants me to be." I sang "Tell America" and "Freedom Prayer," then closed with a challenging message about our ministry and future plans. While still on tour in the Washington, D.C. area, we went to the Pentagon where I showed them my Capitol Records album with the songs "Tell America" and "Freedom Prayer," and they quickly assigned Becky and me to travel to Vietnam for a musical and inspirational tour for our troops. But for our last few appearances on the family programs, Pat got extremely ill with migraines, had to be hospitalized, and the rest of us had to go on with our commitments until she recovered.

On August 21, 1967, Lieutenant Colonel Roland C. Beasley, USAF, wrote me a letter, some of which I quote:

"Dear Mr. Vernon: This letter with enclosures completes processing procedures for your forthcoming tour of Vietnam with your daughter. Enclosed are your passports, travel orders, and airline tickets. You are scheduled to depart Springfield Airport on 27 August 1967 at 11:44 AM on Delta Flight 454, arriving Kansas City at 12:38 PM. You change to United Flight 293 departing Kansas City at 1:45 PM, arriving San Francisco at 3:53 PM. We have arranged for a staff car to transport you to Travis Air Force Base. You are further scheduled to depart there on 28 August 1967 at 3:00 AM on Flight H-243 for Saigon."

So this is the schedule we followed, with stopovers at Wake Island, Guam, and Clark Airfield Base in the Philippines. As we approached Saigon, I wrote:

"We're now starting our descent at about 20,000 feet. Through the fleecy, scattered clouds, everything looks so peaceful down there, the rice paddies, the winding river, the patterned fields, and the wooded area. You'd never guess that a war was going on!"

At the Saigon Air Terminal, we were met by Captain Carl Lillvik, who was to be our escort officer, and the entertainment coordinator, Charlie Neal, who took us to the Protocol Lounge. They quickly got us through the customs regulations and drove us to the Meyerkord Hotel, surrounded by a huge fence, sandbags for mortar attack protection, and guarded by military policemen. After getting settled in our rooms, our escort officer and Mr. Neal briefed us on several important items for touring South Vietnam. Here are a few of these important points:

"1-"You are in a war zone. Don't forget it.
2-Though the city of Saigon is heavily populated, and the citizenry friendly, avoid crowds. Keep moving, if you walk anywhere.
3-Don't pick up any objects or bundles on the streets under any circumstances. It could contain a terrorist bomb.
4-Don't accept rides in the little three-wheeled cycles. Since they are lower than automobiles, it would be a very simple thing for a V.C. to hurl a grenade at you from a passing vehicle.
5-In the event of a mortar attack, get to a shelter if you can. If it should come while you're in your hotel room, get

under the bed. If you're in a barracks or office room, lie down, next to the wall.

6-While on your tour, you will have the priority of Colonel. We give you this rating because of the importance of the mission you are serving. As you present your programs to the troops in the field and at the bases, we offer you the best we have. Sometimes for your program, your stage will be the back of a truck, and for your accommodations, you might have a tent and a cot. But you will always get the best we have.

7-Your travel will consist almost exclusively of flight by helicopter. Your priority is second only to generals and to combat flights, so when you are assigned to a flight, be there on time, for space has been reserved for you.

8-After you have received your tour schedule, don't tell anyone – not a soul – where you are going. The V.C. likes crowds. So, by necessity, your appearances are advertised by word of mouth and low-key promotion on bases only. Sometimes you will appear before a hundred, sometimes a thousand, and sometimes may be ten thousand. But 'Charlie' will never know it. We have a very good security system, and we will take every precaution possible. We want you to also do your best in protecting yourselves.

9-The morale of our fighting men here in Vietnam is very high. This is due primarily to three factors: (a) Every man, when he comes here, knows that he is assigned for just one year. He can ask for extension if he wants to, and when this happens, the government flies him home for a month before his return; (b) Every uniformed man is flown at government expense for periodic rest periods to choice vacation spots such as Hawaii. This is a tremendous morale booster; (c) Entertainment tours as yours are a real factor in the morale of our men. In this program, every service individual gets to attend such a gathering once a month. So your presence is greatly appreciated, and you are contributing in a very effective way to the inspiration and well-being of our men."

After absorbing all of these precautions and letting the excitement and amazement of actually being in a war zone hit me, I prayed for God's protection and blessing, and went to bed.

The next day we were to pick up all of our equipment and our fatigues for traveling. The following morning we took off, fully equipped and ready to go!

Here is a list of the appearances we made on our three-week Vietnam Mission:

3rd Field Hospital in Saigon
79th Maintenance Battalion in Saigon
13th Aviation Battalion at Can Tho
D Company 5th Special Forces Group at Can Tho
Chapel Services at Can Tho
36th Evacuation Hospital at Vung Tau
Naval Support Activity Detachment at Vung Tau
USS *Tutuila* in the South China Sea
IVWG Coastal Defense Group at Cat Lo
Buon Ea Yang Sub Sector at Ban Me Thout
MACV Advisory Team #33 at Ban Me Thout
Detachment B-24 of C Company Special Forces Group at Kontum
MACV Advisory Team at Kontum
Chapel at Bien Hoa Air Base
159th Engineers Group at Long Binh
3rd Brigade of 1st Infantry Division at Lai Khe
Multi-units of 1st Infantry Division at Lai Khe

One of the most exciting and dangerous episodes took place on September 6th while we were flying via helicopter over the jungle near Ban Me Thout. We were on our way to do a program at a combat outpost, when suddenly we spotted a smoking village under attack by the Viet Cong. Our helicopter was desperately needed, so we spiraled down very swiftly, and were hustled to a large underground bunker approximately 30 feet long, 20 feet wide, and 10 feet high. About a dozen armed Special Forces group boarded the helicopter, making it too heavy to take off, so two of the men jumped off, and the chopper with those aboard lifted and swooped over the trees to lend assistance and fight off the foes attacking the villagers. I had my movie camera out catching all of this on film while Becky was hurried into the bunker, with me joining her a few minutes later. I was told that some sixty Vietnamese had been killed a couple of days before this, and we were seeing firsthand the fierce terrorist tactics of the Viet Cong and the North Vietnam Army. When the troops returned, with others joining them in the bunker, we put on our most emotion-packed performance, though unscheduled it was, in the underground "chapel!" A huge American flag covered one wall of the bunker, and with artillery fire booming, I tell you, hearts throbbed and choked as I sang "Freedom Prayer" and "Tell America!" The whole area here was a perimeter controlled by the Americans, and surrounding the hill containing this bunker were "claymore" mines, machine gun positions, and three lines of barbed wire.

The Viet Cong got within two miles of the air strip when we were at Can Tho, and extra precautions were taken at night, such as putting blankets over the windows. Being a radioman as a Submariner in World War II, I spent two action-packed nights in the radio shack, keeping tabs on the movements of the communist insurgents.

As a Navy man, I must say that it was a thrill for me to get to board the USS *Tutuila*! It was a packed house in the ship's large interior gathering area, where our show was received with rousing applause and ovations.

Aside from our USO shows, we were privileged to visit the hospitals and personally talk with U.S. soldiers who had been wounded in battle, listening to their stories and offering our encouragement and support. Then sometimes on the bases, how the guys loved it when Becky got to serve up their meals in the chow line! We also visited a South Vietnamese hospital where American doctors were attending to patient needs. And we were humbled when, after a long and bumpy jeep ride, we got to visit with caregivers at a leper colony.

When Becky and I got home from Vietnam, it was amazing how we were treated like heroes, which of course we weren't. In my hometown of Lebanon, at a high school assembly, they cheered and applauded loudly at the conclusion of our program there. The principal when I graduated twenty-three years earlier, Mr. Ellis C. Rainey, still served in that position, speaking highly of one of his former students! And in Springfield, where the *Daily News* had carried my news reports I had written each day and sent back for publication, we were honored and gained such notoriety. It was so humbling to us. I had made a prior commitment for a month-long mission to South Africa, so I wasn't able to participate in the special assembly at Becky's high school, where she was a senior. But dressed in her fatigues, singing and telling the dramatic account of her Vietnam venture, she was a big hit as television cameras, and also the Springfield newspapers, covered the event. The superintendent of Glendale High, Mr. Willard Graff, said it was the most outstanding and impressive assembly program he had ever seen!

Stuart Cook, a missionary in South Africa, had written me months earlier, stating that he had been viewing *Back to Jerusalem* and asked if I could come there to speak and show the film in theaters. So I went, witnessing and screening the movie in some twenty theaters, then in a question and answer session, explaining the teachings of the New Testament Church. It publicized his work well!

CHAPTER 27

Missions, Migraines, Mayo Clinic, And Moving

IN 1968, THE four of us brothers, besides meeting occasionally for television board meetings and special events like revivals, had the highlight of joining Gene Dulin and John Huk on a mission trip to Russia. We were gone from June 2nd through the 22nd with them and a group of others, ministering and singing at churches in Leningrad, Moscow, Minsk, and Warsaw. It was so fulfilling to fellowship with and encourage these saints who meet and worship under such restrictive circumstances. Much later, we, with some family members also, took a trip from June 12 through July 2, 1985, to Poland at the invitation of dear friends, Paul Bajko and Kostek Jakoniuk. What a rich time this was of preaching, singing, and ministering in so many Polish cities.

But beginning in year 1968, Pat's migraines started coming with more frequency, accompanied by terrible nausea. She would have these attacks three or four times each year, requiring heavy medication and hospitalization when they wouldn't let up. It got so bad that both she and I dreaded the moment symptoms would begin. In between those periods, she would be so happy, enjoying her home life, family, and church activities. I would be able to join my brothers in revivals and rallies, but sometimes I would get a call and have to return home prematurely in order to get her treatment. The first time that either of us could recall her having a migraine was when in pain during a very difficult childbirth, she required an epidural spinal block, and came home with a horrific migraine headache that lasted for three days. But after that, she might have one or two a year, that is, until 1967 while we were on our family's two-month TELL AMERICA TOUR, when she had a migraine and nausea that lasted a whole week. From 1968 through 1971, her condition got so bad several times each year that I was almost beside myself, taking her to the doctor or to hospitals in Springfield and Lebanon, trying to get her help. Of course, it deeply affected our lives, our home, and our ministry, as I desperately tried to keep revival and rally appointments with my brothers, who after some eight years in located ministries had re-joined the Mission on a full-time basis.

Interspersed with these discouraging bouts, I did have some reprieve at times from all this pressure that was mounting and the dilemma I felt. One such was going to a Christian service camp with my young daughter, Debbie, and getting to baptize her. Another, in 1970, was taking our son, Gregg, who also had become a Christian, to a camp in the Rocky Mountains, and later flying with him to Ecuador to meet and witness to a family whose daughter, Rocio Castillo, had spent a whole school year as a foreign exchange student in the home of my older brother, Dallas Jr., and his wife, Mabel. They had planned to make this trip themselves, but Mabel became critically ill with cancer, so I was asked if I could go. Being from South America, Rocio and her family were traditional Catholics, and the hope was that they could be led to become New Testament Christians. Gregg and I had no idea how we would be received and had not even made hotel reservations. When we arrived in Guayaquill, they met us at the airport, we hit it right off, and they insisted that we stay in their home. In spite of the language barrier, things went so well in visiting and simply being together, that I, with my English Bible, and the mother especially, Asusana, with her Catholic Bible, was able to explain to everyone the teachings of the New Testament Church. It was almost too much for them to comprehend it all in the few days we had, but they felt the love we had for them, and more good things were to follow. Gregg and I were taken up into the beautiful Andes in an ancient, rickety train, where we spent a couple days with colorful native Indians, after which we were shown all around scenic and historic sights. We felt we had succeeded in our "get acquainted" mission, and it was truly a sad goodbye when we left for home. But to finish the story, when Rocio came on a visit to Missouri shortly after that, at Dallas Jr.'s home, I was so burdened for Rocio that I took my Bible in hand, poured out my heart and the Scriptures about the conversions in Acts of the Apostles, and it suddenly dawned on her that she needed to be baptized. The Lord dramatically opened her heart, and we went that midnight hour and baptized her!

I opened a nice and spacious office in Springfield during this time, planning to be close to home with my Christell projects so I could help and oversee Pat's medical needs. This way, I wouldn't have to travel and be gone when I was needed so badly because of Pat's condition, my peace of mind, and for my children's sake. When I did this, we were still operating the Mission on a part-time basis. B.J. and Don had not re-joined our television mission work yet, nor had they resigned from their churches. When they did, I gave my office over to the TV Mission, and did my best to once again go forward "full steam ahead" with renewed vision, rallies, and revivals. But I was drained emotionally again, trying to keep going strong, while Pat was going downhill fast.

I got so low after taking Pat to the Mayo Clinic the first time in 1971 to be hopefully diagnosed and treated, but still having the migraines, that I sat down, and in tears, wrote the following:

"An almost unbearable burden has been thrust upon me and my family. Heavy indebtedness, taking on new obligations, increased promotional and evangelistic activity, all meant go, go, and more go, while all the time I was desperately needed at home, and often would have to be called home to the hospital. I grew weary, oh so weary! Really, I felt I was just hanging on, trying to bear a triple load – the obligations of our Christell beginnings, the needs of the Mission, and the great heart-cry of my family – my wife and my family's needs. I got so low and so discouraged, I really did. That's when I really started writing songs and poems, heavy material about suffering, and hope, and the need of the human heart. The weeks grew into months, and the months crawled into years, and finally during the last trip to the Mayo Clinic, after Pat had come so close to death, we both cried out to God and said, 'O God, help us, help us, HELP US! Don't they realize we are perishing, in spirit as well as in body? Oh, to be in solitude for a few months, and away from all the oppressive harried and hurried goings! Oh, to slow down and live, instead of rushing to DEATH!"

On this second and last trip to the Mayo Clinic with Pat, they did three days of exhaustive tests, but at the concluding session, we were told that there was no physiological factor they could find that caused her migraines. The report was that maybe it was the overload of responsibility and deep frustration that had built up in Pat over the years, with my type of work and obligations taking me away from home so much. Family-raising, program and singing demands, making ends meet – all could weigh on her sense of self-worth and well-being, but they couldn't be sure. This made me feel so guilty, thinking that I, in reality, was to blame for all her suffering. But what to do was the big question!

The reason we had gone to Mayo's for help was because of a hopeful letter of concern from Gail Boatman, the wonderful wife of President Don Earl Boatman, President of Ozark Christian

College, our alma mater. We had been receiving letters of concern and encouragement from people all over the country ever since 1967, when the migraines started hitting with a vengeance. But this correspondence was so thoughtful, I want to quote it here in full:

"Joplin, Missouri, March 26, 1971. Dear Bob and Pat: You folk have been in our thoughts and prayers. We do hope that Pat has relief from her headaches. If not, we have friends in Indianapolis who have been through the same ordeal as Pat, in and out of hospitals, hysterectomy, etc. Finally they asked her doctor about Mayos, and he said, 'If you go and they help you, I'll pay all your bill.' She went to Mayos and has had no severe headache since. There is a special department there for such problems. Dr. G.A. Peters is the Migraine specialist at Rochester. Our friend is Mrs. Lawrence Shippey of Indianapolis, who was cured by Rx of her headaches. She said she tried Christian Science, and finally got so depressed and depleted of strength that she wanted to die and forget it all. Now she travels with her husband, lives a normal life, and enjoys it. I just wish you could talk to them about their experience. Sounds exactly like yours! They urged you to go to Dr. Peters for help. There is a new drug which affects the vascular system and relieves pressure in the brain. I don't understand why other doctors do not have success with it. But specialists seem to understand how to administer certain drugs for the best results. If we can help in any way just let us know. In Christian love, Gail and Don Earl."

We followed up on Gail's letter, went to Mayo Clinic in October of 1971, with no results at all; then again for a week in January of 1972. Dr. Peters suggested that perhaps a leave of absence, a climate change, and living a more calm, less stressful life might help. I had happened to pick up Pat Boone's book called *A New Song*, in which he had written about a breakdown and collapse he had suffered in his life, and the new-found peace and strength he had discovered. It really spoke to my heart. I had met Pat twice, attending a TV show and getting to talk to him on the set afterwards, both in Hollywood and New York. Thoughts ran through my mind as I sat there listening to Dr. Peters, not giving us much encouragement from a medical standpoint, but hope with some old-fashioned, sound, and sensible advice. But was I in a position, wise and courageous enough, to really hear and heed these words of the good doctor? He wished us well, and on January 25, 1972, wrote this letter to us:

> "Enclosed is a 'To Whom It May Concern' letter which may be of help in your future care. I hope as time goes along your headaches will begin to remit and be improved. I wish to thank you for coming to see me for investigation of your headaches. I don't know whether I have helped you or not, but at least I made an effort in that direction. It may be that with a leave of absence with your husband things might improve. Sincerely yours, Gustavus A. Peters, M.D."

When we got home, Pat and I talked, cried, and prayed fervently about what to do. We both knew, without a doubt, that we simply couldn't go on with life the way it was. It was about to kill us both, and we had to make a change. But it was a huge shock to my parents, and especially to Bill, B.J., and Don, when I let them know we were locking up our house, loading up a small U-Haul trailer, and would soon be heading west.

When we arrived in California, we stayed the first few days with our daughter, Becky, and looked up Pat Boone. He and his wife, Shirley, graciously invited us into their home, where we poured out our story to them. They listened with great sympathy, praying for Pat with deep fervency, and asking the Lord for His blessing in our search for a place to live. We all went to church together that Sunday evening in their station wagon, with their four young girls crammed in the back. Afterward, we enjoyed further fellowship at their house, with another season of prayer.

The next morning at Becky's apartment, I searched the newspaper for the listings of houses for rent. To my great joy, I found an ad stating that a two-bedroom house with maid's quarters in the Beverly Hills post office area would be available in a week at $500.00 a month. I quickly underlined it, drove up the hills and canyons above Beverly Hills, and rented it from a dear lady named Mildred Volz. I told her our story, and she was so impressed with us and our ministry, that in a few months, she sold the house to us for $67,500.00! She put us in touch with her bank which financed the loan for $50,000.00. In addition, she let us borrow all the remaining $17,500.00 from her, and gave us her baby grand piano and all the furniture! All of this, plus Pat's amazing relief for the first few months we had been in California, made us know we had been led and blessed by God with these miraculous results!

But we had a problem. We received wide criticism from Brotherhood leaders for having any association with Pat Boone, since he had left the Church of Christ to take fellowship with the "Charismatic Movement." I made a thorough study of the Scriptures about the whole "gifts" issue, and while I respected the zeal and fervor of fellow believers, I had no intention of forsaking my roots and ministry of unity in the Restoration Movement.

This criticism hurt my darling Pat and me deeply, in that the Brethren seemed to have no feeling for the very difficult time we had endured. And sure enough, I think all of this controversy perhaps was a factor in Pat having to be hospitalized in late October of that year with another migraine attack.

Pat knew immediately when migraines would come over the next few years, but they struck less often, though with intensity before being able to get relief. Later on, she had a very sudden and dramatic experience, which she described as a visitation from the Lord in her hospital room. She was reading the 11th chapter of Romans, concentrating especially on the last four verses:

"Oh, the depth of the riches both of the wisdom and knowledge of God! How unsearchable are His judgments and unfathomable His ways! FOR WHO HAS KNOWN THE MIND OF THE LORD, OR WHO BECAME HIS COUNSELOR? OR WHO HAS FIRST GIVEN TO HIM THAT IT MIGHT BE PAID BACK TO HIM AGAIN? For from Him and through Him and to Him are all things. To Him *be* the glory forever. Amen" (Romans 11:33-36, NASB).

Moved so deeply and weeping with joy, she had underlined the last verse. Then she said a voice whispered in her ear, "Be patient, my dear. You will soon be healed!" She never had another migraine headache after that glorious event! It was such a deeply spiritual and overwhelming happening she experienced that when she told me about it, tears of joy were streaming down her cheeks. I couldn't contain myself and wept with her in our rejoicing and praising God, as we tightly held each other. Pat has always been a very private person, not wanting to be in the public eye, or making a display of her good works, her deep faith, or her personal experiences. At first, this was such a private and precious moment, but so full of bliss and awe, she would break out in tears, and couldn't talk about it. But as time passed, after our son Gregg had started the Refuge Church, she went to him and asked to share her story with the congregation. He was simply overjoyed! And then when she told me, I said, "Wonderful! ... So you'll want to prepare your notes about things you want to cover." "Notes?" Pat said. "I don't need notes! I just want to speak from my heart." Well, she absolutely astounded our whole family, all of whom were present with the large crowd there, with her boldness, joy, and great poise, as she spoke so forcefully and movingly about her life, her faith, her blessings, the years of agony and depression, and finally, dwelling in detail about the deliverance and victory she received over the agonizing years of pain she had endured. One day she showed me what she had written, describing just how hopeless and despondent she had become: "It was like I had sunk into a deep, dark pit, and try as hard as I could, I wasn't able to climb up out of the awful, black hole. I clawed and clawed to get out, but finally I realized it was to no avail. There was simply no way out." As I recall, she must have penned those agonizing feelings shortly after my remembering the time when she had locked herself in the bathroom, trying to take her life. I fortunately was home at the time, and finally convinced her to unlock the door. I hugged and hugged her so tightly, consoling her and crying to the Lord for his compassion and help. Surely He saw this scene and heard my pleadings, for shortly after this, He intervened, poured out His mercy upon us, and gave total deliverance to Pat, once and for all time! Glory to God on High!

CHAPTER 28

Inspiration Of Bob Vernon
Television Show And Holy Land Tour

BUT BACK TO February of 1972, as we arrived in California and were so blessed with a new home and Pat initially relieved, I had a big decision facing me. Should I follow through with an extended leave of absence from the TV Mission and concentrate solely on a ministry in California? Thinking through everything and praying for wisdom, I came to the conclusion that I could keep pursuing my separate interests in California, but retain a part-time ministry participation with Christian Television Mission, which Pat and I had started and invested so much of our lives in. All along, even in the difficult days of getting the Mission off the ground, I had in mind that it would include Bill, B.J., and Don, and their wives. And now, with their renewed participation and vision, I loved my brothers and the Mission too much to walk away, despite the burdens of our situation. And too, settled in the peaceful canyon above Beverly Hills, in a home surrounded by flowers, shrubs, and cedars, where deer and possums played, it was an ideal setting and haven for Pat to have well-deserved peace and solitude, and hopefully regain her health. So with Becky nearby, and Gregg and Debbie with her, in a few days I drove to Missouri to rejoin my brothers and keep a speaking engagement at the Ozark Bible College annual preaching and teaching convention, followed by a Vernon Brothers rally at Lamar, Missouri. Before returning to

California, I had a joyful reunion with my parents and brothers, gave up my position as executive director, we worked on TV programming, and set a future schedule for us brothers.

The University Christian Church in Los Angeles became our family's home church, and soon without a minister, they asked me to serve as an interim minister, which I did for some time. Pat continued to feel well until late that year, and I was able to keep scheduled appearances with my brothers. One of those meetings that year of 1972 was a revival we held at the Christian Church in Butler, Pennsylvania, where Mildred Welshimer Phillips was a member. In fact, it was her influence that led to the invitation to conduct the crusade. So we all stayed in her mansion called "Elm Court." Her husband, whom she had wanted to become a supporter of our work, had died, and the Phillips Trust Fund that he had set up, of which Mildred was the chairman, met with us and became a great benefactor of both Christian TV Mission and my Christell organization. Mildred was in the stands way back when Bill, B.J., and I were on Ozark's basketball team that beat Milligan College. She was dean of women at Milligan for seventeen years before she met and married B.D. Phillips. It was B.D.'s father, Thomas W. Phillips, who had made a fortune with his Phillips Gas and Oil Company. He had also been a prominent and dedicated member of the Christian Church. When I was a young lad in Submarine Service during World War II, Mother had sent me the famous book he had written about the Restoration Movement, called *The Church of Christ*. I met a Phillips Trust Fund member while at Bethany College in 1964, researching for *Back to Jerusalem*.

I had a great desire to produce a television program that showed how God had surely blessed our family through our struggles. So I got Pat Boone's consent to be on the show, then contacted the Warren Stitt Company to map out the hour-long production with me. His associate, Gary Evans, assisted me with all the details, and on February 21, 1973, wrote the following letter:

"Mr. Jack Spina, Cooga-Mooga, Inc., 9255 Sunset Boulevard, Suite 706, Los Angeles, CA 90069. Dear Jack, I am enclosing a production schedule for the Bob Vernon Special to be shot this coming Monday, February 26. There are two times when Pat Boone will be on the set. The first is at Bob's home, 2241 Bowmont Drive, Beverly Hills, at 9:30 A.M. until 10:30 A.M. This is a casual setting in Bob's patio when Pat, Bob, and his wife will be discussing events and circumstances of their meeting, and the real meaning of 'a friend in need is a friend indeed.' The second time period will be 7:00 P.M. to 9:30 P.M. During that time we will tape Pat singing two songs (lip-sync), a short Bob and Pat chat, and a 'live' all-cast closing song 'Amazing Grace.' The two lip-sync songs Bob would like Pat to sing are 'One Way' and 'Begin to be Free.' The evening taping is with an audience so Pat should dress for 'evening appearance.' If you have any questions, feel free to call me."

I also asked and arranged for a bright and talented young singing group from Pacific Christian College called "The New Creations" to sing on the program.

The early morning of February 26, 1973, fortunately dawned with bright and warm sunshine, ideal for out-of-doors filming. The film crew and the trucks carrying all of the equipment arrived, and we were soon ready to begin shooting our "INSPIRATION" production. I asked everyone to join me in a prayer, asking the Lord to give us favor for the day, and that what we were about to do would glorify His Name and be a blessing to multitudes. Pat and I, with Pat Boone present, took our seats at the table, and before the cameras recounted our story in the scenic setting of our back patio. Next, with the flowered hillside in the background, Becky sang "Sweet Little Jesus Boy," followed by a brief testimony by Gregg. The next scene showed me singing, with Ralph Carmichael's orchestrated background, "Bless This House" as I walked from inside the house, down the front steps to the front lawn. Everything went well during the whole morning, and we made the move and transition to the studio that afternoon, with 11-year-old Debbie singing, accompanied by Becky at the piano, Larry Norman's "Wish We'd All Been Ready." We had a "live" audience, the New Creations' song, and mine and Pat's music. From my Capitol Records album, I sang, again with orchestration accompanying, my song "Tell America," followed by "No Man Is An Island." Pat Boone did a great job with singing "One Way" and "Begin To Be Free," then he and I, seated on the set, had a conversation about life's challenges and the help that God provides. I closed the show with a Gospel message, using a lot of my poetry.

In the meantime, when I told Bill, B.J., and Don that I was doing a special family TV program with Pat Boone as a guest, they asked me, since the Mission needed a special, could we do it in March with Pat again to appear on it? So I talked to Pat, he agreed, and since my videotaped program had to be edited anyway and funds were short, I shelved it for a while to help oversee and plan for a joint Mission production with all four Vernon families. What a great time we had as they all arrived at our house! In the special were my new songs, "Song of Victory," "Vision," "Soul of the Young and Free," "The Golden Way," and "Go Tell." Our family of 19, with Pat Boone as guest singer, provided the musical numbers. Other guests were Dan Issel, a star basketball player with the Kentucky Colonels and a dedicated Christian, and

Dr. Ard Hoven, who delivered a scholarly and moving message on "The Restoration Movement." We called the show "Sing a New Song, Live a New Life," featuring Don's message on "The New Life," and my new songs our family had recorded in an album. The show received wide acclaim as it was syndicated to TV stations all over the country. My son Gregg, who had been a student at Cincinnati Bible Seminary, but had transferred to San Jose Bible College when we moved to California, came down especially to be on the family program. The car had broken down, and he even had to hitch-hike 200 miles to be on time. What he remembers about the program, and it was so obvious, is that every time the camera panned over his way, one of the Mission's board members in the control room had the director stop short of Gregg, because he had "longish" hair!

Gregg grew up in the Beatles era, with culture drastically changing, controversy over the Vietnam War raging, and the drug scene coming on strong and influencing so many young lives. That minister had no idea of what Gregg had overcome to dedicate his life to the Lord and His service. I'm so proud that while that attitude and action truly hurt my son, he was able to eventually overlook it, and even with his not so "longish" hair, go on to reach so many for Christ with his love, his preaching, and his song writing, which he is still so effectively doing with his Refuge band and church.

Another highlight for the four of us brothers and our parents, plus thirteen others who joined us, was a Holy Land Tour, September 11-22, 1973. What a thrill it was for Mother and Dad to be able to visit these Biblical scenes they had read about, especially at their advanced ages of 83 and 82. Mother, who was an excellent writer, had an article published in *The Lebanon, Missouri Record* of December 21, in which she had described the trip. Here are excerpts from her account:

"'For a great door and effectual is opened unto me ...' (I Corinthians 16:9, KJV). A door is an opening through which we pass. I've had so many doors opened for me that although I am, in the modern vernacular, a senior citizen, life is no humdrum existence. When my sons, the Vernon Brothers of Christian Television Mission, announced plans last spring to sponsor a tour to the Holy Land, I began toying with the idea of going along. And as the summer wore on, my plan crystallized into action. I applied for my passport, received it; and that was just too much for my husband, Dallas, who had tried all along to talk me out of going. If you can't 'lick' 'em, 'j'in' 'em, and that is just what he did. We made a trip to the passport office in Springfield to apply for his passport. When we walked in, the fellow in charge began to laugh, 'I knew you'd be back.' We kept our fingers crossed as it was just two weeks until the tour was scheduled to begin. But lady luck was with us and eight days later here came his passport. We left Springfield Tuesday morning, September 11, and arrived in Tel Aviv on Wednesday morning after a ten-hour non-stop flight. Here we were met by our guide and were driven directly to our hotel in Jerusalem. We visited the historic places in Jerusalem (starting at) the Dome of the Rock mosque, built by Moslems on the site of Solomon's Temple. To enter, we were asked to remove our shoes and cover our arms. We traveled the Via Dolorosa, the path to Calvary, and walking the paved, narrow streets, we thought of how our Lord had trudged the dusty roads up to the Mount of Olives located on one of the highest hills. Jerusalem is built on hills and in valleys, and up there on this summit, we thought of how our Lord looked out over the city and wept; and with so much love and pathos in his voice had cried, 'O Jerusalem, Jerusalem, thou that killest the prophets, and stonest them which are sent unto thee, how often would I have gathered thy children together, even as a hen gathereth her chickens under her wings, and ye would not!' (Matthew 23:37, KJV).

"Another never-to-be-forgotten spot was the Garden of Gethsemane where Jesus spent His last agonizing night in prayer. We came to the garden on Sunday morning at 7:00, and as we gathered under an old olive tree probably 2500 years old, the boys sang 'Neath the Old Olive Tree' and 'In the Garden.' We had prayer here, along with having a period of deep contemplation and reflection. The prior day, we had visited the Garden Tomb, where excavations had unearthed an empty tomb in the rocks and said to be the only empty tomb found. It is located near a high hill resembling a skull. Bible scholars are quite sure this location is authentic. It is outside the Walls, the terrain fits the description, and the tomb has all appearances of having belonged to a rich man. We had an impressive devotional period here and the boys sang 'Were You There When They Crucified My Lord.' We spent Sunday afternoon in the vicinity of the Sea of Galilee. Crossing it, we stopped in the middle and had our Communion service, and the boys sang 'Master the Tempest is Raging.' We viewed the ruins of the synagogue at Capernaum where Jesus preached and declared that He was the fulfillment of Isaiah's prophecy concerning the Messiah. Also, on the sloping shore of the Sea of Galilee, we saw where He had preached the Sermon on the Mount and too, where the miracle of the feeding of the 5,000 had taken place. We visited the ruins of Caesarea Philippi, where Jesus asked his disciples the burning question, '… whom say ye that I am? …' (Mark 8:29, KJV)."

Mother went on accurately describing in detail the rest of the tour, but for brevity's sake, I will just mention our visits to the following sights: Bethany, home of Mary and Martha; the Dead Sea; Masada; Qumran, where the Dead Sea Scrolls were discovered; the Wailing Wall; the Jordan River, where Jesus was baptized; Nazareth, the boyhood home of Jesus; Bethlehem, where He was born; Caesarea on the Mediterranean, where we saw the ruins of a Roman aqueduct and an amphitheater quite well preserved; and finally, the ruins at Athens and Corinth, where Paul preached. I left the group in Athens to fly to Frankfurt, Germany, to visit my niece Sue Vernon, who was teaching at Bitburg Air Force Base. I rejoined everyone in London for our flight to New York. On the way home, Mother and Dad had one more stopover, and she described it this way:

"As an added bonus we spent two days as guests of Mrs. Mildred Welshimer Phillips (who had been on the tour with us) at her home, Elm Court, in Butler, Pennsylvania. Little did I ever dream that I would have the opportunity to visit the Phillips family who over the past century had contributed so much to the cause of New Testament Christianity and the Restoration Movement. And to have as my good friend, Mildred Welshimer Phillips whose father, the late P.H. Welshimer, had in his 60 years of ministry built a congregation of 25 members to 6,000 dedicated people at the First Christian Church in Canton, Ohio. For me, another door had been opened!"

With our Vernon Brothers TV special and the Holy Land tour now behind us, I turned my attention to the needed funding and editing of our family's INSPIRATION Special and getting it aired. I was so encouraged and thankful when I received a wonderful letter from Mildred Phillips, which in part reads:

> "I wish you could give the messages you delivered in your revival here at Butler on the Restoration Movement to every college and convention in the Brotherhood. I was deeply impressed with your knowledge and presentation of New Testament Christianity more than anything I have heard in years. Because of your dedication to the Restoration Cause, our Trust was unanimous in wanting to help you in your INSPIRATION TV SPECIAL with Pat Boone. We believe it will be a marvelous production and one that will be a great witness for the Cause of Christ as it is telecast soon to the great city of Los Angeles and elsewhere. We're behind you 100 percent, and we encourage more of our congregations and Christian people to support your Christell outreach."
> It was signed, Mildred Welshimer Phillips, B.D. Phillips Charitable Trust.

Oh! How we praised God for the exceedingly generous check we received in the mail that allowed us to get the program edited and aired on KHJ-TV, Channel 9, Los Angeles, from 8:30 to 9:30 p.m. on February 3, 1974! In the program, I tried to emphasize the necessity that FAITH must remain steadfast in spite of trials such as we had experienced, faithful in our trust in God and His revealed will of New Testament Christianity. We also had segments showing the importance of FAMILY, FRIENDS, AND FREEDOM in living out our lives. Pat Boone wrote, "We're still one nation under God, and His basic building block is the family in these crisis times. We really need to rebuild our confidence in the family. Bob Vernon's Special is a real spiritual transfusion at a time when we need it most. I'm proud to be a part of it." G. Russell Barber, minister of the First Christian Church in Pico Rivera, had this notation in his church paper, "Bob Vernon sings and takes New Testament Christianity into every heart and home. You'll enjoy it for sure."

It's apparent that we succeeded in providing inspiration to multitudes of people, for in a few days after the INSPIRATION Special was aired, we got a ton of mail from viewers. I still have in my files letters and comments of appreciation from 94 different cities, villages, and communities in Southern California. Following are just a few excerpts from those letters:

"It was a real pleasure and treat to watch your INSPIRATION Special last night on KHJ-TV. The entire program was highly inspirational. As always, Pat Boone was great, and your family was in top form. But you knocked the ball out of the park with your closing comments. It was so deeply moving that I'm certain most people watching couldn't help but feel the Lord's presence in your life."

From Medford Jones, President of Pacific Christian College, came this letter: "I saw your program the other evening and was pleased to see your excellent presentation. I just pray that God is continuing to bless and that we will see a continuing succession of your programs."

We received letters from Bakersfield, including this one: "We were blessed by your beautiful program. We have long been thankful for Pat Boone's Christian influence in the entertainment world, and now feel that we will receive blessings and inspiration from you."

From Ventura, we got this comment:

"I was searching this evening on my TV for something really good, and was I ever so glad when I turned to your fine and thrilling program! It was so heartwarming and indeed inspiring. I so enjoyed your singing accompanied by your beautiful and inspiring personality, so is it any wonder that I was so pleasantly surprised? Much success to you and your beautiful family."

From San Pedro: "I watched your special with Pat Boone, and it was one of the most beautiful shows I have ever seen. The way you sang BLESS THIS HOUSE brought tears to my eyes. Do have more shows!"

This very encouraging article, written by Gene Carter, minister of the University Christian Church in Los Angeles, appeared in their church paper:

"The special INSPIRATION TV production by Bob Vernon lived up to its name this past Sunday evening when it was viewed on Channel 9. If you missed the program, you missed a very special hour. The songs and presentations of Bob and Pat and their children, Becky, Gregg, and Debbie, plus that of Pat Boone and the NEW CREATIONS, was a happy blend of bright and thoughtful music and inspiration. A special attraction for University people was seeing themselves in the audience. Joan Manahl was especially noteworthy for her enthusiastic singing with Pat Boone. There was even a shot of the bus driver (Gene Carter) from PCC who later turned out to be the minister of University Christian Church. Our congratulations to Bob Vernon on an especially effective production."

Another letter which was so special, came addressed to my darling wife and me:

"Just wanted to send you a note of encouragement and love to let you know how much your ministry and your sweet spirit mean to us. You both have been an inspiration to our family as you strive to share your faith in such a beautiful and meaningful way. You may not realize the deep influence you have on so many with your gentleness and love which God has given you. You both are in our prayers as we all step out to meet new challenges, strengthened by the love God provides abundantly."

More excerpts from some of the hundreds of viewer letters:

- Upland: "Enjoyed the HOUR OF INSPIRATION … and especially your singing of beautiful songs … I want to tell you how beautiful the poem TELL AMERICA is …"
- Pasadena: "I watched your TV program last nite, and I enjoyed it very much. Also I was so pleased with your poetry you recited …"
- Artesia: "I saw your program, and was very inspired by the story told, but mainly the music praising God … Your program has brought me closer to God …"
- San Clemente: "I really enjoyed your program INSPIRATION on Channel 9. Am enclosing a contribution towards your worthwhile ministry …"
- Cudahy: "God bless you and your lovely family for the work you are doing to help bring the Word of God to the people …"
- El Monte: "Listened to your program for the first time last evening. I just want to tell you your poems are beautiful, and the last one as a prayer was wonderful!"

- Long Beach: "I saw your telecast Sunday night on KHJ, Channel 9, and enjoyed it so much. It was really inspiring, and you have a beautiful voice. God bless you in your work ..."
- L.A.: "We heard your Hour of Inspiration last nite, and want to say 'thank you' for a lovely evening. I loved the way you sang. Thank you and bless you and your family ..."
- Escondido: "Your program last Sunday evening was magnificent! I come from one of the Iron Curtain countries. Will you please send me a copy of your poem on America, also a copy of your song TELL AMERICA. Thank you again for a most outstanding and inspiring Sunday evening ..."
- Bellflower: "Please pray for us ... I am watching your TV program, and my family needs your prayers very much ..."
- Simi Valley: "Enjoyed your beautiful program on Channel 9 Sunday evening. God bless you. Enclosed is a small token of appreciation ..."
- Whittier: "Oh, what a beautiful program ..."
- Orange: "Oh how we enjoyed your program Sunday night ..."
- San Pedro: "I watched your Special ... It was one of the most beautiful Christian shows I have seen ..."
- Riverside: "I have just watched your program of inspiration, and I am not able to tell you how much I enjoyed it ..."
- San Luis Obispo: "Our hearts were deeply touched by the inspiration hour last night. I need much prayer as I've become bitter ... I know satan is very much alive, but know there is one that will set my heart straight. Thank you for the beautiful program ..."

- San Bernardino: "I was so impressed with the sweet simplicity of your message on TV …"
- Rosemead: "My husband and I enjoyed the program on TV very much. I sincerely hope this will help me, in some way, to know the Lord …"
- Wasco: "I saw your special on TV tonight, and truly enjoyed it very much. It's a real blessing to see someone with so much love for our Lord …"
- Tustin: "I would just like to say I saw your beautiful and inspirational program tonight. I saw the Lord on your face and shining through you, and I pray that I may radiate that same glow …"
- Hollywood composer: "Enjoyed your TV Inspiration show very much … I'd like to get together with you …"
- Hemet: "My wife and I heard you over TV on Channel 9, and you certainly have the experience and good judgment in your presentation …"
- Bellflower: "Enjoyed your program …"
- Vista: "I hope the program goes on …"
- Chula Vista: "Enjoyed your singing and message …"
- Taft: "God's blessings upon you! …"
- Inglewood: "I'm such a fan of your show …"
- Compton: "The program was good, and the singing wonderful …"
- Ridgecrest: "Surely appreciate …"
- Bakersfield: "Thoroughly enjoyed it …"
- Eugene, Oregon: "Enjoyed it …"
- Santa Barbara: "Bless you and your ministry …"
- Costa Mesa: "Would love the album …"
- San Diego: "Enjoyed your program …"
- Indio: "Really enjoyed it immensely …"

On February 14, 1974, I wrote the following letter to all of those who had viewed the program and had responded:

"Thank you so much for watching our INSPIRATION TV program, and for taking the time to write us. We have simply been overwhelmed at the highly favorable response, and at the way the program reached deep into hearts. I know one thing. The contents of the show came out of genuineness and love, inspired by the Lord. It was honest, and though we were on camera a lot – much more than we would have preferred – we now know from the scores of comments and letters that most people could tell that we were glorifying the Lord and not ourselves. Only two people wrote otherwise, and we are deeply sorry that they missed the depth and reality of what we and all the others felt. We want to encourage you in your life to follow in the Lord's way, and we hope you feel a partnership with us in this vast undertaking to spread the Word of God."

CHAPTER 29

More TV Specials, Sad Farewell

Two months after our TV film aired, Mother and Dad, Bill, B.J., and Don, with their wives and kids, all returned to California to make another TV special. It was a great family reunion, having fun and rehearsing at our house in Beverly Hills. The title of this show was "In All Things Love," and we had as guests, Dale Evans Rogers, Carl Ketcherside, and John Wooden, famous basketball coach at UCLA, interviewing them all about their faith. Also included on the program was a delightful segment where our big family celebrated the 56th wedding anniversary of our parents, with cake and tributes to them. Vernon Family songs were "What the World Needs Now is Love, Sweet Love," "Love Lifted Me," "Love is Surrender," "Everything is Beautiful," "There's Something About that Name," and "They'll Know We Are Christians By Our Love." The Vernon wives sang "Love Was When," we brothers sang "If That Isn't Love" and "Singing Love Songs," and Dale Evans sang "Faith, Hope and Charity," followed by her comments. Don closed the program with a devotional based on the great Love chapter of First Corinthians 13. Again this TV special gained notoriety as it was syndicated to stations all across the country.

I kept a record of all my ministry trips and appearances through the years, and it almost makes my head swim now to even look at my busy schedule. It looks like I hadn't slowed down or taken the advice of our Mayo Clinic doctor. I won't begin to try listing all the individual speaking and singing dates I had, but in the rest of 1974, I gave three messages in chapel at St. Louis Christian College; spoke and sang with my brothers in the Bi-lingual three-day Convention at Collegio Biblico; had a Vernon Brothers Concert and missions presentation at Ozark Bible College; spoke and sang with my brothers in a three-day Homecoming Gospel Rally at Roanoke Bible College; made an appearance at a state-wide Indiana Christian Convention in Indianapolis; and gave a message and sang with my brothers in the annual Week of the Ministry at Milligan College, Tennessee.

1975 was a full, enjoyable, but towards the end, very sad year. I flew to Butler, Pennsylvania to talk to the Phillips Family Trust members about doing a four-film bicentennial project in that year but to be aired in 1976. They gave their approval, and my son and I through our Christell Productions, set about producing it for Christian Television Mission, with my other brothers and wives coming out to California to join in appearing in the films.

But long before they arrived, Gregg and I were busy making preparations, selecting a studio, hiring a director, contacting actors, and then conceiving and scripting ideas for the four shows. For Show No. 1, the title would be UNITED WE STAND, and we would show how freedom came about through justified revolt against tyranny. Show No. 2 would be called RISE UP AND RESTORE, and then we would demonstrate how through the last resort of war, unity in the nation would be restored. Show No. 3 had the title ONE PRESIDENT'S FAITH, where we would see how renovation of society is achieved as good people of faith shine as lights in a dark world. Show No. 4, GIVE LIBERTY ... GIVE LIFE, would show how the incarnate Son of God, Jesus of Nazareth, the resurrected Lord of Heaven, is the One elected by God, and the only being who can give freedom from sin and life eternal as we obey Him in faith, repentance, confession, baptism, and faithfulness in keeping the teachings of New Testament

Christianity. Restoration of the unity for which Christ prayed, recorded in John's Gospel narrative, chapter 17, verses 20 and 21, would be greatly beneficial in the Church's program of world evangelism.

In a letter to various actors in Hollywood, I described our background in filming *Homestead USA* and our plans for this project, and I wrote:

"In this series, we brothers and our wives will sing patriotic songs and spirituals, and each segment will feature a short dramatization of both an early patriot and a pioneer preacher speaking of the need for liberty, divine guidance, and unity. We will be filming the week of February 2-7, and would be most grateful to have your participation in one of the dramatizations. Due to the non-profit, non-commercial nature of this significant fare, we can offer you your scale salary plus the satisfaction of contributing your artistry to a cause that is so dear to so many of us. Please give us a call if you are available."

We needed actors to play the parts of George Washington, Abraham Lincoln, Betsy Ross, Ben Franklin, Alexander Campbell, Thomas Campbell, and "Raccoon" John Smith. We had film clips of President Garfield and Barton W. Stone. Fred Wayne, Joanna Moore, John Ingle, and Mike Stepanic took roles, and Rick Jason, star of the *Combat* television series, acted in the role of Lincoln for us. Gregg and I went to 20th Century Fox to see if the famous makeup artist, John Chambers, would do the makeup on Rick Jason, to make him look exactly like Abe Lincoln. At first he quoted a fee that was beyond our ability to pay. Of course he deserved it, because he was an Academy Award winner as a makeup artist then, as well as later for the movie *Argo*, which won the Academy Award in 2012. I explained the nature of our work as a non-profit organization, and he joyfully cut his fee. He did a fantastic job for us and was so pleasant to work with. I also had asked Robert Goulet if he might appear on the program, and I received this very nice letter back:

"Thank you for your letter and kind invitation, and I am so sorry I am tardy in replying. I was away in Acapulco, then went direct to Vegas for my engagement there, so only today have I had a moment to even check my mail. Due to my bookings and being out of town, I'm sorry it's impossible for me to do it, but may I wish you and all concerned every success with Homestead U.S.A. and thank you for asking me. I remain, sincerely, (signed) Robert Goulet."

I had made quartet arrangements of my patriotic songs from my solo albums, and we Vernon Brothers sang "Tell America," "God Bless America," "Born Free," "Freedom Prayer," "This Is My Country," "Vision Christian Vision," and "Song Of Victory." We included the Vernon wives on "Great Day," "I Want To Be Ready," "They'll Know We Are Christians By Our Love," "Old Time Religion," "Fairest Lord Jesus," "Standin' In The Need Of Prayer," and "God Of Our Fathers." Of course, we all sang our theme song, "Homestead USA."

We asked Edwin Hayden, Knofel Staton, Ralph Dornette, and Paul Benjamin to write and deliver on the program a five-minute bi-centennial address. Paul had another commitment, but all the others gave a good and inspiring presentation. Each of us brothers in turn wrote and gave a brief closing message and plea for unity, patriotism, and obedience to the Gospel in one of the four programs. I don't have the other writings, but following is what I wrote and delivered. I called it "THE INVISIBLE CANDIDATE":

"The candidate walks the crowded streets and lonely lanes of our Nation, seeking election as representative-at-large. He is the very personification of justice, mercy, and truth. He seeks to set men free of empty words and creeds and hypocrisies. He does not come to bring cold laws, but to create new hearts. Hearts free of prejudice and hatred and enslaving evils. Hearts that will bring new spirit to the individual, the community, and the Nation. Though wealthy, he divested himself of his riches and became a friend of the poor and oppressed. He sacrificed himself for his people, but he lives on, though the Nation has a tendency to exile him from our borders. It was in firm reliance on him that the Mayflower sailed, that our Constitution was ratified, and later that our Union was preserved. We dated our calendar from his birth. In his name, our first colleges, universities, and hospitals were founded. And it was from his sayings and laws that many of our pioneer children first learned to read in their log-cabin schoolhouses. He came to bring peace, to break down walls and divisions, and to create a new temple of familyhood, a new community of love which upholds the rights of all. We believed in him and trusted him. We said so on our coins and we chiseled his name over doorways and arches in our magnificent, marble edifices. This candidate is the great 'I AM,' 'Emanuel,' 'God With Us.' Oh! We need him again, desperately! Let's ask him to come back into our hearts, our homes, and our halls. Voluntarily, let's draft him and elect him to be our supreme representative. Out of our historic diversity, and in our quest to preserve and guarantee freedom for all – both politically and religiously – let us truly strive to be ONE NATION UNDER GOD. Let us give diligence to keep the unity of the Spirit in the bond of peace. For as Paul said, '[There is] one body, and one Spirit, even as also ye were called in one hope of your calling; one Lord, one faith, one baptism, one God and Father of all, who is over all, and through all, and in all' (Ephesians 4:4-6, ASV). Our invisible candidate stands before us and calls for us to live the motto: IN FAITH, UNITY; IN OPINIONS, LIBERTY; AND IN ALL THINGS, CHARITY. He asks us, as a Nation of men and the Family of God, to stand together. UNITED WE MUST STAND!"

During the 200th year of our celebration as a Nation, 1976, Christian Television Mission syndicated these four bicentennial specials to TV stations all over the Nation, receiving wide acclaim and plaudits. To God be the glory!

Also, our Christell production organization had another showing of our family in the INSPIRATION Special, this time pre-empting "Love, American Style" in the prime time of 7:30 p.m. for the showing of our program on KTLA-TV, July 5, 1976. Again, we got lots of mail with encouraging letters, and it really helped publicize our ministry.

I then got a call from Karla Kallen, a producer for KNBC-TV, inquiring about our work and family, and out of that came an interview on that station with Jess Marlow, one of their anchors. It was obvious that God was blessing us with his very generous favor!

But in addition to the hard work and success of producing the four bicentennial films in 1975, I drove from L.A. to Detroit where I met my brothers for our appearance at the North American Christian Convention in July. Then, driving my car, the four of us held Mission banquets or rallies in Michigan, Ohio, Pennsylvania, and West Virginia. Leaving home on June 27th, I traveled for appearances until July 24th.

That summer, our darling daughter, Becky, who worked for a major airline, sent Pat and me to Hawaii as a gift in honor of our 25th wedding anniversary. What a welcome vacation that was, staying for a week at the Sheraton Waikiki right on the beach. It was "just what the doctor ordered" for Pat, relaxing and soaking up the sunshine. And did I ever delight in the balmy breezes, the warm, turquoise-colored waves, and in the Polynesian "aloha" friendliness! What a lush, Pacific Paradise and string of pearls God had created out in the sea! It inspired me to write one of my songs, "Aloha to Hawaii."

But back to business for the Lord, I plunged into writing scripts and working on new programs, both for our ministry on the West Coast and the TV Mission. We brothers held more fund-raising banquets, including at Cincinnati, Washington, D.C. (where we also sang a concert on the Capitol steps), Pittsburgh, and Springfield, Missouri. That tour ended for me when I arrived home on November 14th of 1975, quite weary from almost a month of travel. But we had a joyous reunion and were planning for a thankful and festive Thanksgiving when three days later, unplanned events swept us up in grief, as explained in this Editor's note about an article I wrote, which follows:

"Today's 'Happenings from the Homestead' was written by Bob J. Vernon for the seven Vernon brothers in memory of their parents, Mr. and Mrs. Dallas Vernon, of Lebanon, Missouri. Mrs. Vernon was a longtime contributor to 'Over the Ozarks.' Following is his article.

"The time we all knew was coming arrived with suddenness and full force, but we never dreamed it would be a double blow and that our beloved parents would take their final flight from this planet of life within three weeks of each other. They were both advanced in years and had lived a full and fruitful life. We wouldn't bring them back to their final frailty and suffering for anything in the world, for they both loved life and laughter and had always enjoyed mental and physical agility. It was not the nature of either 'to be ministered to, but to minister …'

"They both had the blessing of accepting the gracious offer of the living and loving Lord of Life to receive the gift of that Great Beyond where there is no suffering, anguish, or death, and they lived out their lives accordingly, able to be active and productive right up to their last year. Mother had contained lymphosarcoma cancer for the past 15 years and had dozens of cobalt and chemotherapy treatments, but you would never know it. To her there was a difference in being overcome and being overtaken. She prepared for dying by a good performance in cheerful and faithful living. She lived life to the fullest, radiant and busy in her home, her church, and her business. Dad, too, lived long and actively, despite aches and pains.

"Married on March 31, 1918, our parents soon discovered farm life on the rocky, gently sloping hills of the 140 acre Homestead was going to be hard, but neither drought nor economic depression could defeat them. And as their seven sons came along, one by one, except for the twins, Bill and myself, they fairly beamed over all of us and the fact that they had seven sons, never mentioning the hardship and sacrifice the feeding and clothing of such a brood brought.

"Mother was never an 'old lady,' or in her own words, a 'knitting grandmother,' but kept up with the times and never wanted to go back to 'the good old days.' She was a successful mother and businesswoman, and an excellent school teacher, writer, and speaker. She had the distinction of being nominated Mother of the Year and served as district president of the Missouri Federated Women's Club and Parent-Teachers Association. Her features 'Reveries from Rambling Rafters' and 'Happenings from the Homestead' endeared her to many 'Over the Ozarks' readers.

"Dad, as a farmer and rural school teacher, had many pressures on him that we seven sons knew nothing about. He had to learn to be the head of a large household without any 'wherewithal' but was always a tender dad. He met with success in the business world as Laclede County Assessor for 16 years, then establishing a land abstract, insurance, and income-tax business after turning 65. For almost 40 years, he and Mother worked together, laboring after most people have retired. They bought and modernized our beloved 'Homestead USA,' where we were raised, nine miles west of Lebanon, and did all they could for their sons and families, their church, and all who crossed their paths.

"Mother slipped away very gently on November 17th, my wife Pat's birthday, and we laid her to rest in the friendly little cemetery just west of the Homestead on November 20th. She had been here since August 24th, 1891. A few days before Mother's passing, when I had been with Dad, bedfast and very weak, he had whispered as I left to go visit Mom in the hospital, 'Tell your mother I still love her.' He was too ill and incapacitated to attend her funeral and told us, 'I don't think I'll be here much longer.' He passed away peacefully on December 7th, Pearl Harbor Day, and on the 9th, we put him to rest beside Mother, 85 years after his birth, February 23rd, 1890.

"The silencing of the voices of Mother and Dad and their not being home makes one, as brother J.P. said, 'want to shut the doors and never go back again.' But we will be drawn back again and again. It will be the permanent home of our brother Ward, 55 and handicapped, who has taught us all many lessons in faith, determination, and courage with his gentleness and quiet strength. So the doors will remain open as a haven for all of us. It will be a retreat for reflection, a place of security for Ward, and a sanctuary for any who want to draw near to nature and to God. We will want to breathe in the friendliness of the comfortable old frame house, built in 1908, to wander in the woods where we played as boys, to contemplate on the banks of the 'sink hole' lake or just to roam the rocky Ozarks hills and fields for the sheer pleasure and soul strengthening it brings. With someone there as caretaker all the time, we will leave most of the furnishings as is, so the house will continue to bear the grace and touch of our dear mother who gave it such warmth and simple elegance. Dad's cap will continue to hang in its accustomed place in honor of his long headship over the Homestead. B.J., Don, Bill, and I will continue our ministry of Christian Television Mission and 'Homestead USA.' On a part-time basis, Bill will operate our folks' business, which he purchased; B.J. and Don had each bought 100 acres adjacent to the Homestead and will continue to operate their cattle business; and I had established and will go on with my Christell ministry, music, and production work; Ward, disabled but able with help to live independently at the Homestead, enjoys working at a Sheltered Workshop; Dallas Jr., with Detroit Tool and Engineering in Lebanon [of which he later became president], and J.P., Head of the Tool Shop at Litton Industries in Springfield, will continue in their engineering careers. All three of our older brothers are active in their Restoration Movement Churches.

"Mom and Dad have said their final earthly 'goodbye,' and in his halting speech, Ward said, 'It will never be the same again here at the Homestead.' But to all of us brothers, this place, as long as we live, will always be 'The Farm,' our 'homeplace,' our 'Homestead U.S.A.' In creating for the seven of us sons, such a wonderful home and haven here in the Ozarks, from the depth of our hearts, we say 'thank you' as we give this loving and enduring tribute to you, our beloved parents!"

CHAPTER 30

Brothers Take Churches, I Continue Fulltime With Missions And TV With Pat And My Kids

THE YEAR 1976 brought such a full schedule for me with my brothers and Christian TV Mission, you would have thought I had gone back to a full-time position! In looking at my record-keeping, I see that I made thirty different appearances for TV banquets, rallies, concerts, conventions, and revivals. They included the Missouri Christian Convention in Columbia; the Kiamichi Christian Clinic in Honobia, Oklahoma; the North American Christian Convention in Denver; chapel services at Milligan, Emanuel, and Johnson Bible Colleges, all in Tennessee; then a concert at Ozark Bible College; our Spiritual Encounter in Branson, Missouri; and concert at the Capitol steps in Washington, D.C. And, of course, we syndicated the four bi-centennial films to TV stations all over the country, where they were heralded by the industry and public alike.

Because I don't want to burden you with the details and dates of all our revivals, TV appearances, concerts, and banquets during the next eighteen years, suffice it to say it was a very full schedule with my brothers and Christian Television Mission until our board retired Bill and me late in 1994. But I will try to highlight some of the most important and memorable matters and events.

As noted before, there was a period when I acceded to all three of my brothers' request to return to preaching for local churches but retain a part-time relationship with the TV Mission. That led me then to set up my Christell ministry, but also to give part time to being with my brothers in the Mission which I had started. Through the Christell services, I was able to record the Word and Capitol solo albums; write some 100 songs and poems; produce and telecast TV specials on the West Coast; make three Christian documentary films; conduct several evangelistic meetings and concerts; and witness abroad in various nations.

My son, Gregg, has been a dedicated and effective associate with me in this work. In fact, while he was about to enter his senior year in high school, that summer I took him with me on a special mission trip to Ecuador and up into the Andes. Through that experience, Rocio Castillo was baptized, entered Ozark Bible College, graduated, and became a missionary herself, along with her husband, Al Williams. Pat and I both always tried to include our children in our Christian activities, Christian service camps, and special trips. As mentioned earlier, when our immediate family took a two-month witnessing tour across the country, in a stop at the Pentagon in Washington, D.C., I requested and received permission from the Officers there to take our 16-year-old daughter, Becky, on my USO tour to the troops in Vietnam. It was in Christian service camp that our youngest daughter, Debbie, made her confession of Christ as her Savior, with me having the privilege of baptizing her into Christ. And for a high school graduation gift to her, since I was a member of the National Academy of Recording Arts and Sciences by virtue of my song writing and recording, I took Debbie to New York with me when the "Grammy" television show was held there at the famous Radio City Music Hall. All three of our children became great worship leaders, with Becky and Debbie proficient pianists, and Gregg a skilled guitarist and band leader, as well as a dedicated minister.

While the daughters pursued their musical interests, occasionally appearing in our television programs, then marrying and raising their families, our son Gregg followed me, his father, in the telecommunication and evangelistic fields. Quoting from our *Christell Communique* of 1986:

"A second generation member of the Vernon family, Gregg, attended Cincinnati Bible Seminary and San Jose Bible College, then continued his studies of Film and Television in Los Angeles. Since 1974, he has become active producing Christian films and television programs. The most recent was the documentary he produced and filmed in Southeast Asia detailing the refugee dilemma and the mission field there in 1986."

The next year, in a return mission tour, I joined him, and on the day before we left, I wrote this letter to our Christell supporters on June 6, 1987:

"As you read this, we are on our way to Southeast Asia. Gregg and I will be spending several days at the Cambodian border ministering in refugee camps, proclaiming the Gospel, and touching needy souls. Then we have been invited to witness from Bangkok on national television to hundreds of thousands in Thailand, Laos, and Cambodia. Our interpreter will be a Native Thai Christian, who is a TV host. Gregg made that contact while he was there last fall. Next, we will fly to northern Thailand, where we will minister with the famed Morse missionary families and do more filming and videotaping. From there we will conclude with brief mission stops in Hong Kong and Japan. As you can see, it is a very special month of ministry with many extra expenses. We thank God for you who are standing with us, and for every gift that helps to meet the needs of this important mission. Please do intercede for us as we go. Prayerfully, Bob J. Vernon."

I kept a daily journal of our three-week mission trip, and on June 7, 1987, wrote this:

"We're on our way! We took off from LAX on Northwest Orient flight #1 at 1:25 pm, and are to arrive in Tokyo at 3:55 pm tomorrow, June 8th, a 10½ hour trip … I was up until 3:00 this morning taking care of last-minute details on finances and arrangements for Pat to look after while I am gone. I was up at 7:15, showered, shaved, and had a period of devotions and prayer with Pat, and a bite of breakfast before leaving for the airport. I feel great and am really excited and thrilled about going."

The next day, I penned:

"We arrived here at Narita Airport in Tokyo on time. I observed the neatly laid-out fields of sprouting green as we approached, and I mused about this 'land of the rising sun,' with my thoughts going back 44 years ago when as an 18 year old sailor boy in the Submarine Service, I was training for what would probably be a sure suicide mission, an invasion by force of this now gentle and friendly island empire of peace-loving people! But at that time, our despised and mortal enemy, and I still vividly recall the 'battle cry' of those dark and ominous days, REMEMBER PEARL HARBOR! I was moved to tears just last week as I watched on TV a reunion of former military men from Japan and America embracing and shaking hands on an island that was the scene of some of the fiercest fighting in World War II. The film was called, 'Return to Okinawa.' Now here I am, finally having set foot on this soil in Nippon, which seemed so soul-less back then. I still shudder when I recall the first reports of a big bomb that flattened, in one hellish moment, first Hiroshima, then Nagasaki. I still wonder about the morality – or the lack of it – of that monstrous and momentous decision by President Truman which incinerated so many thousands of innocent Japanese, even though it saved probably a million or more lives, both Japanese and American, including mine. I'm glad my long-last 'invasion' of Japan was from 'friendly skies' and not through hostile, mine-filled, murky waters! Long live our friendship, Japan! May God crown your good with brotherhood if and when your land of the rising sun more and more enjoys the dawn's early light of the RISEN SON!!"

After about a two-hour delayed departure time, we left Tokyo for the six-hour flight to Bangkok, arriving there just past midnight, 12:15 a.m., June 9th, on a hot, muggy night, getting to bed at 2:00 a.m.

In our tour all around Thailand, we found out that the country is somewhat smaller than Texas, and had a population of some 50 million. Formerly known as Siam until the 1940's, the first Thai kingdom dates back to the 13th century, although it is said that Buddhist missionaries from India in the second or third century B.C. were sent to a land called Suvarnabhumi (Land of Gold) to introduce Theravada Buddhism into the fertile region which today encompasses central Thailand.

Thailand is both modern and primitive. In Bangkok and Chiang Mai, we found bustling cities of commerce and culture. In the villages and tribal areas, we saw ancient farming methods, thatched roofs, water buffalo-drawn two-wheeled carts, and tiny but well-tended rice paddies. Per capita income was about $600.00 per year, but there was an 85% literacy rate, and we found an air of culture, politeness, and hospitality everywhere. Thais, as is their custom, greeted us with the word "sawadee," and instead of shaking hands, they put their two palms together under the chin and bowed slightly. We returned the gesture, and it was always very moving to me. Normally, one never touches another's head, and the foot is never to be pointed towards another person when seated. Entering a Thai house, we would make sure our shoes were removed beforehand. A mat would be rolled out, and our host or hostess would then give an open-palmed, sweeping gesture with the right hand to be seated on the floor. A monarchy, Thailand's king and queen are dearly loved. But spiritually, Thailand is so lost! Our hearts cried with what we saw. She is so steeped in centuries of Buddhism, animism, and spiritism. In Bangkok alone, there are 400 ornately designed and constructed wats (Buddhist temples), and in all of Thailand there are 20,000 Buddhist monasteries and 150,000 orange-robed monks. We saw them everywhere. And there is a "spirit house" (a bird house-sized miniature temple) prominently displayed on a pedestal adjacent to about every house, every shop and mall, and every public building. Offerings of flowers, food, and drink are made to the spirits, as well as to the finely sculptured idol of the omni-present Buddha. In this way, merit is made for one's self, as well as for relatives and departed ancestors, to ward off evil spirits and to guarantee rebirth after this life into a better form of existence. Ninety-five percent of the people are practicing Buddhists, but even most of those who are not, still make merit as a social custom, and reincarnation is almost universally adhered to as a belief.

We felt like the Apostle Paul in ancient Athens! But by reaching out in a spirit of compassion, through music and through a Thai TV producer and interpreter with whom Gregg had made friends the year before, we were able to videotape segments for telecasting on Thai TV as well as for Christian Television Mission. At that time, TV pretty well covered all of Thailand with four network stations in Bangkok.

On our first Sunday in Bangkok, we worshipped, spoke, and filmed at a small church in a poor, slum area of the city. After a delicious rice-noodle basket dinner with them, we piled into a pick-up with all of our filming equipment and drove some ten miles to visit and film at a storefront to be used as a student Christian Center at Rom Phra Khun, near the University. Then we went to Chachoengsao where it was so emotional for us to meet with and also minister to lepers, who invited us to film there in their settlement. Following that, it was arranged for us to meet Dr. Sompon Su Malnop, a native Thai Christian doctor, who invited us to sing and speak at a Christian hospital in Bangkla. This doctor's dedication and influence reached far and wide in that whole section. The doctor's mother and her driver took us to a refugee camp where she worked, and though it was very difficult to gain admittance, especially with video cameras, she was able to get us in. There were 20,000 uprooted and homeless refugees, hoping to be relocated in America. We were there quite a while, ministering and filming. The next day we drove to the Cambodian border and had to be very careful as the Vietnamese soldiers occasionally made incursions into Thailand, and we actually saw armed sentries perched in the trees. Before leaving the area, we heard enemy fire, so we didn't linger! Following this we flew to the northeast and ministered in Sakon Nakhon, fellowshipping in the tribal home of Som Pit, meeting and ministering with New Tribes missionaries Gene and Nancy Gutwein, and sharing out in the countryside with a joyful rice farmer who walked out of his tiny irrigated paddy to meet us. He had a big smile as he greeted us, and was overjoyed as he, through our interpreter, expressed how wonderful it was as a Christian to be freed from all the false and soul-bound superstitions of Buddhism. As we shared our common faith in Jesus, he spoke, and I quote from my journal, "… of the fact that the Creator-God could now be called his loving Heavenly Father. He just beamed and tears glistened in his smiling eyes. And he was overcome to think that we would come to fellowship with him."

The next day, Saturday, June 20, 1987, after having devotions, we flew from Sakon Nakhon back to Bangkok, then changing planes went to Chiang Mai "on an Airbus, a very nice, large European jetliner." I further penned in my journal:

"Chiang Mai is located in a lush green basin surrounded by mountains that are so scenic with tropical vegetation and trees. I like the 'feel' here, it seems to be a sleepy plantation-like Hawaiian village, and we find many missionary compounds here. A friendly taxi driver (who turned out to be a nuisance later) took us to our hotel, the Dusit Inn. It's so nice and has a Waldorf-Astoria appearance. Only $36.00 for the night! But I'm concerned and have been because I can't get hold of any of the famed missionary Morse families or David and Deloris Filbeck, who also labor here along with other American missionaries. Finally, after making inquiries, two Lisu young men, named Hamel and Aleujah, came to our hotel and drove us three miles or so to the Tribal Children's Hostel."

CHAPTER 31

Mission And Filming In Thailand
And TV Broadcasts To Asia

WHEN WE ARRIVED at the Tribal Children's Hostel, we immediately knew we were where we should be! There we found kids, adults, and missionaries faithfully serving the Lord, and who welcomed us with open arms. Some 450 tribal kids were being taught and cared for there. A wedding had just been held, and we were in the midst of lots of merry-making and music at the happy couple's reception. Dr. Stephen Morse greeted us warmly. I described in my journal:

> "He introduced us, telling the others about our history and ministry, got Gregg up on the stage where a few tribal, Western-dressed young men were singing. One of them placed a guitar in Gregg's hands and asked him to sing, so Gregg strummed and sang 'If You Want Love in Your Heart' and 'Rainbow of Love,' one of his own compositions. The crowd loved it and applauded wildly! Steve interpreted the words to the audience, and more applause broke out. Then Gregg started videotaping and had a hey-day, what with all the youngsters and many adults dressed in their native attire.
>
> "Afterward, we went from the large dining hall to the very spacious and well-built staff living quarters where

Steve and his wife, Linda, live with their cute three-year-old Jimmie. We shared and visited until 11:00 p.m. with the Morses and Kathy Grieme, a young woman from the South Side Christian Church in Springfield, Illinois, who is here teaching the kids Bible stories and organizing Bible Bowl groups. She is also instructing the newly married Lisu couple in what the Scriptures have to say about the responsibilities of a husband and wife."

The next day, Sunday June 21, 1987, before going to bed, I described our activities this way:

"What a day we've had! A glorious day! We woke up at 6:45, looked out our window on the sixth floor and viewed a refreshing rain-drenched city. After showering and dressing, we went down and had a 'rai' (delicious) buffet breakfast of watermelon, pineapple, bacon, ham and eggs, pancakes, orange juice, sweet roll and coffee."

By this time on our trip, we were in need of a lot of energy! I continued my account:

"At 10:00 Steve and Linda picked us up, and with our luggage and film equipment, drove us just a short distance to check in at another hotel, the Diamond, a first-class room, only $16.00 a night. Then we went to the Mission Compound for church services, which were already underway. What a beautiful scene it was, 450 or so quiet, well-disciplined tribal kids and a few adult leaders and teachers packed together and worshipping, seated on the floor and singing praises to God! Such sweet faces and voices! I sat next to a Thai interpreter about my age, who filled me in on everything being said. Unobtrusively and with great pleasure, Gregg filmed the worship and Communion service."

With an interpreter assisting, I delivered a message based on Ephesians the first chapter, but since there were so many kids in the audience, I kept it on their level, including references to our family and how we brothers grew up and dedicated our lives to the Lord. Steve then asked me to sing, so I sang one of the songs I had written, which I had sung in Vietnam in 1967, called "Freedom Prayer." I explained to the kids that the greatest freedom we could experience in life is the freedom from sin that we get when we confess Jesus our Savior as the Christ, the Son of the living God and are baptized for the forgiveness of our sins.

After a delicious lunch, Gregg and I journeyed with others up into the beautiful, scenic Ozark-type hills to a sparkling stream for a baptismal service. Several were immersed, and it was such a joyous but reverent occasion, with much singing. Gregg was able to capture it all on film, to be used later on a program we produced for showing in this country and back home in America.

On Monday, June 22, 1987, still at Chiang Mai, I wrote: "Samuel Mani, a 42-year old local Thai minister we had arranged to be our guide, picked us up at 11:00 a.m. and took us on what turned out to be a routine 'tourist trap' tour. We did make a stop at a leper village, and we insisted on tarrying there to minister awhile."

We found many of those afflicted with leprosy crafting and painting with their stubby fingers. It was quite a moving sight, and their friendly faces belied the ancient and dreaded disease they suffered. Three hundred of them live in the several dozen, white, two-room, colonial-style houses, row upon row. What a privilege to visit and minister among these segregated and often neglected, precious souls! Our guide then hurried us out a few miles to what appeared to be a self-serving commercial interest of an "umbrella village," where the locals make hundreds of hand-painted, different styles of parasols.

That evening, we enjoyed a wonderful meal and more sharing at Steve and Linda's house. He greatly desired to take Gregg and me on a surreptitious three or four day trip over the mountains and then by boat down and across the flooded and rushing river to a militant rebel conference in Burma. Steve was born in that country and was intensely interested in not only the mission work there, but also the survival and welfare of the hill tribes in their brave fight against the central Communist government. We would be "slipping" into Burma without legal visas. But Steve had his contacts and connections there, and even though we would have to go through several military, jungle checkpoints, he was confident we could successfully and safely make it. I was eager to change our schedule and also accompany Steve on the clandestine and adventurous mission, but after some long and frank discussion, Gregg convinced me that it would be much too risky and dangerous!

While at Chiang Mai, we gathered with many of the missionaries and took in a musical program with Rich Mullins and a Christ In Youth group. We visited with David and Deloris Filbeck, Tom Love, Jerry Headon, Walter Ridgley, and Tom Morse, all of them very dedicated and involved in the mission work there. Gregg and I also visited the Chiang Mai Bible Institute, where I spoke to the tribal students on the subject, "To Make All Men See," using Ephesians 3:1-10 as a text. My interpreter was Tom Headon, mentioned before, who was a graduate of Cincinnati Bible Seminary, where two of our children, Becky and Gregg, had attended. Tom was serving in the important role as president of the Institute, which majored in leadership training. We also visited with one of the missionary teachers, Peter Sutjaibun, a native Thai whom I had met earlier in the States, who also had graduated from Cincinnati Bible Seminary.

On our return trip, with stopovers at Bangkok, Hong Kong, Tokyo, and Honolulu, I wrote on Monday, June 29, 1987, these words:

"Thank you Lord, for making it [the mission trip] possible for us to do what we could in these short weeks, and help us do even more in the coming months and years. We landed in Los Angeles at 12:35 a.m., just past midnight, safe and sound and planning, the Lord willing, to return to Thailand next year. But for now, it's so good to be back at home, sweet home!"

CHAPTER 32

Joys, Tribulations, And The Bells
Ring At Pepperdine University

THE FIRST TEN years of our marriage were idyllic, pain-free, and so productive in our lives and ministry. Pat, my darling wife, was a perfect and ideal first lady of our student-ministry congregation at Conway, Missouri, giving great support to me in pursuing my college degree at Ozark Christian College. Following that was our full-time located ministry at Cassville, Missouri, where we were both treated like royalty! My deep love for preaching and evangelism then caused me to lead out in the formation of the Gospel Messengers Evangelistic Party, consisting of three of us Vernon brothers with our wives, plus Willis and Lora Harrison. By this time, our first child, Becky Jo, had been born, so there were nine of us launching out to travel full time in two and three week revivals, traveling in two cars, and staying in the homes of members of the churches! Our schedule rapidly filled up, and we did this for three happy and fruitful years. Willis was our excellent pianist, Pat was our chalk artist, I did most of the preaching, the four wives had their singing quartet, and we four men had our quartet. It was quite a challenging but rewarding period of soul-stirring and soul-saving evangelistic meetings, and we were so well received and in great demand by the Brethren. But after this, with three more babies added (our son Gregg, B.J. and Lodi's little Linda, and Bill and Joy's boy Richard), and with families being worn down, we all decided it was time to wrap it up.

It was so refreshing and productive to settle down in located ministries that Pat and I held in new churches we started in Eldon, Missouri, and Joplin, Missouri. At the latter, we bought our first home, and in the basement, organized and launched out in 1956, starting Christian Television Mission. Since 1954, Bill, B.J., and now brother Don, had traveled with me from each of the churches where we ministered, to appear weekly on television. The program originated from KOAM-TV, a powerful station midway between Pittsburg, Kansas, and Joplin, Missouri, that beamed into the four states of Missouri, Kansas, Oklahoma, and Arkansas. Our support and audience grew so large that by 1958, we produced our first *Homestead USA* TV series at Universal Studios and started syndicating the program all over the country. It was a thrilling but challenging time, for it included our wives, our children, and our parents. But it was also during this time that Pat and I lost our baby, Karen, to a rare and incurable muscular disease.

Starting and continuing this expanding ministry meant a lot of travel, fund-raising, rehearsing, appearances, and family filming. Whether all of this was a factor in Pat beginning to have ferocious and frequent migraine attacks over the next fifteen or so years will never be known, I guess. But it nevertheless became an unbearable burden of intense suffering for her and very difficult for our immediate family, to see our loved one in such anguish. Hospitals, doctors, and untold prescriptions provided no answers. Many times, with Pat in the hospital, I would have to take our three small children for Carol or Joy to keep and look after for a few days, while we four brothers would be gone for a revival or a series of fund-raising dates. I started feeling guilty and very discouraged that perhaps I had thrust too much of a burden on my young wife, and was responsible for her illness in the demands of our ministry and heavy lifestyle. For years, it just felt like there was no answer or escape, and I was nearing a complete breakdown myself. Finally, after taking Pat to the Mayo Clinic for the second time and returning to our home in Springfield, we loaded up a U-Haul trailer and made the break for relief, leaving for a hopeful new beginning. As I have described earlier, we ended up in sunny California, where through deep prayer, sunshine, a relaxed lifestyle, and a compassionate doctor, Pat's condition dramatically improved with much longer periods of pain-free living. And at long last, our blessed Lord intervened, totally eliminating her migraines, and with her exceptional charm and grace, enjoyed the next twenty years serving as hostess of our son Gregg's church.

The families in Missouri would return to the West Coast for more filming, and it was such a joy for Pat and me to have them all in our home for rehearsing and fun times, and then go to the studio to participate in the TV specials. What a relief and joy it was, especially after 1980, to be able to join my brothers in revivals, TV banquets, and continued television production on a half-time basis. In this way, we had more family time in California, and Gregg and I carried on our Christell and Refuge ministries, occasionally taking a short-term mission trip, which we did to Australia, New Zealand, Russia, England, Israel, Thailand, and earlier to Ecuador and Africa.

One of the providential and very helpful circumstances that made it possible to continue our Christian Television Mission production was the construction and development of the Good News Production Studios and their satellite outreach. We can thank and give credit to our dear friend, Ziden Nutt, whose vision and generosity led to this important milestone during the last several years of our ministry. We filmed all of our *Homestead USA* programs there by videotape, and they were aired through the use of their satellite dish. All praise to God and deep gratitude to Ziden and Good New Productions International for their benevolent assistance! And we Vernon Brothers and our families give heartfelt thanks to God for His blessings of wisdom, vision, and strength to carry out His Great Commission, and to all the contributors and churches who gave sacrificially through the years to make it happen.

Besides all the vital mission tours and trips Pat and I (and sometimes with our children) took on missions, revivals, filming, and concerts, it was very special when just the two of us could get away for a short vacation by ourselves. At least two times were in Hawaii, where we were so refreshed by the balmy, aloha breezes and the blue, sunny skies, not to mention the sand and surf! Another such renewal of our spirits was a visit to the Bahamas in 1988 to celebrate our 39th wedding anniversary. And in 1990, Debbie, Pat, and I vacationed in England and France. Then, sparing no detail, our son Gregg planned, with Becky and Debbie in on the secret, a glorious surprise 50th wedding anniversary celebration and party for us in 1999. So many of our friends and relatives honored us with their presence and anniversary cards, including my dear twin brother, Bill, and his beautiful wife, Joy, who flew out from Missouri to be with us for this happy event.

I want to mention Bill and Joy, B.J. and Lodi, Don and Carol – all of them – in their love and concern for us, especially their concern about Pat and her years of migraines. It proved to be such a long and difficult time for all of us. I want to say here that I couldn't have had brothers and sisters-in-law that in our struggles could have been more compassionate and loving than they have been! And that goes for my parents, my other three brothers, and their families. And as I have described, what a new lease on life it was when Pat got complete relief and so many joyful and rewarding experiences occurred for our family and ministry.

As far as the weekly programs for television, we would come together over the next several years as a team on an average of once a month. The four of us brothers would each prepare a couple of messages for presentation along with the scripts, and the whole group would select and rehearse the songs to be used for the shows. Then we would drive from Springfield to Joplin and, at Good News Productions, make eight programs that would be aired one by one each week by satellite.

For example, in the record I kept through the years of our TV production, revivals, banquets, and other appearances, I note this account dated January 15 to 25, 1980:

> "Flight from Los Angeles to Springfield, Missouri, Sunday afternoon, January 17th. Production at Good News Studios in Joplin January 18th and 19th. Back to Springfield the next day working on more scripts, then more programs at Good News the 21st and 22nd. Videotaping altogether included making eight new HOMESTEAD USA episodes. The two scripts I prepared and spoke on were entitled 'A Lost Book, A Lost People,' including footage I had shot in Thailand, and 'Suffering Humanity,' with a poem I had penned of that title. The next day we traveled to Johnson County Christian Church, and on the 24th spoke and sang for three services there in Kansas City, enjoying the fellowship and hospitality of the minister, our good friend, Ronnie Epps."

This was a procedure and formula that worked well for us brothers and our families. Coming together to produce films would be followed by traveling to a revival or a series of fund-raising banquets, and then free us up for some family time. This is the life and ministry to which we were committed, dating back to the time in 1947 when we publicly dedicated our lives to full-time Christian service. The four of us brothers held student churches during our college days, as well as preaching in separate ministries for several years prior to three years of evangelism and finally forming a television ministry. Preaching the Gospel has always been our first love and passion, and the fact that God gave us and our wives the gift of singing, wonderfully and providentially enhanced the message of salvation we have proclaimed for more than sixty years! All praise and glory to God that we have been privileged to herald this Gospel of redemption in our located ministries, in hundreds of revivals, in conventions, in Christian colleges, on television, in foreign nations, in civic clubs, in banquets as well as concerts, and by recordings of our own compositions and favorite hymns. This was all God's doing, lived out in our lives through the influence that began with our parents in the home, and continued later with the training we received.

We were so honored by hundreds and hundreds of our fellow ministers to come to the congregations where they ministered to preach in revivals, to hold rallies, and to host fund-raising banquets in support of the television ministry. Many of these men we had met when we were just kids on Ozark's basketball team years before when we played against lots of the other Christian colleges, and in many cases, got to sing in their chapel services.

If I started to name all of these ministers and Christians who befriended and supported us, it would take pages and pages of this book. But one elder statesman and aged minister I met and heard speak only once when I was in Bible college, I will mention. That name is P.H. Welshimer, heroic symbol of success in the annals of Restoration Movement history, and long-time minister of the historic First Christian Church in Canton, Ohio. He was a featured writer in the *Christian Standard* and *Lookout* publications, which my mother made sure were kept subscribed to and read in our home year after year. When we began our television ministry, I wrote to Brother Welshimer, and received back in his own handwriting a short but gracious reply commending us in the endeavor we set out to accomplish. As we progressed in our work, and after his passing, what an honor and privilege it was for us when Harold Davis followed him as the minister, to be invited to preach a revival there "in the House that Welshimer built!" And later, at the invitation of Richard Crabtree, with crowds of 2,000 and more, we preached two more revivals, televising to the whole city of Canton.

My family and I have lived in California from 1972 through the writing of this book, which at the present date is March of 2016. For the first twenty-one of those years, on an average, I was halftime with my brothers in the work of Christian Television Mission producing programs, holding revivals, and promoting the ministry. The TV Mission Board retired Bill and me, and our wives, honoring us with a nice plaque late in 1993, not long before Bill and I reached our 67th birthday on January 4, 1994. Our plaque was inscribed with these words, "Presented to Bob and Pat Vernon, by Christian Television Mission, to honor their years of constant and faithful service to the Lord." Following that is this verse of Scripture, "A dear brother and sister, a faithful minister and fellow servant in the Lord."

In California for forty-four years since 1972, besides the important work I continued in production and ministry with my brothers, many wonderful things have happened in our family and Christell ministry. Though it took time, lots of prayer, and patience, Pat regained her health. I have already described the ministry that my son Gregg and I have enjoyed, working together here on the West Coast and abroad on short-term mission trips. I have written and recorded lots of music, and during the eighties especially, what joy it was for our daughter Debbie and me to sing and do music workshops together. One of our appearances was at the Hollywood Roosevelt! And our talented daughter Becky joined the family in our TV specials.

Another rich blessing that came about with our move to California was the great reception and warm welcome I received at the gorgeous and picturesque seaside campus of Pepperdine University in Malibu. This was possible through the influence of Mildred Welshimer Phillips on one of her many visits to our home in Beverly Hills. I was invited to speak and share some of my history and writings at a noon luncheon there, following the dedication of one of the buildings Mildred's Trust Fund had built. I received a very nice letter from C.B. Runnels Jr., the Vice Chancellor, about the occasion. Following is the correspondence, dated October 22, 1973:

"Mr. Bob J. Vernon, 2241 Bowmont Drive, Beverly Hills, CA 90210. Dear Bob: Thanks so much, Friend, for being our guest today at the lunch where we were honoring our mutual friend Mrs. Mildred Phillips. Your presence added to our little family party and your presentation and kind thoughts helped to make our day complete. Later this afternoon and again tonight I was talking with Mrs. Frank Seaver [a benefactor who was also at the luncheon], and she asked me to remind you of her kind thoughts of you. It's obvious that people like you and Mrs. Seaver who are music composers think alike in many ways. I have an admiration for both of you because of your Christian thoughts and the talents you have and the ways you use them for Christ's sake. Bob, you will be hearing from us again. Today is a day we will long remember. God bless you. Cordially, Charlie."

Seven months later, I was asked to write and present a dedication poem for ceremonies dedicating the Phillips Theme Tower at Pepperdine University, to be held May 7, 1974. A dozen days before the event, I received a letter from M. Norvel Young, the Chancellor, dated April 26, 1974, as follows:

"Dear Bob and Mrs. Vernon: On Tuesday afternoon, May 7, at 5:30, we will have the dedication ceremonies for the Phillips Theme Tower on our Malibu campus. Mrs. B.D. Phillips will be here, and it will be a brief but very meaningful ceremony to pay tribute to our donor, to express our appreciation, and to recount what this very beautiful symbol can mean to the future of Christian education at Pepperdine. We cordially invite you to come, and Bob, we are delighted that you are going to participate on the program. I know that Mrs. Phillips will be pleased with your poem of dedication. Cordially, Norvel."

Shortly after the ceremony, I received this thoughtful letter, dated May 24, 1974:

"Mr. Bob Vernon, President, Christell Productions, Inc., 9255 West Sunset, Los Angeles, California. Dear Bob: Thank you so much for participating in such a special way, in the dedication of the Phillips Theme Tower on our Malibu campus. Your poem and thoughts were most inspiring and appropriate for the occasion, and I know it meant much to Mildred. Best wishes in the fine work you are doing. Sincerely (signed), Bill, William S. Banowsky, President, Pepperdine University."

Following is the dedication poem I had the privilege and honor of writing and presenting at Dedication Ceremonies for the Pepperdine University Phillips Theme Tower at Malibu, California on May 7, 1974:

THE PHILLIPS THEME TOWER
By Bob J. Vernon
Copyrighted 1974

This Memorial Tower...
Made possible by people of faith and destiny,
Reaches Heavenward,
Standing tall and free;
Ever smiling at her friend, the Sea,
Always calling weary passersby of humanity
To look up and see that life can be full of beauty,
Even as this Paradise-like University
Which would free the mind of ignorance and vanity,
Of sectarianism and strifely enmity.
And thus, this Spire, elegant and queenly,
Whispers distinctly and eloquently
The words of her kind plea,
She speaks ... listen closely ...
"I am the Tower of ..." the words are three ...
"Unity ... Liberty ... Charity ..."

The next year, Pat and I received, with the presidential seal, an official invitation to be present at a speech to be given by President Gerald R. Ford at Pepperdine University. Following is the inscription on the invitation:

Pepperdine University
Invites you to the dedication of the
LEONARD K. FIRESTONE FIELDHOUSE
11:00 a.m., Saturday, September 20, 1975
Malibu, California
Address by
Gerald R. Ford
President of the United States

On the Pacific Coast Highway, about a mile before getting to the turn-off to the campus, we found ourselves behind a long line of cars traveling at a snail's pace. And lo and behold, Pat and I were right behind Pat and Shirley Boone's Rolls Royce, stuck in the traffic. They recognized us and signaled that he was veering over to the right shoulder, and off we zoomed following them the rest of the way past the cars on our left, with the dust flying behind us on the dirt shoulder! We found parking places, hurried in to the Fieldhouse, and enjoyed the speech and fellowship following. It was a day never to be forgotten!

In a letter dated July 6, 1976, I got this gracious letter from Chancellor Norvel Young of Pepperdine:

"Mr. Bob Vernon, 2241 Bowmont Drive, Beverly Hills, California 90210, Dear Bob: Our family saw your INSPIRATION TV program on Channel 5, and sure enjoyed it! I thank God for the witness that you are giving in this way. Thank you for your word of encouragement. If you are able to, we would be delighted to have you at our conference on 'Alcoholism' next Monday. I'll enclose a note about it. I am also sending you a clipping from our student newspaper indicating something of the progress that I am making on my project. Thank you for your prayers. Devotedly yours (signed), Norvel, M. Norvel Young."

On August 24th, the next month, Norvel wrote again after they had been listening to my Capitol Records solo album. He penned:

"It is beautiful with some stirring songs that I love so much. Also I saw your Bible lesson in the CHRISTIAN STANDARD which was well done. God bless you in your continued good work. Thank you for your prayers and concern for me. I am thankful that the Lord has held me up through all my difficulties and I am now able to go back to work as I complete my research. Cordially, (signed) Norvel."

Our contact and fellowship with Pepperdine University has continued through the years, and their influence and first-rate educational commitment is felt widely in the local community and all the world. Pepperdine's encouraging love and commendation of our family's ministry, music, and mission work on the Coast and elsewhere in the world, is seen in this letter, written December 22, 1983:

"Pepperdine University, Office of the Senior Vice President, December 22, 1983, Dear Bob: It has been a long time since we have been together and visited about our mutual interests. We would be pleased to have you come and share with us the many accomplishments of your life since you last spoke here. Look at your calendar and call my Executive Assistant, Laurie Suber, for an appointment. In the meantime, have a wonderful holiday season and may 1984 be filled with blessings and fulfillment. Sincerely, (signed) Larry. Larry D. Hornbaker, Senior Vice President. LDH:ls, Mr. Bob J. Vernon, Christell, Inc., P.O. Box 1654, Beverly Hills, CA 90213, Pepperdine University Campus, Malibu, CA 90265, Tel. 213/436-4564."

To this day, we have appreciated not only the excellent training and education they are giving to young minds from all over the world, but especially from a personal standpoint, the kindness and sweet rapport we've enjoyed with Brethren of like precious faith!

Remembrances And Reflections

CHAPTER 33

Mildred Welshimer Phillips

IN THAT MILDRED Welshimer Phillips had such confidence in us and proved to be such a close friend and benefactor of our ministry, I want to devote several pages to how this developed and continued until her death in 1983.

First, as I have mentioned, she was in the bleachers of the gymnasium at Milligan College when Bill, B.J., and I (Don was still in high school) were on Ozark's basketball team and beat Milligan in 1950, I recall. She was the Dean of Women there for seventeen years before she met and eventually married B.D. Phillips, aged son and heir of the rich T.W. Phillips Gas and Oil Company in Butler, Pennsylvania. She had read in the *Christian Standard* and *Lookout*, I believe, about the success of our evangelistic meetings when we preached and sang all over the country in 1951, 1952, and 1953. At the North American Christian Convention in the mid-sixties, we exchanged pleasantries when we met the two of them the first time after they were married. Mildred was extremely friendly and aware that we had established Christian Television Mission, and as I remember, had seen a fifteen-minute film we showed at the first National Christian Education Convention in Cincinnati, Ohio, in August of 1956. Then later when we crossed paths again, she pulled me aside and whispered, "I'm trying to persuade my husband to help you in your television work." I was thrilled to "high Heaven" but tried not to show my elation too much! That was the beginning of several conversations and a very close relationship with Mildred.

When B.D. Phillips died in October of 1968, Mildred became Chairman of the large Phillips Trust, and our friendship deepened. By 1972, it had resulted, by Mildred's influence, in an invitation to us brothers to preach and lead the music in a revival at North Street Christian Church in Butler, Pennsylvania, with us all staying at her mansion, Elm Court! She made sure that all the Trust members were in attendance. Our preaching and singing were lauded, the crowds and converts came in great number, and we had many wonderful after-church meals and discussions with Mildred and Trust members about our Vernon history and ministry. From that time on, our families became close friends, and we were blessed and showered with ministry gifts from time to time.

I have previously mentioned how much Pat and I enjoyed Mildred's visit in our home at Beverly Hills in October of 1973, during which we went to Pepperdine for a luncheon honoring Mildred, where I got to speak. Our kids especially loved it when she stayed over Sunday, and after church, treated us to a fancy and luscious meal at the famed Beverly Hills Hotel!

Prior to that was our Vernon Brothers Holy Land tour, on which Mildred, our parents, and a dozen others traveled with us for a time of glorious fellowship and walking in the steps of our Lord. Mother and Dad overnighted with Mildred at Elm Court, then she accompanied them for a visit to the Homestead on the last leg home. When Mildred returned home to Elm Court in Butler, she wrote the following letter to my mother at the Homestead in Missouri:

"September 29, 1973, Dear Mrs. Vernon: This is one of the times when I wish I had my sister's [Helen, a great published poet] gift of words so I could tell you how much I enjoyed being at the homestead. Your home, so home-like, is the kind that everyone would like to drop in when lonely or weary. You can tell it is a home that has been <u>lived</u> in. And your table looked like a Thanksgiving feast! I'll never forget it. Everything was so good. Your speech at the table meant a lot to me, and that <u>beautiful</u> walnut bowl I'll always cherish. Many ministers will be served from it, and I'll always tell who gave it to me. I am so glad I got to know you and Mr. Vernon. You both added so much to our tour in the Holy Land. As Helen wrote in one of her poems, 'You're a Mother-Queen of the earth.' And after all, that is the greatest thing that can be said about a woman. From now on I hope our paths will cross often. Fondly, (signed) Mildred. Mildred Welshimer Phillips, Elm Court, Butler, PA 16001."

Prior to our tour, right after the noon luncheon at Pepperdine, before we would travel to be at Elm Court, I got the following letter from Mildred:

"Dear Bob: Elm Court seems like a big place tonight with only Raymond [Mildred's driver and grounds-keeper] and me rattling around in it. I have found a new cook who I think will be good. Her son, a senior in high school, has worked for me for two summers. They will move in to be with me at night. Raymond and I are counting the days until you come! Frank Wiegand [a Phillips Trust member and husband of one of the daughters of B.D. Phillips] and I had a good visit for a half-hour over the phone. He is completely sold on helping you. So I think it might be well if you stay a day or two more than the others when you come. I am so pleased over the Pepperdine luncheon! I was so proud of you, and Frank was pleased to hear about it. I fly to Milligan Tuesday noon and will be there until

Sunday afternoon when I go to Nashville for the meeting of the trustees of the Historical Society. If you should need to get in touch with me, I'll be staying at the Inns of America in Johnson City. I always do enjoy being on the campus. The Wiegands will be there too, so Frank and I will get a chance to talk. Be sure to let me know when you will arrive in Pittsburgh on the 10th, so Raymond and I can meet you. I have your record on now and at this minute you are singing, 'If you know the Lord, you need nobody else.' How true that is! Yet sometimes you like to have someone near to talk to who is human too. At least I do. I am enclosing a snow scene in front of Elm Court …
I know you will have a good evangelistic meeting in Eden, North Carolina. Goodnight, and a big God bless you! (signed) Mildred."

I have already referred to the glowing letter I received from Mildred after our revival there, prior to our Holy Land tour. It is God I have always sought to please when I preach, but it encouraged me to no end when Mildred wrote, "I wish you could give the messages you delivered in your revival here at Butler on the Restoration Movement to every college and convention in the Brotherhood."

I have dozens of letters where we corresponded with each other, but of course space prohibits me from sharing them all in this book. I'll include, however, a few more, then conclude with a heartfelt tribute I wrote when she passed on to her Heavenly reward.

On January 24, 1976, I wrote this letter:

"Dear Mildred, It was so good of you to call and let me know what's going on there. Talking on the phone is not like speaking face to face, but it's the next best thing. In case you can come out during our filming, the dates are February 12, 13, and 14. I really am thrilled about the way things are falling into place concerning the programs. I have my hands full trying to take care of all the little details, as well as the big ones, in preparing for production. I hired a script writer today to help Gregg and me put the screenplays into scene sequence for the lines that will be spoken by us Vernons and the actors. The four films are 'United We Must Stand,' featuring Thomas Campbell and unity; 'Rise Up and Restore,' covering Alexander Campbell and restoration; 'One President's Faith,' telling of James A. Garfield and the New Testament Church; and 'Give Liberty … Give Life,' featuring Barton Stone and evangelism. We will have dramatizations of both patriotic and restoration pioneers, using actors. The eight of us brothers and wives will sing patriotic songs and national hymns, and each of us men will speak on one of the programs. We have also asked Edwin Hayden, Knofel Staton, Ralph Dornette, and Paul Benjamin to write and deliver a message, each one for a different topic and film. This is really quite an undertaking, and we need much prayer and help to complete and air the programs. You and the Trust have been so good to us … so very generous, Mildred! Don't slip and fall on all that snow you're getting. It's so sunny and warm out here, you better come out and spend the rest of the winter! At any rate, thanks again, Mildred, for all the inspiration you continue to be for me and the Cause. As ever, (signed) Bob."

In a couple of notes from Mildred I found these expressions: "Just a few lines to tell you again how much I appreciated coming out and being with you and your family." Again: "Your visit here gave me just the lift I needed! I think you know how much I enjoy our talks together. You're a kindred spirit! You will always be welcome here. I value your friendship! Always, (signed) Mildred."

In October of 1979, I was invited to speak at the Christian Church in Pittsburgh where Frank Wiegand was an Elder, so I flew there late on Saturday, stayed all night at the Wiegands, and delivered the Sunday morning message. I was received royally, and it was such a pleasure to be together again, and enjoy lunch with them. As I recall, that was the time I drove over to Butler for another visit with Mildred. A few days after I got back home, I received this letter, as follows:

"Dear Bob: It's always lonely after you leave. You were here such a short time. Your tapes bring you back! I certainly thank you for them. I stayed awake playing them last night. A week from Sunday there will be a good article in the LOOKOUT about my father. Be sure to read it. Mark Taylor sent me an advance copy. I hope you found Pat well when you returned home. Thank you for coming to see us. The best ornaments in my home are the friends who come to see me! Hope you'll be back soon and stay longer. Fondly, (signed) Mildred."

The plumbing and other major structural problems in the aged mansion of Elm Court caused Mildred to have to move to an apartment in Butler late in the 1970's. Then early in 1980, she made her home in Johnson City, Tennessee. On March 17, 1980, she mailed me this letter:

"Dear Bob: Appreciated your phone call and your letter. I really have been rushed since moving. I think this apartment is nicer than my Butler one. I believe I told you what a good 'send-off' the Butler people gave me. Was really touched! Jean did not come with me. I have a wonderful woman who drives for me and acts as housekeeper and cook. I eat many of my meals at the college [Milligan]. Spent the weekend of four days in Newnan, Georgia with Paul [Jones]. We still talk every night. Will write more after things are settled here. Still have my books to unpack. As ever, (signed) Mildred."

I pretty well kept all my correspondence through the years, including letters sent to me, plus copies of letters I wrote. Here is another one I wrote to Mildred on July 23, 1980:

"Dear Mildred: I'm sure you must think I've broken both wrists! No, only one knee! I had to cancel all my speaking engagements and concerts for the last three months. I didn't get to go to the North American or World Conventions. I fell on steps here and twisted and snapped my knee terribly. It's been very painful. But I'm hobbling around again, and was able to go to Westwood Hills Christian Church on Sunday with the family. Lord willing, I'll be going to our annual Spiritual Encounter in Branson. Bill Lown will be the featured speaker. Do come if you can! Sorry I wasn't able to come down there as I had planned to, but will make it later. Debbie decided not to go to Pepperdine this fall, because she's continuing on with her music and working part-time for a law firm. She may go later. Thanks a lot for writing a letter of recommendation for her. Must close. As you can see by my writing, I'm still a little shaky. Hope you are well and happy there. Write me all the latest. Miss seeing you. As ever, (signed) Bob."

I note that the last letter in my files before Mildred's death is one in which I told about a long and successful Christian Television Mission series of meetings with my brothers. Then I wrote:

"... The tour was [also] very productive in that during it, I composed ten new songs and poems. They were on the following subjects: FLIGHT ON HIGH, PEACE AFTER THE STORM, SUNSHINE OF GOD'S LOVE, FOREVER A FRIEND, PRAISE AND ADORATION, WEEP LIKE JESUS, REST FOR A MOMENT, CELEBRATE THE DATE, THE CALL OF THE WATER, and LIGHT THE WORLD WITH THE WORD OF LIGHT. I must close now. I do appreciate your concern for me, but our needs here are being met, so I prefer that you send future support to our TV Mission in Springfield or to the colleges you love and believe in. I will always be a friend, and it is friendship and spiritual support that means the most. As ever, (signed) Bob."

Soon after, Mildred was involved in a tragic automobile accident the first week of May, 1983, and shortly thereafter died from her injuries. From California, I flew to be at Mildred's funeral, and in the May-June issue of the *Christian TV News*, headed with her picture, I wrote and eulogized our dear friend with the caption, TRIBUTE TO MILDRED WELSHIMER PHILLIPS, by Bob J. Vernon, for the Vernon Brothers:

"Mildred Welshimer Phillips is gone. This dear, sturdy, stalwart friend and defender of the 'Plea' fell victim to the Grim Reaper, and was laid to rest May 10, 1983. Mildred was 'true blue.' A friend to the end. Queenly, but very much a 'commoner,' with deep human feelings. Analytical and critical, but courteous, kind, thoughtful, and generous through and through. Mildred was saintly but not at all 'sanctimonious.' She was cheerful and fun-loving, and how she loved to entertain the Brethren, especially at Elm Court. But she herself, as she once wrote me, 'would rather enjoy a good, juicy hot dog than have someone fuss over me with a big, fancy meal.' She had many women friends, and took great delight in teaching her Monday women's Bible group while she lived in Butler, Pennsylvania, but she was turned off by idle chatter. The great loves of her life were her father, P.H. Welshimer, her husband, B.D. Phillips, Sr., her Lord Jesus Christ, and the Restoration Movement. She loved to be in the company of men, discussing great issues of consequence, and she served with distinction on many boards of the Brotherhood. The Vernon Family and Christian Television Mission will miss Mildred greatly. She was a special friend and benefactor. Our paths first crossed in 1950, when she was on the staff at Milligan, and we were there as students of Ozark Bible College to play basketball and sing in Chapel. Her father wrote and encouraged us when we began the Mission in 1956. Steady correspondence with Mr. Phillips and Mildred began twenty years ago, and they were very enthusiastic and complimentary about our films, 'Philippian Jailer' and 'Back to Jerusalem.' Because of that, after his death, Mildred was influential in getting the B.D. Phillips Trust Fund to back Christian TV Mission and Christell Productions in many projects here and in California. On a personal level, she was like 'family,' especially in the lonely and transitional years after Mr. Phillips died. She visited the Homestead, and wrote afterward to Mother, 'this is one of the times when I wish I had my sister's [Helen] gift of words so I could tell you how much I enjoyed being at the Homestead. Your home – so homelike – is the kind that everyone would like to drop in when lonely or weary.' She visited many times over the past ten years in Missouri and California, and called on the phone frequently, out of her deep Christian love and concern. Mildred was very strong in her decisiveness and in the courage of her convictions. But she would reminisce for hours about her 'growing up' years in Canton, about her dear mother and father, who called her his 'John.' About her sister Helen, a great poet, who suffered so much before her death, and her love for brother Ralph as well as for her only nephew and niece, Mark and Paula, her pride and joy. About her escapades and studies at Hiram College, her Alma Mater, and the 'glory' years at the CHRISTIAN STANDARD and at Milligan college where she was Dean of Women for seventeen years. But the gleam really came in her eyes when she told the details of her fairy-tale romance and wedding to B.D. Phillips and their perfect five years of blissful marriage. She spoke of her deep caring for the entire Phillips family for the way they took her in and received her and loved her as one of their own. She appreciated everyone in the Phillips family: Ben Jr., Victor, and Don, and their wives, Rollie and Stella Ehrman, Frank and Undine Wiegand, and Joe and Clarinda Sprangles. What a privilege it was to get to know them all personally. Mildred and I drove up the hill more than once when I was in Butler, to visit the gravesite where Mr. Phillips was buried. 'Now I'm going to get a little misty,' I recall her saying. One time we drove to Newcastle, and spent a half-day looking at the inscriptions on the grave markers of many of the Phillips' forebears, and talking about T.W. Phillips and his book, THE CHURCH OF CHRIST. But then her thoughts turned to her beloved mother and father, and the Welshimer sentimentality that she deeply felt. And weeping softly, she said, 'As deeply as I love my husband – even still – and as much as I care for everyone in the Phillips family, when I go, my heart tells me that I want to be laid to rest beside father and mother. But,' she whispered, 'Do you think everyone will understand?' I replied quietly, 'I'm sure they will.' One of my most recent songs that Mildred loved, and would call me up long distance and ask me to sing to her over the phone was THE PROMISE OF TOMORROW. Here's the chorus:

> There's a promise of tomorrow
> And an end to ache and sorrow,
> Don't lose sight of glorious daybreak just ahead;
> Though the world is full of sadness,
> There's a lot of love and gladness
> That awaits you,
> So lift your weary head!

"Yes, Mildred Welshimer Phillips is gone, but never forgotten. Her TODAY is over … her TOMORROW has just begun!"

CHAPTER 34

Vernon Reunions

TOWARD THE MIDDLE of July in 1993, we had a glorious, never-to-be-forgotten happening at the old Vernon farm Homestead where we seven brothers were raised. Several months before it came about, all of us got a letter from our very thoughtful, loving, and organizer extraordinaire sister-in-law, Carol Vernon, Don's wife. Here are some excerpts from her letter:

"Dear Family and loved ones, This letter comes as an announcement of a wonderful event that you surely will want to attend, so read closely. There has been a great deal of talk and interest recently in having a Dallas Vernon Sr. family reunion this year, so we've decided to get the ball rolling and make it happen! We'll share below the tentative plans that have been made so far and would encourage each of you to come up with some of your own ideas and send them to us. Dates: July 11-13, 1993. This would appear to be a good time for a majority of the families since the North American Christian Convention will be bringing many to St. Louis during the week of July 3 to 8, and the week following the proposed reunion is the Vernon Brothers Spiritual Encounter at Branson. In order to minimize travel time and expenses, this week in between looks appealing. We're a big and busy family and finding time when everyone can participate will be virtually impossible, yet we'd like to try to accommodate as many schedules as we can, so let us know if these dates are unworkable. Mark your calendars anyway! Location: Homestead U.S.A. ... The farm will take a lot of fixing up, so if any of you would be willing to make time for this needy project, your contribution would be greatly appreciated. [I volunteered on one of my trips from California to help paint the house.] ... We are planning for a Sunday evening service and would appreciate any suggestion as to who we might get to sing and preach. Ha! Ha! ... May your holidays be full of joy and peace as you spend time with friends and family, remembering Him who brought joy and peace to us. You are loved, Carol, wife of Don, the 7th son."

Pat and I, plus our kids and grandkids, were so thrilled when we got Carol's letter and started making plans to join all the other Vernons in this very special occasion! We replied excitedly, thanking Carol for all her time and work in organizing the reunion, and volunteered whatever might be needed in preparation for the big event. And as I mentioned, how I enjoyed getting into some old clothes and a crumpled hat to help scrape and paint the house on one of my trips back before the reunion. Someone snapped a picture of me in that garb, a snapshot which I still have!

By 1993, I'd built up more than 200,000 frequent-flyer miles going for television production, evangelistic meetings, banquets, concerts, and overseas missions, so we had more than enough points to be able to have Pat, me, Gregg, Debbie, Becky and Stephen plus their little kids Jeremy and Jessica, to fly round-trip free for the North American Christian Convention in St. Louis, then on for the reunion! I can't begin to tell what a blessing it was for us all to be together back-to-back for both events! It took some time and doing working out our schedules and getting our free travel tickets, but I did it and also made reservations for our hotel in St. Louis and our cabin at Bennett Spring State Park, not far from the Homestead, for our stay at the reunion. The large picturesque park, noted for and named after its huge, sparkling round spring some fifty or so feet across, bubbling up and flowing in a winding stream a few miles into the Niangua River and amply supplied with rainbow trout, has always been an attraction and favorite recreational spot for our family.

It was so wonderful in St. Louis for us four Vernon Brothers, our wives, and our brood to enjoy the inspiring sessions of the convention from July 6th to 9th. We had a Mission booth, sang on the program, and fellowshipped with the Brethren from all over the country. At the conclusion there, we rented cars and drove the 180 miles to Lebanon, Missouri, our hometown, then out the nine miles to the Homestead for hugs with dozens of other welcoming Vernons arriving for the reunion. Late that night, tired but excited, we drove the short distance to Bennett Spring, checked in at our cabin, and anticipated the three days of special pleasure beginning the next morning. And, needing rest, we all slept soundly.

July 11, 12, and 13 was such a glory-filled period that we wished time could stand still, that it would never end. It was like a bit of Heaven on earth! Everything pretty well clicked off according to the plan that Carol had mapped out. The weather cooperated with sunny skies smiling and beaming its bright rays down on the joyful clan mingling together in heavenly unity. The huge tent, erected to the eastern side of the house, shielded the happy reunioners seated on the long benches from the sunrays and the few typical, summertime Midwest showers that cooled the atmosphere. Here we had our entertaining programs with lots of laughter and applause. And here, Sunday at dusk, we ate a great meal fixed by B.J.'s and Don's clan. The next gathering, however, in the cool of the Sunday evening under the stars, took place as we were all seated in lawn chairs at the big front yard for our Praise Service. It surely must have been very pleasing to our Heavenly Father to see such a scene as this, a gigantic and devoted family of families coming together to start their reunion with a worship service!

Our oldest brother of the seven, J.P., acted as host and leader, welcoming everyone and lifting up his voice to Heaven in a fervent and heartfelt prayer. Bill made introductions, Doug led the singing, B.J. read Mother's favorite Scripture, there was lots of special music, and Don brought a brief devotional. Topping it all off was partaking in Communion, with Joe, Bob, Ken, and Gregg serving the group. The service was closed with another special, a hymn, and the benediction.

The next day, Monday, saw separate families enjoying their breakfast and noon lunch together, with pleasurable activities in between. That afternoon, we got together visiting, sharing stories, hiking in the woods, the kiddos splashing in their kiddie pool, playing games, and you name it!

As planned, we all got together under the tent for the evening meal fixed by mine, Bill's, and J.P.'s families. This period of good food, fun, and fellowship around the tables proved to be a favorite and joyous time for everyone.

Shortly after the meal, the entertainment for the evening began. First was a lively game of Family Feud, led by Denise's husband, funny man Tim Harlow, with competing teams from each Vernon brother family. Next was Dallas Jr., who took the microphone as emcee and out-did Tim with the hilarious antics of this genteel, retired, long-time president of the Detroit Tool and Engineering Firm in Lebanon! He did get on the more serious side, reading a very descriptive poem he had written about being raised on the Farm, titled "Junior Grows Up." He then emceed the show called, "GRANDPA, TELL US 'BOUT THE GOOD OLE DAYS." Each of us seven brothers was listed, with the following instructions given to all the on-lookers: "Write out ahead of time a question you want to ask, then one at a time, direct your question to a specific Grandpa about the good ole days in growing up on the Farm." You can just imagine all the hysterical laughing that went on for the next couple of hours as incident after incident was recalled and related to the kids, grandkids, cousins, uncles, and aunts!

The final day of the reunion, Tuesday the 13th, followed the same pattern as the first two, with most everyone gathering in the afternoon for games and various activities. In early evening, a luscious meal was provided by the Dallas Jr. clan, followed by a full evening of top entertainment. I made sure of that since I was chosen to be the emcee! But before giving a line-up of all that good stuff, let me share with you Dallas Jr.'s very descriptive poem about growing up on the Farm:

JUNIOR GROWS UP
Written by Dallas Vernon Jr.
On November 9, 1992

Along with six brothers,
And Mother and Dad,
Growing up on the Homestead
Wasn't all that bad.

Horses and cows,
Chickens and hogs,
Turkeys and geese,
And don't forget the dogs.

Horse-drawn machinery,
Collars and bits,
Harness and doubletrees
Can all give you fits.

Plowin' and plantin',
And puttin' up hay,
With mules and horses,
All without pay.

Cows to milk,
Hogs to slop,
Eggs to gather,
No place to stop.

Wood to split,
Water to draw,
Lamps to fill,
Just some of the law.

Ridin' Ole Fly
As fast as she could go,
It was fun till she fell,
Then country boy's woe!

Roamin' the woods,
Swimmin' in the ponds,
Stumped toes and grasshoppers
Make a farm and boy bond.

Wood-burnin' cook stove,
Kerosene lamps,
Dipper and water bucket,
And 3-cent stamps.

Homemade light bread,
Tenderloin and bacon,
Blackberry cobbler,
Mighty good makin'!

Strawticks and featherbeds,
Split bottom chairs,
A two-holer outhouse,
And a cold upstairs.

Blackfoot school,
Marbles and books,
Barefoot and bib overalls,
We weren't much for looks!

At Oak Grove Baptist,
We learned about the Lord,
From singin' and preachin'
And drills from the Sword.

A Model T Ford,
Then a Model A
With side curtains floppin'
Every cold winter day.

With an Assessor's election
Came a '37 V-8,
And a new Zenith radio
To keep us up late.

Two years in the 8th grade
Because we were poor,
Finally finished high school,
And there isn't much more.

So as bad as it sounds,
It was fun for us all
To have such memories

We now can recall.

My name now is not the same,
The change was kinda sad,
We had to overcome first
Objections from my dad.

"We've always called him Junior,
At school and everywhere.
If I can't call him that
I'll call him 'George,' so there!"

Now there you have it,
My early life to see
Things you'll never find
On a Family Tree.

First, I arranged for a pre-session, in which J.P. and I belted out as a duet, songs that we sang on the radio when I was only 13 years of age, backed by a country band. The songs were "Home on the Range," "Beautiful Texas," and "My Little Girl." The crowd went wild! Then Debbie, at the keyboard, sang a couple of beautiful songs she had written, "Without Love" and "Wait for the Harvest." Michele's husband, Jack Ward, with his huge vocal range, warmed our hearts with song. Then, from a child's perspective, Pat's and my dear little 6-year-young grandson, Jeremy Walker, brought a lot of smiles and applause as, without hesitation, he clearly voiced in childish terms how he loved being at the reunion and getting to know his cousins, then singing a few lines of the song "A Whole New World" from the latest Disney movie.

For the start of the main session, I asked everyone to join in singing the theme song of our television series, *Homestead USA*:

There's a Homestead in the valley
That recalls fond memories,
There's a deep old well by a strong old house
Nestled there beneath the trees.
There I learned to love my neighbor,
It was there I learned to pray,
Is it any wonder that I should love my Homestead USA.
When the Folks we love headed for the West
In search of a land that would suit them best,
They believed in God and He led them through
To a land of promise new.
So here we lived and labored,
And here our vows were made,
Is it any wonder that we should love
Our Homestead USA.

What a rousing, harmonious, and heavenly chorus of "Homestead" voices it was that rang out over those Ozark hills and valleys! Next, I thought it appropriate to quote the words of a song I had written, called, "Homeplace Yesterday:"

This is the homeplace where I was born,
Where I first saw the light of morn.
The mem'ries flood my soul
Of childhood long ago,
Of laughter and love
That were gifts of God above.
This is my homeplace, my home, sweet home,
I won't forget it no matter where I roam,
I'll have this heritage until
Heaven's great homecoming day,
My homeplace in the Ozarks,

My homeplace yesterday.

Here lived our Mother and Dad
And seven sons in all,
In the friendly hills of Springhollow
Where quail and whip-poor-will call.
And mockingbirds sing sweetly
Out the wooded way
That leads to the place
Where we learned to work and pray.
We labored and neighbored,
And sang from day to day
As we were plowing and planting
Or working in the hay.
There was time for baseball and swimming,
Oh how we loved to play
On our homeplace in the Ozarks,
Our homeplace yesterday.

There's the oak grove and the church house
Where the neighbors gathered 'round
For Sunday school on the Lord's Day,
And dinner on the ground.
We heard the choir and the sermons
On love and the Gospel way.
We'd worship and pray,
Oh it seems but yesterday!
See the dirt road to the schoolhouse
Where I learned to read and write.
And across the valley through the little lane
Is the sacred graveyard site
Where lies Sweet Mother and Dad

Waiting Resurrection Day.
They rest now from their labors
Near Homestead USA.

Next, our first cousin, Alma Vernon Stickler, oldest daughter of Uncle Owen and Aunt Exie Vernon, gave some reflections and remembrances about Grandma Etta Vernon and Homestead history. The Joe and Beth Milan family then favored us with some special music, followed by Judy Vernon Gilmore and her daughter, Stephanie, singing and sharing. Homemade movies of the 1961-62 era delighted us, and everything was capped off by screening excerpts of the first *Homestead USA* film that was made at Universal International Studios in 1958, and the "Philippian Jailer" special episode produced at Desilu Studios in Hollywood two years later. The films featured us Vernon Brothers and our wives, but Mother and Dad had an important role in both productions. In the former, looking at old pictures, Mom was reminiscing about meeting Dad, their courtship in the horse and buggy days, their marriage, and raising seven boys. They were "hits" of the evening, especially to the youngest ones who had never seen these films. Who would ever have imagined that our parents, both in their late 60's, would become Hollywood stars! What a way to end our reunion! The happy crowd applauding, giving honor, and paying homage to the kind and devoted couple who started it all, Dallas Sr. and Beulah Tribble Vernon! Mother and Dad have always been stars to us seven sons and our families, but that great night they became stars to all the newest little "Homesteaders," even as they had been stars to television viewers all over the country.

After getting home, I wrote this letter to each of my brothers:

"August 23, 1993
From me, your brother Bob
To you, my dear brother of the Seven

Hi from here:

"Didn't we have a great time at the Reunion! It just couldn't have been better, with the exception that we missed those few who couldn't make it.

"Personally, from our family, we want to thank you and yours for all your love, and for all you did to make it such a success.

"The whole Vernon Family is so blessed to have such a caring and considerate clan. I could really sense Mother and Dad's presence with us those three days. It's as though the clouds parted and there they were, saying, 'We're so proud of you!'

"I'm sending along a few historical items and enlargements I got done to add to the collection I presented to you in person. I know you'll enjoy and cherish them.

"I guess I should let you know I'm still having a good bit of dizziness and discomfort, but I'll get it whipped! Have been ordered to take it easy, take medication, and get some R&R. So I'll try to pay attention and be a good boy!

All our love, Bob & Family"

In 1998, we had another wonderful reunion at the Homestead. I'm including a rather lengthy poem I wrote and gave the first night, plus an outstanding tribute that Tim Harlow, Denise's husband, penned about it in his church paper after he got home. Tim is the great minister of a mega-church near Chicago.

HOMESTEAD MYSTERY ... VERNON HISTORY
By Bob J. Vernon
July 3, 1998 – 12:30 a.m.
The Vernon Reunion

There's a question intriguing, forever unknown,
Who settled this land, using tools of stone?
Was it Asians or Alaskans or the Blackfoot tribe?
It's all a mys'try we can't trace or describe.
It must have been something living wild in these hills,
Hunting buffalo and deer, knowing the barest of skills.
Planting maize and beans, and fishing the stream
Of Niangua, White Bluff, and Bennett Spring.
Recorded Vernon his'try, so full of lore,
Goes back to Duke William, the Conqueror.
I found our genealogy displayed on a wall
There at Vernon France, in City Hall.
I gasped in disbelief at this document rare,
This chart of ancestors whose name I wear.
And in Westminster Abbey I saw a statue of fame,
Admiral Edward Vernon, his royal name.
Our new world was settled and explored by our kin
Facing hardships but believing that with faith they'd win.
In 1844, Vernons left from Tennessee,
Hoping and praying that Missouri they'd see,
Bride Sarah by the side of young Obadiah,
A godly pioneer, no prince but no pariah.
They came by Covered Wagon, this man and wife aboard,
Little Joe taggin' 'longside, how his spirits must have soared!
At this Oaktree knoll, with no more trav'lin'
Obadiah said, "I'll build a log cabin."
He labored and farmed for sixteen years,

Then at thirty-nine, died, midst cries and tears.
Eight children and Sarah, grieving to the brim,
Got help from the elder boys, 'specially Jim.
As a teen he served in the Civil War,
Bringing peace with a cry, "War no more!"
With his dear wife, Liza, little Ruth and Ed,
Jim's joy turned to anguish when he found his wife dead.
Young Etta, when sixteen, met and married Jim,
And life no longer seemed to be grim.
They had Lena and Oda, then Dallas and Owen,
Dad's fame as a pitcher for years kept a-growin'.
At a movie that cost just a little moola,
Dad was nudged by a lady, who turned out to be Beulah.
"Are you Dallas, the fast pitcher?" He answered, "I am."
She said, "My name is Beulah, and I'm a big fan!"
Cupid struck with a wedding, leading them to Hornhollow,
Born were J.P. and Ward; Grandpa Jim's death followed.
So they moved to the Homestead, trusting God in their woe,
Worked hard and created this haven we know.
Way out in the country, nine miles west of Lebanon,
They made Grandma's Homestead a place worth remembrin'.
The Depression made it hard, but they had God's blessing.
Teaching school and farming, and later assessing.
Horse and buggy would carry them to church ev'ry Sunday,
Then a picnic or ballgame to make it a fun day!
But the lovebirds had the feeling that something was missing,
More kids were needed to round out the blessing.
Mom and Dad solved the problem, oh wow, did they ever!
Five boys were added, making seven altogether.

J.P., the reader, and Ward, so bright but lame,
Soon had a dimpled brother, Dallas Jr., his name.
Then twins, Bill and Bob, born a little after,
Cut a funny caper that brought a burst of laughter.
We crawled and dived into the blackberry cobbler,
'Til our noses and faces matched the ol' turkey gobbler!
Big B.J. joined the clan, hazel eyes of expression,
His smile and quick wit offset the Great Depression.
And last but not least, came Donnie bringing joy,
I got to rock the cradle of this handsome baby boy!
So there you have it, seven boys and our parents,
It's the heart God looks on, not the outward appearance.
That's what we were taught, that brought faith, hope, and love,
With blessings on earth, then Heaven above,
After losing two elections, Dad won three as Assessor,
He got a brand new Ford, 'cause finances were better.
He purchased the old Homestead, a radio, and more cows,
Took us all to church on Sundays, to the Lord paid our vows.
Mom and Dad, up there, how moved you must be,
Viewing this big reunion of your large family.
Seven boys who reached manhood, each following his dream,
Knowing life is fleeting, like the tea-kettle steam.
Oh the beauty and charm of our faithful Vernon women,
It appears that we men really knew how to pick 'em!
Mabel and Mary Jo, Pat and Oleta,
Lodi and Carol, Joy and Patricia.
We're the seven Vernon brothers, wives and offspring you see,
From a lineage of love passed to you and to me.
What a heritage of honor and faith have we,
The Vernon clan in this big Fam'ly Tree!

AS FOR ME AND MY HOUSE
WE WILL SERVE THE LORD
THE DALLAS AND BEULAH VERNON FAMILY REUNION
JULY 3 – 8, 1998
By Tim Harlow

"Greetings from the Homestead near Lebanon, Missouri. We spent the 4th of July weekend there for Denise's family reunion. There Dallas and Beulah Vernon raised 7 sons, of which my father-in-law was the youngest. From the family that grew up in this farmhouse, faith in God has been preserved for 3 generations that have followed, and many more to come. There are over 120 people in this family, and almost 90 of them were at the reunion. Yes, it was hot, and yes, we got chiggers, ticks, and poison ivy, but what a time of celebration for a family of God!

"I admit, I was initially attracted to my wife because she is gorgeous (I am a man), but I found that she came with quite a dowry. When I got to know her family and the heritage she came from, I realized a lucky man would marry this girl. When (if) most families get together, there is drinking, cussing, and fighting. When the Vernons get together, there is testimony of God's power, worship, tears of joy, and knowledge that this family reunion will never end. From what I know, every one of the descendants in this family are Christians. A majority of the adults have been or are involved in vocational ministry, and the rest are actively involved in ministry in their churches. I told several of them I'd love to have them in our church. Good, solid, Christ-like people – from Pennsylvania, California, Maryland, Colorado and Missouri – who serve God, love their families, and make the world a better place.

"Thank God that Dallas and Beulah had the determination to teach their 7 sons about the ways of the Lord! I am a lucky recipient of that gift, as are the thousands of people that have been ministered to by them. Someone said we should just paint the words, 'As for me and my house, we will serve the Lord' on top of the house, because that was their motto. I hope it is for your house. If you don't come from a family heritage that you can be proud of, IT'S TIME TO START A NEW ONE! Put 'As for me and my house, we will serve the Lord' on your house and take steps to making sure it happens. Be involved in church, and not just a participant. Model servanthood, teach giving, live a life of example, and make sure your kids know the importance of church. Get them to VBS, camp, CIY, children's church, Team Kids, and everything you can to combat the influence of the world. But more importantly, show them what it means to live for Jesus."

CHAPTER 35

The Big Los Angeles Earthquake!

On January 17, 1994, while it was still pitch-black at approximately 4:30 in the morning, we were suddenly jolted and rudely awakened out of our deep sleep by the violent shaking of the "big one," a long-predicted earthquake. Needless to say, never do I want us to have to go through such a deafening and earth-shattering experience again as that which we survived that ominous morning! I described it in a long and graphic letter I later wrote and sent to family and friends across the country, an account which I will include for you, the reader. But first, I'd like to refer to, and quote from, a very sweet and gracious answer I received from Mae Bolles, elderly wife of Vernon Bolles, a dear first cousin who passed away some time before. Vernon was just a little boy when his mother, Oda Vernon Bolles, had died in the world-wide flu epidemic of 1919, which my mother, also critically ill, had barely survived. Aunt Oda, dying seven years before I was born, was a sister of my father, and she had been married to Rob Bolles. Their young son, Vernon, went to live with my parents for some time in the second year of their marriage. Mae's letter follows:

"Dear Bob and Pat, My wheels turn slow … and slower. I do manage to get things done, even if some come along a few months late. I have thought of you MANY times, and have re-read your graphic account of your terrifying experience in the earthquake, and goodness sake, what an experience! Only to live through it, would one ever know! And thank God you all came through it safe and sound. Your descriptive letter makes it come closer to home than I could imagine, and the noise, I just didn't realize there would be such deafening noise associated with an earthquake, other than that which came with everything falling apart all around you. I truly appreciate your including me when you sent your letter. That means a lot to me. Vernon's family has always been like part of my family. You have been so good to me, and I love you all. Your letter will be something I will keep, it is so 'for real!' Pat and John [Mae's daughter and son-in-law] were here when it arrived and of course read it. Then my sister, Dorothy, and two of her daughters came for a visit and read it, and were really impressed with your account. Now since I am getting your letter answered, I will send a copy to my sister, Eva, in Lebanon, for I know she and her family would like to read your account of the earthquake experience.

"I share your joy and thankfulness that little Topy survived. These little (and big like my dog, Frosty) human-like dogs are so precious to us. Pat and John spent most of the fall and winter with me, looking after me mostly. I was quite ill – very ill – with pneumonia and flu last October, and spent the next few months recuperating. I am doing pretty well now, though I've lost some ground. But I'm pretty lively for a lady of eighty as of April 9!

"I am so thankful for the fact that I have Pat and John, and of course our Frosty, who was also loved by Vernon before his death [in 1988]. When the storm clouds come rolling in around here, and there are these dire tornado warnings on television, I often wonder how I would ever get big Frosty to the safety of the basement. He doesn't like the open stairway, and that is one place he won't follow me.

"The log cabin in Lebanon [their home for years before moving to St. Louis] still beckons to me. I had spent a month there last fall before I took sick.

"I do pray that you have been able, or will be, to purchase a home. This check I'm sending will perhaps help in some small way toward that goal or in getting your lives back together, maybe buying a door-knob to open your way to the warmth of your own home. With it comes my love and my thankfulness to God for keeping watch over you. And Pat, I am so thankful that your health is improved. My love to you both and your dear loved ones. Thank you for letting me hear from you, (signed), Mae."

Now following is my account of the harrowing survival in the huge earthquake that very well could have taken our lives.

"February 12, 1994
Earthquake Reflections
From Bob and Pat Vernon

"Dear Family and Friends:
"It hit with such sudden, violent, crashing, thunderous force! Like some extra-terrestrial giant from outer space angrily shaking the bed and building, kicking in the doors, cracking the walls, shattering the windows, and smashing crystal, pictures, dishes, and our prized life-sized sculptured bust and head of David we had owned since early in our marriage. No doubt, this was a tyrant on a tirade!

"The noise was deafening, the room pitch-black, and the heart pounding. Jolted so rudely and unceremoniously out of my heavy slumber, I immediately and instinctively knew this was a huge, unwelcome and unwanted visitation from the deep, a 'big one' from the inner regions of the earth. This was totally different from any of the several mildly rolling or gently waving quakes I had experienced. Pajama clad, at the first motion and piercing of the nocturnal silence, I scrambled to the foot of the bed and barely could manage to crawl amid falling shelves and drawers to a crouching position in the upstairs hallway.

"'Pat, Pat!' I shouted at the top of my lungs to my wife downstairs, 'Are you all right?' Evidently, she couldn't hear me above the deafening noise for there was no answer. I was deeply concerned. It was because of Pat's painful health problem that we had moved from Missouri to California back in 1972. We had weathered many illnesses and crises. There had been drought, floods, fires, mudslides and mild quakes. But nothing like this! God had brought us through every trial, and these past years had seen Pat almost totally regaining her health and vitality. But would we survive this, I wondered as I knelt there and prayed.

"Just then, our son Gregg stumbled into the hallway from the other upstairs bedroom. 'Dad,' his voice quivered, 'I think this is the big one,' as he fell on his knees beside me. 'I'm afraid you're right,' I blurted out as the heavy, incessant shaking continued.

"As the long seconds ticked off their frightening cadence, we held on to the door jam and to the Lord's hand for dear life. 'Will this never end?' I asked myself. 'Yes,' I remember thinking, 'earthquakes have a short span, and we will come through this if the building doesn't totally collapse.'

"'Mom!' Gregg thundered out, 'Are you okay?' Barely, above the noise that Gregg later described as being like a 747 crashing, we heard her cry out, 'I'm safe, but where's Topy (our beloved benji-like pup we call Topaz)?'

"After what seemed to be an eternity of the jack-hammer motion (experts now speculate that the fault line under us experienced two periods of gigantic, successive seismic pulsations with a magnitude of more than 7 on the Richter scale), the 45 seconds of extreme quaking tapered off gradually to another 15 seconds or so of 'winding down' vibrations.

"In still midnight blackness (the quake had struck at 4:31 in the morning, and we know it's a true saying, 'It's always darkest just before the dawn'), Gregg felt and fumbled for the flashlight which should be just inches away on the bathroom cabinet top where we had left it the night before. 'Where's that flashlight?' Gregg moaned as he kept groping for it amidst all the rubble on the floor. Finally he grasped it, and we had light. Ah, the blessing and comfort that light brings, physically and spiritually!

"We cried out to God our thanksgiving that we had not been harmed. Pat said she got up from the couch downstairs and started out to call and search for Topaz while still barefooted. But there was so much shattered glass, debris, and overturned furniture that she realized she must get her shoes on. She somehow made it to the door of the kitchen to try to retrieve another flashlight. But the doorway was almost totally blocked by the refrigerator, which had bounced all the way across the kitchen from its normal setting. She managed to reach and force it back just enough to stretch to the drawer and get her hand on the flashlight. Then climbing over and around piled up furniture, she side-stepped poor David's fallen and shattered head (let it be a lesson to us, 'How fallen are the mighty'), and made her way up the stairs. Frantically she was pleading, 'Topy! Topy! Where are you? Oh Bob, I'm afraid she's dead. I can't find her anywhere!' Of a truth, Topaz is almost more human than dog, or so we think. We kept calling out to her and soon found her huddled and shivering in a corner of the bathroom, the safest place she could have been!

"I made my way back through the pile of fallen shelves of books, broken lamps, and cluttered furniture, to the bedside to try to find my socks and shoes and a pair of pants. Everything was buried under an avalanche of clothes and shelf items that had come crashing down from the closet. What a mess! It looked like Fibber McGee's must have when he opened the closet door and everything came roaring down! For you younger ones, that was back in the good old days of radio. I'm really showing my age!

"Anyway, back to my real-life drama, I could only find a pair of jeans, no socks, and some old tennis shoes that cramped my toes. 'We've got to get out fast,' Gregg yelled. 'There'll be aftershocks maybe as big as this one!' Hurriedly I tugged my jeans on over my pajamas, wiggled into my tennis shoes, pulled on a jacket and rushed down the stairs with Pat, Gregg, and Topy.

"The front door was broken and jammed, so Gregg smashed the entryway glass with some flower pots so we could maneuver our way through and out to the street. By now, sirens were screaming. The stench of gas filled the air. Fire and smoke could be seen in the distance. Neighbors were scrambling out onto the sidewalk, frightened and shivering. It was really a scary scene.

"Our neighbors, Jackie and Tony, were trapped upstairs on their outer balcony. 'A flashlight, please somebody, we need a flashlight!' By stretching up my full 6-feet 2-inch figure, and on tip-toes reaching another 3½ feet, I managed to hand her mine. Though I needed it, 'share and share alike,' I thought. The Good Book says, 'It is more blessed to give than to receive.'

"We pounded on two more neighbors' doors, but heard nothing. Joyce, a dear widow, lived alone. And Oly, a dedicated single mother, had two lively teenagers, Dino and Andrea. After some anxious moments, they all appeared, shaken and petrified. We comforted and led them out to the street.

"We decided that we should all soon go to an open parking lot, away from buildings and high wires. But first, Pat and I knew that if possible at all, we simply must drive the 3 or 4 miles over to our daughter Debbie's apartment to check on her. On the way, we saw lots of damaged buildings and some buckled streets. But we made it rather easily, and she was safe, thank God. Her fiancé Randy (they are to be married June 11th at the Westwood Hills Christian Church) had already arrived from his nearby apartment. Damage in this section of Los Angeles seemed to be minimal.

"Fortunately, our other daughter Becky and her husband Stephen, with their little ones, Jeremy 7, and Jessica 5, had just moved to Phoenix right after Christmas. They are associated with Family Entertainment (animated Bible videos). Gregg's apartment, which had been rented for a while by his friend Jessica, was also severely damaged. But she and her daughter Nalani had been spared.

"Back to our neighborhood we drove, deeply grateful to God that our whole family had survived the worst earthquake in modern L.A. history. Prayerfully, we awaited the dawn with our neighbors in the parking lot, as the aftershocks came in waves.

"After sunrise, we cautiously went back into our home to survey the damage. It was catastrophic! Pat's cherished antique glassware, her crystal, and other items from her folks and mine, had all been destroyed. Our baby grand was banged up, but still standing. Furnishings were overturned and scattered all over. Broken dishes, pots and pans, and groceries were strewn out on the kitchen floor. Mementos and pictures littered the rug in the living room. We stood in disbelief before huge cracks in the walls and the foundation.

"Not being able to rent a truck 'til Wednesday (because of the heavy demand), we decided to load the cars with things we most urgently needed: a few clothes, quilts, food and water, financial files, keys, purses, a checkbook, and toiletries. It was quite a task to unpile and locate everything, and somewhat unnerving too as the aftershocks continued. Several times we found ourselves running outside when the building would shake, rattle, and roll.

"I don't know what we would have done without Randy and his friend, John, who came to help sort through everything, do some heavy lifting, and start the endless process of boxing up all the loose and undamaged belongings in all the rooms. Authorities had set a 7:00 p.m. curfew, and it was about that time when the last load was unpacked and set in Randy's garage. Debbie went to buy groceries and assist John at his home in preparing a delicious and most welcome dinner for us. It was a needed and enjoyable respite for the weary around that table.

"The day had been long and so full of uncertainties. We realized as the hours had worn on that we were going on nerve, grit, and lots of faith. The enormity of what we were experiencing didn't fully hit home until a week later. At that time, we couldn't 'let up' or 'let down.'

"When the earthquake hit, our minds were flooded with questions. What to do? How to survive? Where to go? Where to sleep? Where to live? How to notify relatives? How widespread the damage? What about utilities? Who to ask for help? How much the cost?

"But slowly, answers had come. There was an outpouring of love and concern. Family, neighbors, and friends pulled together. Plans and decisions took shape.

"When Debbie first arrived at our place and saw the extent of the damage, she was so shocked, she burst into tears. She immediately said Pat and I would stay in her 1-room apartment. Bless her! Randy would have Gregg, Debbie, Jessica, and Nalani all stay in his 2-room place! What a guy! He's the greatest, most generous, gentle-hearted future son-in-law that I could have picked for my daughter!

"Besides, Randy had said, 'I'll get in touch with my landlord who has a 3 bedroom house on the same property as ours. He's got it crammed full of stored antique furniture, but maybe in this crisis I can get him to move enough out so that you can put your things there, and perhaps even live there soon.' In vain, Randy had tried to reach Allan, his landlord all day Monday. But early Tuesday morning he took me with him to try to find his house. Finally, we succeeded, and he kindly agreed to our request. I then drove back over to our place along with Pat, Debbie, and Gregg, and we spent the day in continuing to rummage through everything and pack our belongings.

"Bless their hearts, Ted Sanchez and his father came with his small truck to help several hours, joined later by his wife Terrie (my sweet niece, my brother Dallas' daughter) and their little Michael. Randy and his landlord in the meantime were working hard moving furniture out of the other house.

"Wednesday at noon, I got the Hertz truck, and with two more of Randy's hale and hearty friends, Terry and Paul, along with all the rest of our crew I have mentioned, we made a big 'dent' in the moving process. Oh what a job moving is, especially under these circumstances. I had thought that perhaps we would have several days to get all our possessions out. But no! Wednesday morning the building inspectors had arrived and 'red-tagged' our building with an 'unsafe' and 'no entry' poster. They said they weren't even supposed to let us go in at all (which in many places was strictly enforced). But if we would hurry, they would allow us to proceed in getting our furnishings out. So everyone pitched in even harder. We beat the curfew again Wednesday night, and God bless them, Ted and Terrie went, unknown to me, and brought in sodas and pizzas to satisfy starving and homeless relatives!

"Thursday saw us completing this humongous task of packing and moving. During this whole process, Pat and I mostly organized, packed, boxed, and taped; letting the younger ones take charge of the heavy lifting, loading, and unloading. What with my recent double hernia surgery and follow-up complications, I had to swallow my manly pride, be a good boy, and let the others take over. And what a job they did! I'm so proud of caring family members and dear friends. Thank you Lord!

"Friday was spent in Gregg and I assisting Jessica in getting things out of her condemned place, and into a nice 3 bedroom house she fortunately found by driving around, in Sherman Oaks. We also went to the disaster center to see about assistance, but so far we have encountered much red tape and conflicting reports from FEMA authorities. We have read that in parts of L.A., many have received checks in the mail for over $3,000.00, and they weren't even made homeless!

"But checks have come in from family, friends, CTM, and a few churches as they hear about our great loss. Bless you all! You know who you are, and we'll try to soon send you a personal letter of thanks. In the meantime, THANK YOU, THANK YOU, THANK YOU!

"We still need all the help we can possibly get. It costs so dearly to be completely displaced, and to get relocated. At our age especially, it's hard to 'start over.' It would be a great blessing if we could get enough in assistance and grants to have a down payment for purchase of a home, instead of having to rent. But we'll wait on time and the Lord, and see what is in store for us.

"These two Sundays since the quake, I have wept in thanksgiving as I have knelt before God in deeply moving worship services at the Valley and Westwood Christian churches, praising Him for His grace, mercy, and eternal lovingkindness. What a great destiny we have in our great God and in His dear Son, Jesus Christ our Lord.

"It is comforting to know, as the earth continues to occasionally quiver and quake in these aftershocks, God's kingdom is solid and everlasting! 'Therefore, since we receive a kingdom which cannot be shaken, let us show gratitude, by which we may offer to God an acceptable service with reverence and awe; ...' (Hebrews 12:28, NASB).

"Shaken, but safe and secure, (signed), Bob and Pat Vernon and Family"

CHAPTER 36

Film Script Of Back To Jerusalem

IN WRITING THIS book, I have decided to include the script of *Back to Jerusalem*. I have already spent an entire chapter which described my desire to make a film showing the unity and power of the first Church ever, established in Jerusalem, the gradual departure from the doctrines and practices pictured in the New Testament, finally followed by the movement to go "back to Jerusalem," so to speak, to restore and recapture in the contemporary world the pattern, unity, heart and spirit of New Testament Christianity. I appointed a panel of well-known scholars and ministers to help me in developing the script, met with my brothers and our Board of Advisors, and with Pat as the Script Continuity Person and a film crew, we set off for Jerusalem. On a rooftop overlooking the city, I narrated the script, as follows:

"I'd like to speak with you about the Christian Church, of which I am a member. Perhaps you've met someone, who when asked what church he belonged to, replied, 'Christian.' But when asked, 'But what denomination?' said 'no denomination, just Christian!' There's a growing group of people in the world today who prefer to call themselves 'Christians' only. We're going to examine this movement and find out why there are in the world, people who want to simply be known as followers of the Christ, or disciples, or Christians, members of the

Christian Church or the Church of Christ. Of course, there's no better place to begin this story than right here in Jerusalem, for it is here that Jesus established the Church through the inspired preaching of his Apostles, as they were filled with the Holy Spirit. It is rewarding to stand in the streets of Jerusalem and sense the history of scenes which look much the same now as they did 2,000 years ago when Jesus walked here. The little town of Bethlehem, where He was born ... the sheep roaming the rocky hills where He played as a boy ... the wilderness where He withstood the temptation of Satan ... the Jericho Road, hot and dusty, which He often traveled ... the village of Cana where He performed His first miracle ... cool Galilee near His home, on whose shores He preached and fed the multitude with loaves and fishes, and where He called his first Apostles, the fishermen, Peter, Andrew, James and John ... Bethany, home of His friends Mary, Martha, and Lazarus ... the Mount of Olives, where He wept over Jerusalem ... Gethsemane, where He prayed, alone ... Golgotha, the place of the skull, where He was crucified ... the Garden Tomb, where He rose from the dead.... All these remind us of the reality of Jesus Christ, by whose name we are called.

"From Jerusalem, He commissioned His Apostles to 'Go ... make disciples ... baptizing them ... teaching them to observe all that I commanded you ...' (Matthew 28:19-20, NASB). And the Spirit of God came upon men, and as a whirlwind, began to move across the world in the form of the Church.

"Paul, who once had persecuted the Church, obeyed the Gospel and carried its message to other places ... to Damascus, where facing danger from those who now would persecute him, he made his escape through a barricaded window in the wall of the fortified city. He traveled throughout Asia Minor, spreading the Gospel and building up the Church in such important cities as Corinth … and Athens, where he answered the philosophers on Mars Hill, in the shadow of the symbol of culture, the famous Acropolis. Then, in Caesarea, Paul was imprisoned, but he continued to win people through the Gospel; and finally, though in custody, he was able to realize the longing of his heart to go across the Mediterranean to Rome, capital of the mighty empire which extended over Europe. Now Christianity had become a threat to Rome, and as they had tried in Palestine to silence Jesus, so they now embarked on a campaign to silence His followers. Then came an ugly period of persecution. Christians were hunted down, and in the Catacombs beneath the city, where they were allowed to bury their dead, many were captured and sentenced to die before the Emperor and the crowds in the arenas. The spectacle of throwing Christians to the lions soon exceeded that of the fights of the Roman gladiators. Despite this fierce persecution, Rome could not stamp out Christianity, and history testifies that 'the blood of the martyrs was the seed of the Church.'

"But then, strangely, the Church became politically powerful. The simple Church of Jesus gradually developed into a hierarchy, with trappings and accoutrements of the most elegant sort. His commands and teachings were all but obscured by non-Biblical traditions and practices. There were those who raised their voices against these distortions, but the would-be reformers were branded heretics. The movement for reformation became a great force, but men, being convinced of one leader or another, divided into groups and denominations until today in America, there are over 250 of them.

"But something happened in America 200 years ago that caused the beginning of what is called 'the Restoration Movement.' There was born in the hearts of men a desire to restore simple, original Christianity before the introduction of man-made creeds and regulations. Early stirrings of the movement were felt in England, Scotland, Ireland, and Wales; but it was in America, shortly after the Revolutionary War, that it began to catch fire. In this new country, without hundreds of years of traditions, it seemed that it might be possible for Christian men to unite in simple New Testament Christianity. And across the new frontiers, this movement began to form. In Kentucky in 1801, there occurred at Cane Ridge one of the great phenomena which characterized this period. Barton Stone, a Presbyterian minister, together with some other preachers, had arrived at the remote settlement to hold services and serve Communion. To their surprise, they found 750 wagon-loads of people waiting for them. No one knows where they all came from. The largest city in Kentucky had only 1700 people at that time. But the crowds became so large that no one man could be heard by all, so other ministers began to preach, as many as six at a time in various parts of the area. Estimates of the crowds range from 3,000 to 25,000 in one day! Those who came stayed for days, until all the surrounding countryside had been exhausted of food. The records are not clear, but one thing is certain: the Spirit of God united these thousands of people in a common spiritual need, and it seemed that God was visiting the American frontier people in a special way. From the time of Cane Ridge on, Barton Stone developed the growing conviction that man-made creeds and confessions tended to divide Christians. So he and others who numbered about 15,000 dissolved their Presbytery and united in an association which called itself simply Christian. At about the same time in western Pennsylvania, Thomas Campbell, a Seceder Presbyterian who had gone to America from Ireland, was disciplined by his Presbytery for administering Communion to those who were not of his group. Thomas Campbell felt that 'closed Communion' was wrong, that the Scriptures clearly taught this was the Lord's Table, and no man had the right to deny it to another Christian. When his denomination declined to assign him a pulpit, he and others formed a group that was called the Christian Association of Washington, Pennsylvania. He was commissioned by the Association to write its aims and purposes. And while living in the farmhouse of Addison Welch, waiting for his family to join him from Europe, wrote his 'Declaration and Address,' one of the most remarkable documents of American religious history. In it, he stressed the need for Christian unity, and the aims of the Movement from that time on were summarized in the phrase, 'in faith, unity; in opinions, liberty; in all things, charity.'

"When his son, Alexander, arrived from the University in Scotland, he found that though they had been separated by an ocean, they had each come to the same conclusion: the authority of Scripture had to surpass any man-made creed or tradition.

"After studying the Scriptures pertaining to baptism, Alexander became convinced that he should be immersed. To make the position clear, a sequence of sermons lasting a total of seven hours was preached. Then the immersion took place in the deep pool of a branch of the Buffalo Creek. His father was not so easily persuaded, but on the day of his son's baptism, he quietly revealed that he had asked his wife to prepare a change of clothing for him too! Alexander was a disciplined scholar and writer, and soon emerged as the leader of the growing group of Christians. During his lifetime, he wrote fifty-nine books and was the editor of two monthly periodicals. He spent hours in his study, a small brick building in the shape of a hexagon, a few steps from his house. It has windows only at the top, which besides giving good light to work by, reminded him, as he put it, of his need for 'light from above!'

"In his home, which was known for many miles around as the Campbell Mansion, because it was the first house west of the Alleghenies with glass windows, he founded a boys' academy, and his interest in education led him to found a college across the creek, in what is now Bethany, West Virginia. Eventually, the Movement encouraged the founding of many schools and colleges across the country. Bethany's first buildings were modeled after those at Glasgow University, the Campbells' alma mater.

"In 1832, the Movement of the Campbells, and that of Barton Stone, united. Other frontier preachers, such as 'Raccoon' John Smith and Walter Scott, became part of the common Cause: restoring the Bible as the only rule of faith and practice. They became known as Christians or Disciples, and from this humble beginning in the Ohio valley, the Movement has grown to now include more than five million believers. The men of this movement came from churches and groups with wide theological backgrounds, but they came together because they felt that the seat of truth and the basis for unity could be found in the New Testament.

"The emphasis of this plea for unity has always marked our Movement, for Christ prayed in his great intercessory prayer, 'Neither for these only do I pray, but for them also that believe on me through their word; that they may all be one; even as thou, Father, *art* in me, and I in thee, that they also may be in us: that the world may believe that thou didst send me' (John 17:20-21, ASV). [*These* in this verse refers to the Apostles.] We believe it was because of this, that ours was the only American church which did not divide over the slavery issue during the Civil War. We still have no written creed, no declaration of faith, except what the Bible says, we believe. In considering all the commandments of Jesus, we must obey them. For example, in the matter of baptism, we believe that it is necessary for a believer to be baptized as a part of God's provision for salvation. Jesus said, '… Except a man be born of water and of the Spirit, he cannot enter into the kingdom of God' (John 3:5, KJV). The Apostles preached that men should '… Repent, and … be baptized … for the remission of sins; and you shall receive the gift of the Holy Spirit' (Acts 2:38, NKJV). We believe that baptism is for those who are old enough to make a confession of their own faith in Christ as Savior, and that therefore the baptism of infants is wrong. Baptism, according to the New Testament, must be preceded by faith and repentance. Jesus was about thirty years old when he submitted Himself to John's baptism, '… to fulfil all righteousness …' (Matthew 3:15, ASV).

"It was awe-inspiring to visit the spot where Jesus went down into the Jordan River to be baptized. The act of baptism was not a discreet wetting of one's brow in a secluded corner of a church. It took all of one's self into the water, in plain view of any who wanted to watch; to visibly, openly, and unconditionally declare that he was giving himself completely into the hands of God. Something happens at baptism…. Paul says, "Therefore we are buried with him by baptism into death: that like as Christ was raised up from the dead by the glory of the Father, even so we also should walk in newness of life' (Romans 6:4, KJV).

"In the matter of Communion, the Lord's Supper was instituted by Jesus as a memorial of His death when He said, '… this do in remembrance of me' (I Corinthians 11:24, ASV). The early Christians did so each Lord's Day as they met to worship, as we read in Acts 20:7 (KJV), 'And upon the first day of the week, … the disciples came together to break bread …' We believe that we need the blessing of this Communion with Christ every bit as much as the early Church.

"On matters where there is no decisive position in the Scriptures, we believe that each Christian should have the liberty to hold his own opinion, without binding that opinion on others. Our church is not characterized by well-known orators or theologians with wide followings, rather we believe the genius of the Church is the individual Christian serving in his local congregation in his own community. We strongly believe in proper and adequate preparation for the Christian ministry, but we do not believe that there should be any distinction between the paid minister and those whose Christian service is volunteer.

"A notable member of our Movement, who believed in serving Christ where he was, was James A. Garfield, a preaching Elder in the Church. When he became President of the United States, he let nothing stand in the way of his devotion to Christ. Once, when he was asked why he had refused to schedule an important meeting of state on a Sunday morning, he replied that he had a standing appointment for that time, around the Lord's Table! And on another occasion, when questioned about his beliefs, he gave this clear statement about the Christian Church:

'1. We call ourselves Christians or Disciples.

2. We believe in God, the Father.

3. We believe that Jesus is the Christ, the Son of the living God, and our Savior. We regard the divinity of Christ the fundamental truth of the Christian system.

4. We believe in the Holy Spirit both as to His agency in conversion, and as dweller in the heart of Christians.

5. We accept the Old and New Testaments as the inspired Word of God.

6. We believe in the future punishment of the wicked, and the future reward of the righteous.

7. We believe that Deity is a prayer-hearing and a prayer-answering God.

8. We observe the institution of the Lord's Supper on every Lord's Day. To this Table, we neither invite nor debar; we say, 'It is the Lord's Table, for all the Lord's children.'

9. We plead for the union of God's people.

10. The Bible is our only discipline.

11. We maintain that all ordinances should be observed as they were in the days of the Apostles.'

"The Christian, the one who wants no other name, is not trying to be difficult; he wants desperately to let people know that he is trying to be a follower of the Christ, and an upholder of His Church. In our desire to return to first century Christianity, we have no wish to wear beards and robes and walk with sandals on dusty highways.... We believe God has put us into an age of speeding cars and jets, and that the Spirit of God can be as present, and as much at home in our hearts today as He was in the lives of the first century Christians. And we believe that the words of Jesus are just as needed, and just as applicable today as when He first spoke them. One of the highlights of my trip in the Holy Land, was a journey to the village of Maloula. Almost 2,000 years ago, a small group of Christians from Palestine came across the Syrian Desert and built their homes into the sides of the cliffs, so they could be free to worship God as they pleased. This is the only community in the world where Aramaic, the native tongue of Jesus, is still spoken. I asked one of the men to repeat something from the Scriptures in Aramaic, and he quoted John 13:34 and 35, words of Jesus, in the language of Jesus. As I heard these ancient words that Jesus spoke, I was reminded of the timelessness of Christ's message of love; and of the fact we today are a living continuation of the Church which He founded ... for the church of Jesus Christ has always been present in the world since He established it, and not always within buildings or beneath steeples. In Jerusalem, where a group of expectant disciples were filled with the Spirit, the Church was there.... In a prison with Paul, the Church was there.... In the grottos beneath the streets of Rome, where Christians met in secret to celebrate the Lord's Supper, the Church was there.... In the prison dungeons of the arenas while believers waited to face the lions, the Church was there.... In Wartburg Castle, where Luther and his associates cried out for reform, the Church was there.... In a clearing in the woods of Kentucky, the Church was there.... In a home in Bethany, where Christians met around God's word, the Church was there. And right now, where you worship ... the Church is there.

"As we go about the work of the Church, may we not forget these moving words of the Apostle Paul: 'If there is therefore any exhortation in Christ, if any consolation of love, if any fellowship of the Spirit, if any tender mercies and compassions, make full my joy, that ye be of the same mind, having the same love, being of one accord, of one mind; *doing* nothing through faction or through vainglory, but in lowliness of mind each counting other better than himself' (Phil. 2:1-3, ASV).

"I think again of the words of Jesus spoken by our friend in Maloula, in the language of Jesus: 'A new commandment I give to you, that you love one another, even as I have loved you, that you also love one another. By this all men will know that you are My disciples, if you have love for one another' (John 13:34-35, NASB).

"Why is the plea for love and unity so important? Because as Jesus Himself prayed to the Father, '… that the world may believe that thou didst send me' (John 17:21, ASV)."

CHAPTER 37

Drury College And An Atheistic Minister!

I HAVE MENTIONED beforehand that after our graduation from high school, and a summer of working at Detroit Tool and Engineering Company in Lebanon, Dad and Mother drove Bill and me to Springfield to get enrolled in Drury College. We got in one semester before volunteering for our war-time service in the Navy. We also attended Drury one full year after the war was finally over.

I thought it might be of interest to quote from a letter I wrote to my parents on September 23, 1944, after that first enrollment:

"Dear Mom and Dad and boys, I'm really sorry I haven't written, I did write one letter to you, but didn't have a place to mail it until a day or so ago. Oh yeah, the Fraternity heading you see at the top, let me explain. Bill and I weren't going to join any, but all the frats had their 'rush week' a few days after we got on campus. The Sigma Nu's took us out to dinner last Sunday, and we thought the fellows were pretty good, but we soon found out differently. Apparently, that is a sports frat mainly, and they all smoke and drink. So Tuesday the Lambda Chi boys took us to a Coffee Shop for dinner, where we met Virgil Anderson, Don Threlkeld, Bill Smith, Rich Fellows, Dick Smith, Bob and Leonard Proncho, and a whole bunch of clean-cut guys. Boy, they're a swell group, and none of them smoke or drink. They offered to help any of us new guys that had the least bit of trouble in our studies or anything. They said they have on file old tests and papers on all the subjects, which might come in handy. Instead of having a frat house this year, there are three suites and rooms each in our dormitory, which is called 'the Barn.' Bill and I joined the Lambda Chi frat, the other two are Kappa Alpha and Sigma Nu. In our first frat suite is a radio, nice furniture, a writing desk with stationery, and oh yeah, two single beds, so B.J. you'll have a bed any time you come up to visit. We also have a free phone for use by us Lambda Chi's. Oh yeah, we got a $50.00 dollar scholarship for our expenses in the frat. And Bill and I got a job at the Commons kitchen and dining room on campus, drying dishes. It takes about 30 minutes each meal and is really easy.

"Our subjects: Algebra, German, Chorus, Chemistry, European History, and English. I am not playing in the band because it interferes with basketball practice, which is from 3:00 to 5:00. All our classes are held in morning hours, except Chemistry Lab on Tuesday p.m., and A Capella on Monday, Wednesday, and Friday afternoons. All of our classes finally started on last Thursday morning. But in reality, we're not really organized yet. Do you want us to send our laundry home every week? I think we had better because I have only two shirts left. I'm trying to be frugal in my expenses, but little things pop up here and there 'til I have found out that College isn't a Savings Bank!

"Tonight there was an All-College mixer at Wallace Hall, and I got acquainted with a lot of nice kids, but it is quite late now as I write this at 12:15 a.m. I am in our frat room writing you while the radio is playing soft music – aah! I guess I'm crazy because I never got to bed before midnight.

Aren't you ashamed of me? There is always something to do – study, read, socialize a little, play ping-pong, learn music, or something! Bill and I are well-known on campus due to the fact that we're the only twins on campus.

"Say Mom, will you please send us our ration books and shoe stamp. And also more <u>letters</u>, you too, Dad, shucks, I know you don't have to walk very far to mail a letter! And B.J. and Donald, at least you could write once a week.

"Oh yeah, we freshmen have to wear little green caps everywhere until we win our first basketball game. Lots of teasing and fun. Bill and I went to town today and bought a couple of tennis rackets which cost only 59 cents each, made in Japan. We've got to buy some shirts and pants soon. I forgot to say that I sang in a quartet and was in a skit at the mixer. Tell J.P. to inform George Carr we won't be able to work weekends, since we have jobs here. Well, it's late, so I'll close. How I would love to be home for a big dinner tomorrow! Your loving son, (signed) Bob. P.S. Please send Jr.'s tennis shoes. [He was in the Air Force.]"

I'm copying here in my book another letter I wrote as a freshman, telling not only about college life, but more importantly, about a matter that shocked me to my core. And that is the fact that I learned firsthand as a young person, how terribly liberal religious departments of colleges and yes, some churches and ministers, have become. Drury was an excellent institution of learning when it came to its secular courses, but it had what is called a Disciples of Christ Christian Church Chair. I wasn't studying there in that Department, and had no idea at that time I would later become a minister. But God used an incident that I experienced there when I met a young ministerial student in studies at Drury, and who was preaching at a small Disciples Church near Springfield.

Following is my letter, first describing mundane activities, but then the conversation I had with the "religious" student so called, that God used to deepen my faith, as I learned that he had no faith:

"Drury College, Springfield, Missouri, October 1, 1944. 4:00 p.m. Hi ya all: Yippee!!! The St. Louis Browns just finished the New York Yankees for their first pennant in history. I bet you all were listening to the game too. We listened in the frat room, and you should have seen us, excited like the old days at home when we would walk the floor during a close game. Say, Dad, you should go up to St. Louis to see the World Series. I would if I could. Life is just about the same here on campus. I haven't had a date yet, but in two weeks, we pledges are having a party for the actives, and we're supposed to have dates. Saturday morning we practiced football for a couple of hours. I'm really sore over it, but it was lots of fun. Then Saturday afternoon, four of us guys mopped the Commons, that is, just the kitchen. We did such a good job that Mrs. Jones, in charge, bragged on us, and fed us all we could eat. The reason we mopped is because we have to get in 22 hours of work per week. Three hours at meal-times for seven days makes only 21 hours, so we have to get in an extra hour of work. I don't mind though, 'cause it's a good deal. I'm told that we'll soon be operating the dishwashers.

"Say, I wanted to tell you about one of the most disturbing and fascinating incidents I have ever experienced. There are several St. Louis students here, most of them Congregationalists. The other day, about 11:00 p.m., I asked … [a fellow student] about his beliefs and why he started preaching. He told me he thought it was the most good that he could do in life. We went on talking, and I learned that he has a church not far from here, where he preaches every Sunday. Then he went on explaining these beliefs: 1. Each person has his own god in his mind, however he thinks; there is not one god, but one for everyone. 2. Jesus Christ wasn't sent from God, nor was he anything that any of us couldn't be. Moreover, he performed no miracles, but imagined them as we imagine ghosts today. 3. There is no Heaven or Hell. When a tree falls, there it stays; so with men. The only reward is in your mind; if you are satisfied with your life when you die, your mind will always be happy, if in torment, your mind will not know it. 4. Nobody can prove that the Bible is holy, or that it is Christ's or the apostles' teaching; therefore all its sayings are false. Human existence and intelligence are so advanced that belief in God, Heaven, and fables is a sign of delusion and ignorance.

"He said that in his first sermon, he told the congregation what he believed in all of these matters, and that there was nothing wrong with drinking alcoholic beverages. After that 'trial' sermon, he said he was hired. He says that when he goes into a home, they have a bottle of beer, talk and discuss problems, and converse about current events. He did say that some people he talks to, tell him he has no religion, and certainly isn't a Christian. I say he isn't about to be one! I told him that, but it was hard to argue with him because he doesn't even accept the Bible as being true. As far as I am concerned, all a person has to do is open their eyes, look up to the heavens, and there is plenty of evidence that God exists! We must have faith. The Bible is the Word of God, and has the inspiration and means, as well as the power, to lead us to salvation by Jesus Christ, the Son of God.

"All for now. Gotta study my German, so Auf Wiedersehen. Love, Bob"

That conversation with such a very liberal and atheistic student minister at Drury College was something I never forgot. It spurred me on more than ever in my own personal faith, with a desire to serve my Lord diligently, and to defend the truth of His divinity and of the inspiration of God's Word. Before leaving for college, during my senior year in high school, I had been baptized into Christ, and it was still fresh in my memory. And even prior to that, the summer before my senior year, my brother J.P. had led me to start memorizing a few Scriptures. And of course being raised by such Godly parents, I had early in life been guided and taught the ways of the Lord. My faith was so real as a child, that I can remember, in learning to pray out loud, how anxious but also how nervous I was to get the words right. So this experience at Drury was shocking to me, and no doubt, though I didn't know it at the time, all along in my life, God had His hand on me preparing me to eventually dedicate my life to full-time service in serving Him and lost humanity. I see now that it was no wonder that I first gave this some thought when my brother Bill lay on that Navy hospital operating table; or later on board in the Submarine Service when I came across the Navigators and started memorizing a lot of Scripture verses, using their little Bible cards; or when the atomic bombs were dropped and I was so moved as a young 18-year-old Navy Radioman, that I looked up to God and committed my life to ministry; or when a Christian Service Camp held by Ozark Bible College took place, and through the influence of our cousin, Roger Tribble, and Dr. F.W. Strong, as well as the overriding providence of God, the four of us youngest

Vernon brothers of the seven attended Bible college and publicly dedicated our lives to the ministry. Truly, as the old saying goes, "God leads in mysterious ways, his wonders to perform." As far as I know, we had no ancestor who was a minister except a great grandfather on the Tribble side of our family. There was nothing special about us; we just happened to be brothers who submitted ourselves to the will of God as individuals, and felt a deep need and passion to preach the Gospel. In essence, each of us, in the words of the Apostle, said then as well as now, "But far be it from me to glory, save in the cross of our Lord Jesus Christ, through which the world hath been crucified unto me, and I unto the world" (Galatians 6:14, ASV).

But don't get me wrong! I am far from perfect. As the old saying goes, "But for the grace of God, there go I." The only perfection I have is that I am clothed with the righteousness of Christ, and look to God for strength, forgiveness, and wisdom to correct my shortcomings, sins, and mistakes.

People look at my accomplishments and successes and think, "Oh, how wonderful it is that you've achieved so much, and lived such a glamorous life!" Yes, I have been so blessed by the Lord, but it certainly has not been all glamour and roses, by any means. There have been many challenges and low points in my life. I was told that I had a case of double pneumonia as a one-year-old baby, and besides all the doctor could do, it took my loving mother praying and hovering over me, applying hot mustard poultices to my chest, to save my life. Then, though I was too young to remember it, they say I pushed out the screen of a window and fell out to the ground below, landing on my head! In the Navy, the dropping of the atomic bombs prevented our having to invade Japan, and probably spared my life. Diagnosed with almost the worst case of prostate cancer in 2001, my son Gregg and the Elders praying over me, with the anointing of oil, plus 43 radiation treatments, pulled me through and made me whole. A misdiagnosed gallbladder infection and eventual emergency surgery helped me survive another near miss with death a few years later. And as I write this, with an MRI and EEG behind me, the neurologists are still trying to figure out what's going on in my head! So most of the time, I'm confined to my bed with my typewriter in front of me on a bed-stand, and fortunately, I'm able to sit up, one finger hitting one key at a time, trying to finish this book.

Then, of course, there was the huge task of raising the necessary finances for our television filming, not to mention the burden of being on the road, away from the family, for evangelistic meetings, rallies, and missionary projects, year after year.

There is no way I could adequately describe the pain Pat and I felt when we discovered that our baby Karen had a very rare incurable malady that eventually took her life while we were filming in Hollywood. Then a decade later, there were the lonely days and nights that extended for some fifteen years into the future, as Pat suffered such atrocious migraines and would be hospitalized dozens and dozens of times. It was during that mystifying period that I wrote so many poems and songs about suffering, despair, trials, and misfortune, but in every one of them I always closed them with hope, faith, and the promise of a better tomorrow. Some of the titles were "Why This Suff'ring," "O Lord I Cry," "Promise Of Tomorrow," "Not The End But A Bend," "When The Savior Passed By," "Suffering Humanity," "When You Get The News Someone Has Died," "You Can Make It," "Lullabye To Such As You," "Morning Glory Feeling," and many, many more. I recorded many of the songs, one of which was "Why This Suff'ring." Following are the words:

Why this suff'ring, why this anguish,
Why this cloud of darkness day by day,
Why this rainfall, why this nightfall,

Why this trouble 'long the way.
These are questions we can't answer,
These are puzzles we can't solve,
But there's One who has the power
Ev'ry heartache to dissolve.

No more suff'ring, no more anguish,
No more clouds to darken up the day,
No more rainfall, no more nightfall,
Is God's promise 'cross the way.
Hear His answer to all people
Who are puzzled and distressed,
Lovingly He sent the Savior
Dying for the worst and best.

He knew suff'ring, He felt anguish,
He saw black clouds darken up His day,
But He conquered death and sorrow,
And He's with us all the way.

Finally came the long six-and-a-quarter years' nightmare, beginning on September 17, 2009, when Pat suffered a massive brain hemorrhage, called a subdural hematoma. I rushed her to the hospital where she underwent an emergency craniotomy. She slowly recovered, and with rehab therapy, was able to regain total cognizance and come home for a very happy family Thanksgiving. But it was short lived, and by Christmas, she was experiencing severe hallucinations and I had to admit her to a nursing home. From then on until January 20, 2016, my main ministry was to her and others there until her passing. Our musical and ministering son, Gregg, led in a loving tribute and celebration service, ably assisted by our musical daughters, Becky and Debbie.

CHAPTER 38

Love Letters

"Lebanon, MO, June 14, 1949. My most wonderful darling Pat: My pretty Patricia, how I miss seeing you! I made it home O.K., but only in the wee hours of this morning. By the time I got to Joplin, it started raining cats and dogs. So I stopped at the Bible College, where I was told I had an urgent message from my brother Bill in Commerce, Oklahoma, 40 miles away. I called him, and he said I needed to back-track and drive there to pick him up for both of us to go on to Lebanon. So I got in my car, slapped my face to stay awake, and headed to Commerce in a down-pour. I made it, picked him up, and from Commerce he drove while I slept. I had told him we would need gas. I had been asleep about an hour, when all of a sudden Bill said, 'Hey Bob, wake up. Looks like we're out of gas,' as the car slowed to a stop. Fortunately the rain had stopped, and we walked about two miles, found a gas station open, bought a can of gas, and a kind trucker gave us a ride back to our car. Soon after we were merrily on our way again, the rain began to come down in torrents! It was 4:00 a.m. when we finally pulled into the driveway at the Vernon residence, known as 'Rambling Rafters' in good old Lebanon, Missouri!

"Tonight, Bill, B.J., Don, and I went over to Jr.'s and Mabel's to see them and the kids. I think I told you how cute Janet Sue and Carol Ann are. They're both growing so fast. While we were there, we sang several songs, and had a swell time together again. It's good to be home again, but how much better if you could be here with me! And to think – I had just about given up all hope of ever meeting my 'dream girl.' And you are so far above all expectations – a very wonderful Christian, a Christ-like personality and character, and so beautiful in appearance and actions. I love you and want you, Pat, because I still believe God made us for each other. I remember one week ago today, when you and I were first together – when we played ball and you hurt your hand, then when we played and sang – and looked at some photographs of an awfully pretty girl. I asked for your picture and you asked me to go with you on a picnic. Then we had our first date by going to prayer meeting together – and how the people stared – but who cared!

"Then Thursday, what a full day, both of us teaching in Vacation Bible School, a picnic lunch, fishing and catching 20 croppie in the boat with Fibber McGhie and Howard Cash, and then that unforgettable and hilarious time at supper. How you ever stood it all afternoon and evening, I don't know, but you were such a good sport. Well, we had to be good sports around such a jolly and joking bunch of people as Mrs. Cash, Fibber and Lucille! Was I ever embarrassed when the car wouldn't start when I was going to take you home! With your strong arms, you were going to help me push it, but finally I got it started and got you home safely. I was so deliriously happy as I drove back to town to Mrs. Roy's Boarding House where I was staying.

"The next morning, Friday, I found out that the battery had a dead cell, so I had to part with $21.00 to buy a new one. I met you then for our classes at VBS, and we were to meet out at Mr. and Mrs. Stamps, near your home in the country, for a big noon dinner. I got there but 'where is Patricia?' I wondered to myself. 'She said she would be here, but I see only three plates at the table,' I continued to myself, half perplexed. I didn't want to appear too inquisitive, so I let it ride until the answer came. Mrs. Stamps burst out laughing, and the teasing started!

"How beautiful you looked when you arrived, in that red-checked dress and the blue scarf, prettier than any girl in all the world. I was completely bowled over! There was only one thing on my mind that was bothering me: 'Will Patricia like me? Oh, how I love her!' We had a sumptuous meal for lunch, then I played the piano as Mr. Stamps was whistling and carrying on in the yard, while you and Mrs. Stamps sat there listening to my silly songs and crazy antics.

"I was so love-sick that I literally started feeling feverish, and you applied cold packs to my brow. You may have cooled my face – and how good it felt – but I know my temperature must have soared! Then at the supper table towards the end of the meal, I got so queasy, that I had to jump up, run outside to the backyard fence, hang my head over and lose everything! How embarrassing! And you all laughed your heads off.

"I recovered, and at the Vacation Bible School program that night, everyone noticed our sitting together, and in fact, they seemed to get as big a kick out of it as we did! That's the night I rocked you to sleep, well, I tried. You just wouldn't go to sleep, and I really didn't want you to. Oh darling, you don't know how happy I was that evening as I drove into town. I just felt as though I had a good reason to believe you cared for me a lot!

"Saturday was another full day, with me preparing a sermon on 'The Call of the Unattainable.' I worked hard on studying for that message. Then on Sunday morning, I put all my feeling into it as I preached, and at the door afterwards, everyone was so complimentary. People must have the goal of Heaven before them at all time, because so many things can come into a person's life which tends to make him forget the purpose of this life. Pat, never, never permit the world to make you feel that Heaven is not attainable, because it is to those who through faith and obedience strive for it. Heaven is so real, and so is Jesus.

"Believe it or not, last night I dreamed that Jesus returned to this earth. He was so fine-looking, so meek and humble in appearance. It seemed as though at first I was startled and scared, and only believed half-way that it was He. But in the dream, He spoke in such a beautiful, sympathetic, but yet authoritative voice, that I knew it was really Jesus. We talked together, then He disappeared, and I woke up. I thought about the dream a long time and wondered just why I dreamed it. I was glad I did though. It is true that Jesus is coming again, and this world will be destroyed in fire. 'Wherefore, beloved, seeing that ye look for these things, give diligence that ye may be found in peace, without spot and blameless in his sight' (II Peter 3:14, ASV). Patricia, before you go to sleep tonight, I wish you would read the first and second epistles of Peter, then get down on your knees and pray that we will both grow in the grace and knowledge of our Lord and Savior Jesus Christ.

"Back to that Sunday morning before church, how I dreaded that this would be the last day I would be with you! But I got up early at 6:00 and went out to the car and practiced preaching my sermon to myself 'til about 8:00. Then breakfast, Church, and dinner out at Wallers. I wanted so bad to be with you all afternoon, but had to study for my sermon which I gave that night with you there inspiring and cheering me on! After the service, I never had so many to tell me how they'd enjoyed my being there. Then we went to your house and spent the next few hours on the porch swing. I didn't see how I could ever leave you, even 'til August, when we planned for you to come up for Camp and College. Never before has it taken me three hours and fifteen minutes to say goodbye! I've been checking up. It was January 24th, 1949, six months ago on a Monday evening, that I first saw you, and have never forgotten. How could I ever forget anyone so beautiful as you are. You're just scrumptious, that's all! Darling, I do love you, with a love that's true, and pray that your love for me will be as deep as the sea.

"Must quit for now, Trish. Take care of yourself, and be a good girl, and I'll try to be good, just for you. You mean a lot to me, don't forget! Always your 'preachuh,' (signed) Bob."

THAT WAS THE first love letter I wrote to Pat, but I wrote several dozen others during the summer, all of them chock-full of my deep feelings for her. In return, I received a lot of loving letters from Patricia, expressing sentiments similar to mine. Then, towards the end of summer, she wrote that one of her admirers tried desperately to woo her back, and it was a scare! But our love prevailed, and I composed and sent her this poem:

PATRICIA ANN ANDERSON
By Bob J. Vernon

Of all the girls in Eternity's span,
There'll never be another like Patricia Ann.
So sweet, so darling, so gentle and meek,
It's just a pleasure to hear her speak.
Her soft, easy voice entices me
To heights of love and fidelity.
Her face has the glow that angels admire
And makes them sing better in the heavenly choir.
Her eyes reveal her soul's shining beauty,
So kind, so searching to sense her duty.
Her lips, her hair, her countenance fair,
Oh Lord, you gave her so much for her share.
You planned to use her in a special way
When you fashioned and made her that glorious day.
It's true, and Lord, you'll be richly repaid
For a holy decision, she's already made,
To place her life in your dear Son's hand
To follow His footsteps all over the land.
Humbly, oh Father, I pray Thee just now,
In Jesus' name, to Thee I bow.
Please Father, reserve her for me,
And make her mine for Eternity.
I love her so dearly with a love so true,
Who else could love her the way I do?
To Thee so perfect, so holy above,
Please keep us united in Thy bond of love.

Here's one more of the dozens of letters of love I poured out of my heart to my new-found angel during my absence from her that long, hot summer:

"Lebanon, MO, June 25, 1949. My most wonderful Darling, I haven't been able to do much thinking about anything except you and what you mean to me. Darling, your letter this morning was so wonderful and is making me go in circles! I've been trying to memorize the funeral sermon I have prepared and will present tomorrow, but how can a guy keep his mind on a funeral when in reality all he's got his mind on is marriage?? Oh, I love you, Pat, and know that you were surely made for me. I would do anything within the bounds of the law of Christ for you!

"So everyone is talking serious now, and not just teasing, huh? I can't understand how they all knew we loved each other so much! Maybe they could see it in our eyes. Darling, I'm so serious that if I thought I could never marry you, I would be the most miserable creature on earth. As far as I am concerned, our engagement was sealed the first night I kissed you, and when I gave you my class ring, I gave you my heart. Of course, they all don't have to know as much as we do, do they? Not that I mind, but let them keep guessing. They tease us, so we'll turn the tables on them! But when they ask you if we're ever going to get married, as far as for my part, you can tell them all, 'Sure we are, but don't get in a hurry!' Oh honey, being married to you would be the grandest thing in the world! I mean it!

"You're not the only one that's being subjected to questioning. All the Vernons (and there's lots of 'em) are wondering. I told them all about you. Mother thinks she's lost another son. The day I got two letters from you,

I really got 'razzed.' Dad said today at the dinner table he thought we'd better move farther south, and I said, 'Suits me fine!' Oh, I do wish I were there with you right at this moment!

"I wish I knew for certain whether or not I'll be back in College this fall for the first semester. I'll know in about a week, but I think I will. If so, I want you – that is if you really want to – to come and be there too. You can finish your high school and graduate in Joplin, but also take some Bible College courses too. So I'm hoping and praying that both of us can work it all out and be together in September. Darling, do you think you'd like to be my wife, my own precious little Trish? Of course, we would have to wait a year or so, but we could do that if we were just together for that period, and how wonderful that would be! I realize that marriage is sacred and holy in the sight of God, and that it is a very serious thing. I've prayed that our relationship would always be holy and would become such that we would know that it was God's will that we be united together in holy matrimony. I've prayed that our relationship might always be such that it would be a blessing to Jesus Christ and His Kingdom. I know my ministry can be so much more effective if I have you for my life companion, if you want to be. Oh Darling, please tell me, do you? Would you be willing to forsake all others for me?!

"Your hair was so beautiful when I was there, I hope the permanent you mentioned in your letter doesn't change it any. I like your hair about the way and length it was. So you already have your bridesmaid and flower girl picked out, and they agreed, huh? Great! Sounds good to me!

"By the way, the meeting I was supposed to preach in Kansas has been postponed, so I might hold a revival at the church down near Competition instead. Tomorrow I'll be comforting a family and preaching the funeral for their loved one. I have to close now, but oh, Patricia, my darling, how I love you, so very, very, very much! Know something? You're the sweetest, most beautiful, most wonderful girl there ever was! It's so hard and painful to wait until August the 8th, when I get to see you again. Always yours in Christ, (signed), Bob. P.S. I'm yours to stay! P.P.S. I love you lots! P.P.P.S. No, I love you more than that!!!"

Following is a wonderful letter of deep love and support I got from Pat when I was in South Africa for a month-long mission with Stuart Cook, a missionary serving there. He had invited me to show *Back to Jerusalem* in theatres and give teachings on "The Restoration Movement." I had made the commitment months before, but it was hard to leave home since I had just returned from a lengthy USO tour in Vietnam:

"Friday morning, October 6, 1967. My darling Bob: Please excuse my writing paper, but this was handy, so I'll use it. I had my mind made up to sit down and write you before I do anything else this morning, and before I'm disowned by someone. Right?!! Oh, how I love you!

"To start things off, we're all a little sad right now. Mimi [our little poodle] became very, very sick yesterday. We took her to see Dr. Gentry, and he had to perform surgery right then to give her a chance to live. He found that she had a ruptured intestine, and was full of blood, so he cut out 8 inches of it that was dead. He told us to keep our fingers crossed, for we won't know how she'll do for a day or two, if she lives. She was in severe pain. [In the next letter, I was told she didn't make it, and there were lots of family tears. One of the big sacrifices of being on the road in the Lord's work so much, is missing our families, their activities, and emergencies.] Cambridge Terrace [the suburb in Springfield, Missouri where, our home was located] had a chili supper last night, and had a pretty big turnout, but ran out of chili before everyone was served.

"The kids are all fine. Debbie still has that loose tooth in front. Becky has been quite busy in school work. Glendale High School is having a special patriotic assembly the last of the month. It will be centered around Becky and her tour of Vietnam with you. She will sing your songs, TELL AMERICA and FREEDOM PRAYER. If you had been home, they were going to have you participate and sing. This is all Mrs. Hemingway's idea, and she's going all out to have city officials and political leaders there, and have it covered by television and newspapers.

"Gregg went to a football game, by bus to Springdale, Arkansas, week before last. Last Friday night was Glendale's homecoming game. I think he's going to get along fine in school this year.

"Debbie gave me a big scare last night. She fell flat on her stomach, with a glass of water in one hand, and when she hit the floor, the glass shattered into hundreds of pieces. Her hand was bleeding an awful lot, and I just knew I would have to rush her to the emergency room to get it sewed up. But I got it bandaged up, everything calmed down, and we didn't have to go. I made sure she was all right.

"Well, how are you doing? Is everything going well? I do hope you have an opportunity to get caught up on your rest. I felt so sorry for you when you left, knowing you hadn't had much sleep or rest since you had been home such a short time from Vietnam. Do take good care of yourself. I love you too much to see you neglect yourself. It still gets pretty lonesome around here for me with you away. But knowing that it is work for the Lord does help to console me some. Recognizing this and how much effort you give to your work, plus all the time, sweat, and endless hours you put forth, I just can't help but be proud of you. I just wish I had half the drive you do in getting things done.

"Thank you, Bob darling, for choosing me to be your life-time partner. I pray that I don't disappoint you too much in this department. God bless you, Bob, and I'm sure He always will. Must close, since I have a couple of errands to do for Becky, and it's pouring down rain. Do take care, hear? I mean it! I love you, darling!! Always, (signed) Pat."

Now that I have presented love letters from me to Pat, and one very sweet letter from her to me, I want next to include very thoughtful and loving letters from each of our three living children, Rebecca Jo, Gregory Mark, and Deborah Elaine. I am so proud of my darling wife and our fabulous kids. So first, here is Becky's letter, written November 2, 1967:

"Dear Daddy, I'm sorry for not writing sooner, but you can't imagine how busy I've been, especially the past week. It's almost the end of the quarter, and we've been having 9 weeks tests. Dad, I think I'm doing pretty good this year in school. Making good grades really is almost an obsession with me this year.

"Tonight is a Campus Life bunking party for all the girls. Daddy, this organization is really outstanding. At our first meeting we had 75, and at our second, 90! Then at our 'Pumpkin Panic,' we had over 100. And the great thing is we're getting responses, and kids are wanting to know Christ in a real way.

"Oh Daddy, everything has been so wonderful for me since I got back from Vietnam. I'm sure Mom told you about the Assembly. Oh, it just couldn't have been more wonderful! I got a standing ovation, and all I could do was cry because I was so happy. Mr. Willard Graff, our Superintendent, was the first to stand up! Ever since then, I've done so many things concerning my trip. I spoke and sang at Evangel College, and also did some numbers with the 'Freedom Singers' there. The Treasurer from the United Nations, who also attended the Assembly program, was there and also spoke. Then, the Rotary Club asked me and the 'Freedom Singers' to put on a program, and again we got a standing ovation. We also did the same for the Springfield Association of the Blind. Dad, I really, really feel great about being an American citizen, and I think I've put this in everyone's heart in all these appearances. And I'm especially thankful that I have Christ to stand by my side during all these times.

"If you could've been here, our Principal, Mr. Ford, said he would have had you on the program, and also to sing. Well, since you weren't here, he said he'd like to have you sing in an Assembly later on. Wouldn't that be groovy?!!! I think so!

"I've got to go eat breakfast and wash my hair, so I better close for now. But first, I'll go right now and mail this so it'll get to you real soon, Okay? I'll try to write again soon! I love you, Daddy. Hurry home! Love, (signed) Becky."

Becky starred in our TV films, excelled as a church pianist at age 14, attended Bible college, and is a talented singer. She is married to a great Messianic Christian, Stephen Walker, and they presented to Pat and me two wonderful grandchildren, Jeremy and Jessica.

Fifteen years later, in November of 2000, Becky wrote the following sweet letter to Pat, after we had driven to be with them for a visit:

"Dear Mom, Happy, happy birthday! I love you so very, very much. I can't even begin to tell you how much I enjoyed our recent visit. It was so wonderful to spend time with you, my mother! I understand a little better now why each of my kids wants personal, individual time alone with me. They are each individuals. Our love and relationship with each other is so precious and important ... And you and Dad brought such a peace into our household at a time it was really needed. You teased and played with the kids and brought your wisdom that life is not so serious but that we can have a 'light heart' and care for one another ... Thank you both, SO MUCH!! I love you, Mom!! Again, HAPPY, HAPPY BIRTHDAY!!!! (signed) Rebecca."

As our first-born, Becky has always had such a pleasing personality and has been a smiling, blue-eyed, blonde doll. And Pat and I have been so blessed that all of our children have been so beautiful, so talented, and so loving! Spoken like a true father, huh? But I have a right to be very proud, and maybe a bit prejudiced!

Here's a very caring letter from our devoted son, Gregg, when he was a student at Cincinnati Bible Seminary. He was there for a couple of years, then transferred to San Jose Bible College when our family moved to Beverly Hills in 1972:

"October 27, 1971. Dear Mom and Dad, I guess it's about time for a letter, right? Write! I'm sorry I'm just now getting around to it. I just want to say that you're the greatest parents in the world and that I love you very much. We certainly have had our hassles, but now that I've been away for a bit, I've grown to appreciate you both all the more ... Dad, your letters have really been encouraging. More and more I find myself identifying with you because I know you've been where I've been, and I'm just super lucky to have a dad like you. I really mean that. You're A-OK! ... Mom, wow! You're super! I'm just really sorry that you've had to be sick so much. Sometimes God works in strange ways and it's hard for us to understand, but all things work together for good, as we're told, 'to them that love God and are called according to His purpose' (Romans 8:28, ASV). I just got your card a couple of days ago. That was really neat! Since I've been up here things haven't exactly been roses. Like the pamphlet said, 'When you're at C.B.S., you'll know you're in College!' And wow, that's the truth! But it's really been an experience. I've really met a lot of neat people. I can just feel God using me. Sometimes I really have my doubts, but things always work out ... Last night I saw Randy Matthews ... Dad, I think he really admires you, but not a millionth of what I do, and you too, Mom! ... I better close now, I have a term paper to get started on. All my love, (signed) Gregg."

Gregg has been a partner with me in the Christell production and mission outreach, in film-making, and in many overseas tours. He also served as an Associate Minister at The Hiding Place, before starting his own Refuge ministry, which continues to this day. He is an excellent guitarist and musician, as well as writer, singer, songwriter, and speaker.

From the time Gregg was five years old, he appeared in our nationwide *Homestead USA* television series filmed at Universal Studios.

Last but not least, for she is a loving and shining light to everyone, I want to quote from some of Debbie's writings. Debbie is a very sweet but vulnerable soul, and it shows in her songs and her writings. She reaches down deep into her heart when she expresses her feelings, as you will see from some inspiring words from her pen.

In August of 1981, when Debbie was just coming through a challenging period in her life, she wrote me, as follows:

"Dear Dad, This trip has ended up being the best thing I could ever have done. I am so eager to get back and really live! I have let so many things pile up while I was wilting away from day to day. I will be extremely busy when I first get back, but that is O.K. I have the faith and backbone that life takes, I know! I would like to take just a moment to thank you for everything you have done for me. I really do love you, Dad, and am concerned about your life as much as you're concerned about mine. I know everything is going to work itself out. We all deserve the best out of life! With all my love, (signed) Debbie."

Then Debbie wrote this about her music:

"I never set out to write songs about God, I just wrote about what I was going through. Moving from the Missouri Ozarks to Los Angeles at a very impressionable age, it was tough and I just wanted to belong. My peers didn't accept a preacher's kid very easily, so I started at age 14 to write about my feelings and experiences, because it seemed to help. I'd sit down at our funky old piano and sing and write all the time. My writing simply mirrors what is going on in my heart at the time I write. My music and lyrics always come from a very deep place. I would perform at local parties and clubs, as well as serving as worship leader at church, and wherever I played I was singing about God. At the clubs and parties, they knew I was singing about God, and it just didn't seem to bother them! They looked to be comfortable. They'd listen, and cry. If music is inspired and sincere, it stretches beyond the walls of a church. I feel my music reaches those vulnerable enough to admit they have emotional needs. We've all asked the question at one time or another, 'Where does the answer lie?' At a very early age, I began appearing with my family in their musical and television series called 'Homestead U.S.A.,' singing on the shows and at conventions and churches."

Debbie says that I influenced her a lot, spiritually and musically, and I am grateful for that, but I'll give God and my darling wife the credit for her talent and success. And she has done a lot of it on her own initiative. For my birthday in January of this year, Debbie wrote, "What a wonderful life you have given me, and what a great father you have been, so loving and giving … I treasure you! Love, (signed) Debbie."

She and Randy, a film and video editor, have given us four beautiful grandchildren, Emma, Colton, Beau, and Baxter Drake.

CHAPTER 39

Family And Ministry Letters

FOR YEARS, WE were quite a letter-writing family. How different today! Here's just one of the many letters I wrote to my folks:

"January 14, 1965. Dear Mother and Dad: You are a darling, Mom! A real gem. Sometimes I don't get to see you as often as I would like to tell you that, but don't ever forget that I think it is true. And of course I think my dad is about the greatest father in the world! But my thoughts turned to you tonight, Mother, as I got the letter you wrote before Aunt Wilma passed on. It was just a note, but it certainly expressed a great deal of warmth and truth in just a few words. You said, 'I'm going by in a few minutes to see how my little sister is making it. It's awfully hard to reconcile myself to life without her. I could always go to her when I had no one else to go to, and everyone has that need some time or other. I never felt unwanted or in the way – take a loaf of bread, a can of jelly, a pie, or just stay a bit, visit, and eat a bite – those are precious memories.'

"I can better see how Pat can feel so all alone sometimes, with her mother gone, and no one else in her family close. It meant so much for her to be in DeWitt just a few days after Christmas. At heart, she is such a wonderful and sweet wife, and an excellent mother to the children, but she does get terribly lonely sometimes with me gone so much. And even when I am home, a man might not be particularly helpful as much as a sister would be.

"I cherish wonderful memories of my sweet Auntie, and of dear Grandmother Minnie and Gramma Ettie. They loved us so much, and were so good to us. And in thinking back on my early life, I am so grateful for being brought up into such a wonderful family. It was the hand of God that made it possible.

"No mother could ever have been so lovely and so sacrificing for her children as you. I know there were many dark, uncertain days, and I marvel that you and Dad could do what you did in rearing seven sons during the Depression. Our generation just does not have the strength of character nor the stamina of heart to do what you did. Thank you, thank you, thank you! A thousand times ... a million times ... times without number!

"I am full of expectant hope for the future. And why not? As heirs of God and joint-heirs of Jesus, we have everything to gain in the future and not a single thing to lose. 'All things are yours,' said Paul!

"I have been trying to get my life better organized. It is exciting, thrilling, and challenging to live in 1965, and I am looking forward by the grace of Heaven to achieving some worthwhile goals this year. The two new films will soon be completed and I have been putting in many hours writing on the books. Speaking of books, how are you doing in getting yours written? I have my little office fixed up quite well here at the house. This is where I work most of the time. I built me two large book-cases, and Pat helped me stain them, and they really look nice. Becky, Gregg, and even little Debbie joined in helping on the project. Stop by and give your approval, and eat with us next time you're in town.

"As I tell you both a loving goodbye for this time, I am looking at your pictures, which I proudly have displayed on my desk. I have to be good, for you look at me all the time! Lovingly and gratefully yours, (signed) Bob. P.S. I'll be going to Philadelphia Tuesday, and be there about a week. It will be the last trip there, for which I am thankful! It's to view the final cuts of 'Back to Jerusalem,' and 'Glimpses of Missions Around the World.' They'll then go to the lab, and I should get the prints the middle of February."

The next two letters I am including in my book tell of the thrill I and my brothers felt as we got letters from people all over the country who wrote about their joy in viewing *Homestead USA* as the films came on the air:

"July 8, 1959. Dear Mom and Dad, We recently received a letter from Paul Neal, minister of the Central Church of Christ in Portsmouth, Ohio, who wrote as follows:

'Last Sunday was the third Sunday 'Homestead U.S.A.' had been viewed on the local station at Huntington, West Virginia, which is WSAZ-TV. Many, many of our people have written the station telling them how much they appreciate it, and Bob, you'll never know how proud it makes me feel to go into the homes of our members and hear them enthusiastically praise the film, reviewing each scene, step by step! Then I am thrilled to talk to people on the street and hear them say, 'We saw your program and we like it so much.' I am so enthused about the whole mission program and I can see its potential possibilities, and anything I can do for the TV Mission, do not hesitate to call on me. My wife says, Bob, that your father is one of the best actors on the program. He seems so happy and relaxed, and so natural! So Bob, convey these thoughts to your parents, and tell them how happy we are each Sunday to have the Vernon Family visit us in our living room.'

"Good letter, isn't it? Now Dad, don't get too big-headed! Ha ha! Pat, the kids, and I will be up Friday afternoon, and will spend the night with you. We will leave early Saturday morning for Illinois. We will be in Flora for a two-week revival crusade. With much love, (signed) Bob."

This correspondence from viewers came to Mom and Dad in Lebanon, after to their total surprise, they tuned in to *Homestead USA* on their TV in Kansas, and recognized my parents. Here is their letter:

"March 16, 1959, Dear Beulah and Dallas: Just happened to turn on our TV set this morning, and much to my happy surprise, I saw you and your family on your TV program. Dad had told us about it when he wrote from Lebanon, but I didn't know it would be on a channel we would be able to see. I looked a couple of times and then said to my sons, 'Those people are very dear friends of mine, we used to work in the same building!' They thought I was kidding for a minute, then they remembered the Vernon boys had rented Mom's and Dad's apartment in the past.

"It's a wonderful program, and my oh my, your family is certainly an inspiration to American families! Are your programs a series? I'm interested and know no better way than to ask you! Ha! It was such a genuine surprise and pleasure for you to come into our home this morning with your Christian testimony, because I knew it wasn't just words, for your lives lived that testimony. Thank God for people like you! Sincerely, (signed) Mary Willard Douglas, 409 S. Sycamore, Ottawa, Kansas."

This is such a sweet and special letter from Emma, our darling granddaughter, when she was just eight years old. When she came to visit us, I would let her use my typewriter, pecking out with one finger at a time, the characters on the keyboard. On this occasion, it took her about an hour to write this. I couldn't believe what a good job she had done, and Pat and I have treasured it ever since. So this is for you, Emma, when you read my book:

"Dear Grandy and Papa, I just want to say that you're the most greatest grandparents in the world, and I just want to say that I absolutely love you and I think that you both look terrific every time I see you and I never stop thinking about you! But whenever I'm sad, all I have to do is think about you in my head and that frown is turned upside down. But every year what I look forward to is Thanksgiving because that's when there's family gathering and everyone has a good time just laughing, talking, and having fun. And that's what I look forward to every year, well, that and Christmas! But what I love the most out of everything is spending time with my family every Thanksgiving and Christmas. And you guys are the greatest grandma and grandpa in my life. I LOVE YOU!! You're the best!

"Also you guys always keep a smile on my face while I'm there and that just makes me feel happy and of course like I'm loved and cared for. Now Grandy, this comment is for you: now I have one thing to say, you make the best pies, gravy, sweet potatoes, and of course fudge!! Now this comment is for you, Papa: whenever I come over to your house you always let me play with my dolly toys, and you take me to the Dollar Tree, the 99 cent store, and the park and I just love that so much. But the most important thing is that we always spend good time together and have fun! Now what I'm trying to say to you both is that you're wonderful, the best, and awesome! Love, your darling granddaughter, (signed) Emma. Love you!!!"

One of the best, if not the very best, friends I and my brothers have had in the ministry, is Doug Willis of Australia. A genial and extremely dedicated evangelist, he looked us up after arriving in America, having come as a deckhand on a cargo ship about 1960. He had heard of our television ministry, and our friendship blossomed immediately upon his visit at that time. When he returned to Australia, he arranged for our films to be shown in churches there, as well as on television. After my tour in making *Back to Jerusalem*, I traveled on ministering in Russia, Africa, and Australia, where I spoke and had sweet fellowship with Doug and Arnold Caldicott. But even prior to that trip in 1964, I had gotten this letter from Doug, dated 24th July, 1963:

"Dear Bob, I heard some wonderful news last night and just had to sit and write you to share the thrill that is in my heart. The Philippian Jailor film you produced has been in the hands of Dave Watt of Melbourne for some time now. Last night he was down to Geelong for the Gospel service and mentioned that the Philippian Jailor is being wonderfully received in the Churches of Melbourne, and he has about six bookings for it besides a booking in our capital city of Australia, Canberra.

"But the most wonderful thing of all is that he tells me that many of the men who are 'on the fence' here in Melbourne have been very impressed by it and you can be sure it is being used to break down a lot of barriers. These people are beginning to think 'Independents' are not such a critical and negative group after all! It is certainly paving the way, Bob, for you to come to Australia and be received in Melbourne churches, and this would mean an open door for the rest of Australia. So we can certainly praise God for this, and I thought you would like to know, hence this brief letter. May the Lord continue to bless you. Yours in His service, (signed) Doug."

After getting home from Australia late in 1964, I received this letter from Doug, written 27 January, 1965:

"Dear Bob, It still seems one big dream to think you thought enough of us to drop in as you did. Hope you had a good trip home and that all is well at Springfield. Joyce was thrilled to meet you and sends her love, and to even the score, please give Pat my love. Margaret Franks has applied to Ozark for August this year. She's desperately trying to save for her fare. I don't know Beverly Bird's plans. Since seeing you at Ballarat, the Lord has opened a wonderful door for us. Next Monday we will shift into a house on my Dad's farm where my family will be settled indefinitely. As Dad has given the house rent free to our Crusades, I can now give my full time to evangelization. Please give my Christian regards to Don and Carol, along with B.J., Bill, and their wives. Will be looking forward to hearing how 'Back to Jerusalem' is getting along. Yours because of Calvary, with love, (signed) Doug."

Doug Willis had desired greatly that our team would be able to evangelize a lot in his home country, to not only win souls to Christ, but to strengthen the churches and counteract the liberalism that had taken over in the Restoration Cause there. But because of our busy schedules of filming and other ministry activity, I greatly regretted that it hadn't happened. My son Gregg and I did tour New Zealand and Australia in 1988 during a short period, where we also attended the World Convention of the Churches of Christ in Auckland, New Zealand, November 2 to 6. Finally, as 1991 rolled around, I felt strongly that our whole group should make the mission become a reality. I wrote the following letter:

"May 15, 1991, Dear Bill and Joy, B.J. and Lodi, and Don and Carol: Enclosed is my idea for a working schedule on a possible Australia and New Zealand tour. I'm also sending a couple of maps and mileage charts I think would be helpful and useful.

"I've spoken to Doug Willis, John Fulford, and Jim Cunningham. They all are excited, and will put in a lot of planning and work, and I don't see how we can back away from this again. I'm working to see if I can't get more time beyond June 15th to pay for the tickets – because of our being pressed financially – and hopefully we'll get until July 10th or so. I suggest that we really proceed by faith, since they are counting on us, based on our talking this all out, and the commitment we gave. They are all arranging for the churches and families to provide accommodations. I think we might want to stay in a hotel in Sydney one night, and of course on our return trip, we'll have two or three at a hotel in Hawaii.

"I suggest that each of us brothers compile a list of 50 individuals and churches immediately, start calling or writing them explaining this opportunity and the urgency, and ask for a $50.00 or $100.00 special missions gift within a week or ten days. I believe if we have the faith that it can be done, it will be Done!

"Since Pat has had this miraculous recovery from her migraines, for almost ten years now, she is excited and looking forward to going on this month-long trip! And Debbie is planning to go also. So we're hoping, praying, and pulling for you all, that God will bless us all with the good health and finances to make this tour possible if it be His will, and that the mission will be very fruitful and enjoyable!"

Well, God did make it possible, and from August 21 through September 21, 1991, things clicked off perfectly, and the tour was a huge success. It was so fulfilling to all of us, and in every appearance we made in New Zealand and Australia, we were received royally and treated like stars! Doug Willis worked so hard lining up our appearances, as did John Fulford and Jim Cunningham. We were hosted beautifully by so many people, including Joyce, Doug's wife, who had prepared a festive and delicious meal for us weary but happy travelers when we arrived at their place. Even before that, when we arrived in Sydney, Doug had arranged for us to pick up a very large Toyota Carry-all, which barely did hold all of us and our luggage. Doug got to accompany us on some of our meetings, and what a sweet fellowship it was! All in all, in looking over the schedule we carried out, I see that we made 31 appearances, and among others besides Doug, John, and Jim, we fellowshipped at churches ministered by two of Doug's sons, Peter and Mark; Ross Heyward; Alex Wilson; Peter Ramahau; Terry Smith; Bruce Roberts; and Delroy Brown at Toowoomba. I can't seem to locate the names of others we were with, for which I'm sorry. We brothers took our turns at preaching, besides joining the girls in concert at every meeting. And Debbie was so pleased to play and sing some of her own compositions.

It was such an emotional and sad time when we said our goodbyes and prayers in leaving Doug, but at the same time, our hearts were full and content that we had been so blessed the entire period of our tour. And to top it off, we had three paradise-like days in balmy Hawaii, relaxing from our wonderful but strenuous trip, before returning home.

How moving it was to read Doug's eloquent and complimentary description of our tour when he wrote later that it was like being "in Paradise with the Vernons!" He went on:

"Having spent one whole week travelling with the Vernon brothers and their wives, during their four-week Australian tour, I have a much clearer picture and a greater desire to go to Heaven than ever before. The fellowship we enjoyed was richer than anything else ever experienced. We really saw Christian and brotherly love in action under the most trying circumstances: living out of suitcases and in private homes; organizing transportation, luggage, and pick-ups; sleeping in a different place almost every night; marshalling sight-seeing, shopping, and wild-life expeditions; keeping to time schedules; driving on the opposite side of the road; coping with those subtle cultural differences; living and travelling on a limited budget; getting to the meetings dressed without too many crinkles and on time; coping with all the bugs in PA systems and electronic equipment; and most importantly, the devotional times for spiritual preparation in the mornings for presentation of the Gospel in song and spoken Word at night! What a mammoth undertaking – the blending of all our individual wills into the Master's plan! But it happened, even with our human frailties. To God be the glory! If Heaven is going to be better than this, then I for one want to go there."

Then further, in a heading he entitled, "The Vernons' New Zealand and Australian Tour," Doug wrote the following:

"Rarely, if ever, has a family been blessed as the Vernons with so much preaching and singing talent. But more than this: their faithfulness to the New Testament teachings; their concern for the lost; their desire to edify the saints and build up the Body of Christ in love; plus their willingness to serve on a non-commercial basis, makes them unique among God's people.

"They have been received with great enthusiasm by both young and old. All their meetings have been a tremendous blessing and benefit to everyone. We have been encouraged to build stronger spiritual homes, stand even firmer for the true New Testament Gospel, and to love more deeply the people of God.

"Their testimony was humble and convincing; their singing was inspiring with meaningful words and contemporary sound; their preaching was strong, loving, sound and challenging, given without hesitation; and their living was exemplary.

"The big question now on everyone's mind is, when will they return? We praise God for you and thank you for making yourselves available, along with Debbie, Bob and Pat's daughter, who sang. We'll never forget you all … come again. The Lord be magnified!"

There were so many ministry experiences I was blessed to have since 1945, and as I write this it is 2016, that I wish I could include them all in my book. But, of course, that is impossible. I will note one more letter telling about very special occurrences and joyful happenings:

"*Christell Communique*, July 15, 1996. Dear family and friends, Praise God!! I can hardly contain myself! Through Gregg's ministry and preaching at his Refuge Christian Church, seven souls came to Christ, and he and I baptized them into Christ according to Galatians 3:26 and 27; Acts 22:16; and Romans 6:3-5. There was much rejoicing!

"Shortly after that, 'Heaven came down' and glory filled the hearts of my son-in-law Stephen's Jewish parents, Morton and Edith Walker. As I was teaching them from the book of Acts, the prophets, and other pertinent Scriptures, heavy conviction came upon Edie first, then Morty said, 'I don't want to be left out, I believe too!' And our grandchildren [Jeremy and Jessica] chimed in that they wanted to be baptized also. So I quickly set up my video-camera beside Stephen and Becky's pool, we had a little Pentecost and revival right there, and I had the glorious privilege of baptizing all four! Mine and Pat's travel to visit Becky and Stephen brought unexpected and heavenly rejoicing to us and the angels in Heaven! To God be the glory! All for now. Yours and His, (signed) Bob."

CHAPTER 40

A Day Of Darkness And A Long Goodbye

Upon awakening but before arising, Pat showed signs of confusion in her speech and memory on the morning of September 17th, 2009. And I quote from an account of that nightmarish day I later recorded:

"We dressed and went downstairs, slower than usual, and I made coffee and prepared our breakfast. Before we completely finished eating, she said, 'I'm so tired and have a slight headache. Let's go back up, I've got to lie down.' So we slowly went back up to the bedroom, and I stayed upstairs where I could keep a watchful eye on her, and do some paper work at the same time.

"In a short time, she was on her knees by the bedside, and I thought she was praying. But seeing that wasn't the case, I helped her back up on the bed. In a few minutes, she slumped to the floor again, almost unconscious. I got her back up on the bed, where she fell asleep. Now sensing something was terribly wrong, I called my son Gregg at his home. He exclaimed, 'Dad, she may have had a stroke! Call 911 or get her to the hospital right now!' I immediately ran outside and hailed two neighbors to help me carry her to the car, and I drove a furious pace to Valley Presbyterian Hospital in five minutes. Upon arriving at the Emergency Room, several nurses and personnel came running out with a gurney, and rushed her in for tests. Inside I explained what had happened and said, 'her doctor has had her on Plavix and baby aspirin to prevent a stroke, but I'm afraid that's exactly what she's had.' About that time, Gregg arrived, and one of the doctors said, 'damned blood thinners!' Quick tests revealed that she had suffered a severe subdural hematoma, not from a fall, but the fact that a tiny, initial trickle of blood from a breakage must have burst into a massive hemorrhage. She was wheeled into the operating room, where Dr. Ayman Salem, a neurosurgeon, performed a craniotomy, while Gregg, Debbie, who had come, and I prayerfully and anxiously waited. After the operation, the doctor came to us and said, 'It went well. Now the dangers are infection and pneumonia.' We never saw him again, and Pat was never quite the same.

"She survived the surgery, was in intensive care, intubated, and kept in an induced coma for three days, and suffering severe hallucinations and confusion. After 13 days, she was admitted to a UCLA Rehab Center, and when I walked in, my heart sank at the close quarters and all the wheel-chair patients in the narrow halls. Our family felt strongly that she was in dire need of expert neurological supervision and treatment, which didn't happen. But by Thanksgiving, with rehabilitation treatment, she was able to come home for a joyous family holiday! But it was short-lived, and by Christmas, the confusion and hallucinations returned. With more facility rehab, hospitalizations, and then a few months of in-home therapy, I tried hard to have her home."

I quote again from my record-keeping of this whole ordeal of attempting to get the very best of medical treatment for Pat and even trying to take care of her at home:

"Patricia (Pat) had the intermittent periods of improvement and set-backs, hallucinations and terrible confusion, but the bad times increased especially in mid-summer to the point that I, her husband, just was not able to take care of her at home. I even moved her to a lower bed so I could lift her and try to walk her to the bathroom, but it became impossible. Two very frightening episodes convinced me that I had to do something totally different and permanent for her safety, welfare, and treatment. Somehow, very late in the night, she had struggled to get up out of bed and go downstairs, open the door, and make her way down the front steps and out into the pitch darkness of the night. All of this without my knowledge. I was frantic when I woke up and discovered she wasn't in her bed. I hurtled down the steps and ran first out to the street, but couldn't find her. So I scurried hastily back past our front steps and down the concrete stairway several yards to our parking lot. There I found her staggering around, muttering to herself, and having no idea where she was or what she was doing. I was so relieved that she was safe, but visibly shaken by what had occurred. A few days later, while I was in my study at home – this time during the day – Rose, a nice neighbor lady who lives not far from us, came to our door with Pat. She had found her headed out to the street, totally unaware of what she was doing. Again, I was so relieved, and I thanked Rose profusely, but I thought, 'That does it. I've learned my lesson! For Pat's sake and safety, we've got to change course immediately.' I remembered that Pat, in one of her clearer moments a few days after she had gotten out of intensive care at the hospital, had plaintively said in a somber tone, 'Bob, what I'm going through may mean that things might never be the same in our lives, and I know this is very hard for you.' Bless her heart, how prophetic she was. And how loving that she was thinking of me, and not herself!"

So the long six-and-a-half-year goodbye began in one nursing home, then a little better one, and finally, five years in the best one of all, the Sherman Oaks Health and Rehab Center where she received such loving care until her passing to the perfect Rest Home, Heaven itself! My long watch-care for Pat had ended; God has taken over 'til I meet her at Heaven's gate.

Now, I want to share a note from my precious wife, and present a few expressions of love and appreciation on cards and letters to Pat and me, then close this book with my loving tribute to Pat, along with her obituary.

I received the sweetest letter from my darling wife, written in her own handwriting, and enclosed in a Father's Day card of 2007. I treasure it so highly, for I think it was the last letter of love from her before a year or so later, when she suffered the debilitating stroke that left her impaired:

"Darling Bob, You are the most caring and loving husband, always looking after your family's needs. You are so thoughtful! I look up to you and love you so very, very much. You are so strong regarding your faith in the Lord. I appreciate that so very much, and wish you a HAPPY FATHER'S DAY. I do so love you with all my heart! All my love, (signed) Pat."

The card was headed, "THANK YOU, LORD, FOR MY HUSBAND," and these meaningful words followed: "In our marriage, we share so many things that make us one in thought, in spirit, and in love. But the most important thing we share is our faith in Jesus. Through Him, we are able to give each other so much more …"

Like most people, we're a card-giving family, including notes of love and appreciation, at every holiday, birthday, and anniversary. I have gone through all of these cards recently, and have picked out a few of the favorites to show you the feelings expressed. First will be cards from Becky's family, then Debbie's, and finally, from Gregg.

From Becky and Family:

"May 10, 1998, Dear Mom, It has been so wonderful to have you here for Mother's Day! You're so much fun – now don't get me tickled! This has been so special to be together and enjoying everything, as well as seeing you so happy. You deserve every happiness … and I'm glad if I can bring you just a little. It's so good to be your firstborn who loves you more than you'll ever know. Love, (signed) Rebecca."

For Father's Day, I got this card from Becky: "Dad, The best guidance you could have ever given to me was your love and commitment to the Lord. I am eternally grateful to you! Thank you and HAPPY FATHER'S DAY! I love you to Heaven and back, (signed) Becky."

On the same day, Stephen, Becky's husband wrote this: "Bob, you are an ongoing inspiration! Your love, compassion, and zeal for the Gospel is wonderful. Thanks for all the blessings you have given to my family, and for being a great father-in-law and friend. Much love, (signed) Stephen."

Their children, on a very nice Father's Day card, penned this: "Poppa, what would I do without your love that is always poured down on me? You are looked up to for your wisdom, and you bring great joy and love to my life! Always, (signed) Jessica."

And Jeremy, my dear little grandson who was ten years young, penned this, and it gave me a chuckle: "Grand Ol' Poppa, I love you. Thank you for your unswerving peace and joy, not to mention, my mother. Merry Fathers Day. Yippee, (signed) Jeremy."

From Debbie and Family:

This Mother's Day card and message was presented to Pat from Debbie in 2003: "Dear Mom, The challenges of motherhood are never too much when love overcomes all obstacles that we face. Your love for me, my husband, and your four gorgeous grandchildren, is deeper than the ocean. The greatest of all mothers is one like you, illustrated by her relentless ability to bring calm to a storm. She is the lightpost and the lighthouse. We look for her light, morning, noon, and night. Happy Mother's Day to you, Grandy. Love, (signed) Debbie, also for Emma, Colton, Beau, and Baxter."

Debbie's husband, Randy, penned this: "Mom, I'm grateful to be a part of this Mother's Day to have a special opportunity so that we can express our love and appreciation towards a very special Mom. Thank you for your presence and the care you show every day for this family. Love, (signed) Randy."

Debbie's and Randy's four children, Emma, Colton, Beau, and Baxter, each wrote a note of love about their Grandy's passing:

"Dear Papa, I'm so sorry for your loss. Grandy was a one of a kind woman. She was always so nurturing, so caring, so loving, and so beautiful. Although she may not be with us anymore, she's in a much better place now with her daughter Karen and her mother Beulah. Grandy will always have a special place in our hearts. I love you very much and will always be there for you. Love, (signed) Emma."

It's not signed, but this printed Scripture verse came from Colton, I believe: John 3:16 – "For God so loved the world that He gave His only begotten Son, that whosoever believed in Him shall not perish, but have eternal life. Amen."

"I love you, Papa. Through the loss of your precious wife and our Grandmother, my heart goes out to you, Papa. And though she's not with you on Earth, you can be comforted in knowing that she is with the Lord today in Heaven. Thank you for being the best grandparents ever. I will be praying for you and Grandy. I miss her so much. Love, (signed) Beau."

"Papa, I am sorry for your loss of Grandy. I know this must be a difficult time for you, and we are here for you. And though we miss her, she is with the Lord. Love, (signed) Drake." [His name is Baxter Drake, now called Drake.]

Our son, Gregg, has been so thoughtful and so considerate of me and my needs, especially during Pat's long periods of illness, and now looking after me in my health problems. He has always shown deep love for his mother. Following are quotes from three of his cards:

"There are so many reasons to thank you, to love you, and to wish you happiness on your anniversary and always. I love you both and appreciate you more than ever! Love you, (signed) Gregg."

The wording printed on a birthday card he gave to Pat reads: "Today's all about telling you how important you are to me and how much it means to me to have you in my life. HAPPY BIRTHDAY." Then he wrote, "I love you, Mommy! (signed) Gregg-y."

It's not his own words on a Father's Day card he gave me, but I think it reflects Gregg's thoughts: "Dad, when I was a little child, you knew everything about everything. Then when I was a teenager, suddenly you didn't know anything at all. Now you know everything again. Happy Father's Day! Love, (signed) your son."

No, I'm far from knowing everything! All I know, and all I am, I owe to God, my parents, my teachers, my brothers, my wife, my kids, my experiences, and last but not least, the Scriptures!

Next are three cards I chose from the many I gave to Pat through the 66 years of our marriage:

"11/17/04. My dear Pat, You are so beautiful inside and out! I feel that God did a very special thing when He created you, a woman so stunningly gorgeous, so full of grace, and so generous in spirit. HAPPY BIRTHDAY!! All my love, (signed) Bob."

"11/17/2010. Pat, How could I be so fortunate and so blessed to marry such a beautiful and caring woman that you are!! I truly married the girl of my dreams!! HAPPY BIRTHDAY! Love forever, (signed) Bob."

Here's the last anniversary card I was privileged to give to the love of my life. On the front is a large, beautiful red rose, with the heading, "Happy Anniversary To My Wife." Inside it reads, "Forever etched in my heart … forever in love." I wrote these words dated 9/30/2015: "Darling, I loved you passionately with all my heart 66 years ago, and I still do!! What an angel you are!! Happy Anniversary with love, (signed) Bob."

She had no awareness at all as I reached down and placed a soft, lingering kiss on her cheek. Almost four months later, the early morning of January 20th, 2016, she quietly slipped away from this earthly scene of activity to the Heavenly realms of Paradise above, greeted by her Lord … "'Til we meet again, goodbye my Love."

I just can't close my book without paying special tribute to someone, who from the very beginning of her childhood and on through life, was so close to and loved Pat so dearly. And that person is her first cousin, Joyce Hornbeck Cooper. They were best friends as girls, went to school and church together, and both fell in love as young women and married Christian men. No one was more encouraging to me, nor more concerned for Pat during her lengthy health ordeal and suffering than Joyce, though they were separated by hundreds of miles. She never missed a holiday or birthday in calling or sending a card of love and concern for both of us. And even before Pat's illness, you can see Joyce's heart in a card she wrote on Monday, June 7, 2004:

"Dear Pat, I've just watched the funeral procession of 'our' Ronald Reagan, and feel a great sadness, not only for Nancy and her family, but for another era passed. I was also reminded that it isn't often you get to watch a teen-age idol become a world leader and powerful president. Maybe our intuition as kids wasn't too bad, huh? Those were great days! I went to the Hornbeck family reunion Saturday and am helping Jeanie Simond

Stone's decoration for our 55th class reunion in July. I am doing O.K. healthwise, and hope you and Bob are both doing all right, too. May the Lord continue to bless you. Much love, (signed) Joyce."

I was deeply moved recently when Carol, my brother Don's wife, sent me a copy of a letter she wrote and gave to her daughter, Michele, after Pat's passing. The letter explains why I feel led to include it in my book. It is titled, "A Letter to Michele," and I'm quoting it with my heartfelt thanks to dear Carol, for it reveals a bit about Pat that I never knew:

"Pat Vernon died three days ago, January 20, 2016, after being in a coma five years. This has been very hard on Bob. This letter is to let you know how special she was. I don't know if I've ever told you about [your] Aunt Pat and Gregg when you were born. Pat and Bob had lost their baby, Karen Elizabeth, about six months before you were born. This was a very hard loss, especially since Karen had a bad disease and could not be cured. She could not move any of her muscles and even drinking her milk from a bottle was a very hard problem. Her disease was called Amyatonia Congenita. She was such a beautiful and good baby, and seldom cried. Her smile was beautiful. Bob and Pat suffered, and I don't think Pat ever recovered from this death. Since you were born so close to her, I think Pat loved you even more than usual. She and Gregg would come over almost every morning, and both of them would hold you and talk to you. You were also a beautiful baby. One day Pat even came with a gift, a beautiful pink sweater, very nicely knit, and a matching dress. It was so pretty! You have it on in the picture of you, taken when you were three months old. When you were eight months old, we all were invited to New York City to be on Garry Moore's show, 'I've Got A Secret.' This was a very famous and popular TV show. Anyway, Bob's family rode in our car with the three of us, from Joplin to New York City, crowded, yes, but fun. We made it and Pat seemed to enjoy being with you so much. The point of this letter is just to let you know how much Pat loved you. You were a real blessing to her! I love you, (signed) Mother."

Jason Brown, a young, bright intern minister from Australia, came to live with us for several months, while assisting our son Gregg in the Refuge Christian Church ministry. At the conclusion when he had to return home, he wrote this card of appreciation:

"Dear Pat and Bob, I want to thank you so much for the kindness and love you have given to me. You made me feel so at home even on the other side of the world. I could not have had the rich experience if you had not made it possible. I love being the 4th Vernon. Thank you for all the meals and a roof over my head. I love you and thank God for your lives and the example to all of us. I'll be missing you terribly. Love, (signed) Jason"

On my birthday, January 4, 2007, I received the following letter from Jennie Silver, a dear friend and dedicated member of the Refuge, Gregg's Church, in which after my retirement, I have assisted in preaching and ministering for 23 years, including the nursing home and Christell ministries:

"Dear Daddy Bob, Where do I start to tell you how much I love and appreciate you! The strength and affection you've given me over the years, plus your support and understanding, is beyond that of anyone I've ever met in my walk with the Lord. You truly emulate the heart and mind of Christ every day of your life. You are an inspiration to all who know you.

"It is the memories of your kindness, love, joy, laughter, spirit, grace, and honest humble love of our Lord that still keeps me tied, like an umbilical cord, to the Refuge. No matter where God sends me or directs me to go in this life, I will take you and all you have taught, with me. I have been so richly blessed to know and love you like a father. I hope you enjoy the book. I'm sure you've had numerous devotionals in your life, but this one is so very special. I've had the 1925 edition of 'Streams in the Desert' for 2½ years. This was my treasured copy … I knew you would appreciate it. Plus it's older than you! I pray for you and my beloved Mama Pat every day.… A gloriously happy and blessed birthday to you and every day that follows. Love always, (signed) Jennie."

Our family received sympathy cards from friends, as well as from my brothers and extended family members across the nation. Space prohibits me from mentioning them all, and distance prevented most of them coming for Pat's funeral. But I so much appreciated my twin brother, Bill, and his son and daughter, Richard and Diane, coming to pay tribute to our loved one. And Bill, with his dramatic reading of Pat's obituary, almost made her come alive! Of course, our children and grandchildren were present to honor their mother and grandmother. Becky, Gregg, and Debbie, though grieving at such a sad and emotional time, made me so proud as they lovingly eulogized, sang, and brought their dear mother to life through a recording of Pat singing, "I got shoes, you got shoes, all God's children got shoes. When I get to Heaven, gonna put on my shoes, gonna walk all over God's Heaven!" How appropriate! And then when Gregg had arranged for a screening of a *Homestead USA* episode, where Pat appeared in close-ups with the other girls singing "Cleanse

Me, Oh God," the pews of people at the funeral exploded with applause! Though somewhat lightheaded from the myoclonic disease I have suffered since mid-December of 2015, with the help of my cane, I was able to get up and speak a few words about my love for Pat. I started by quoting from memory, verbalizing it in the feminine form, two passages of Scripture pertaining to Pat's life:

"Finally, *be* ye all likeminded, compassionate, loving as brethren, tenderhearted, humbleminded: not rendering evil for evil, or reviling for reviling; but contrariwise blessing; for hereunto were ye called, that ye should inherit a blessing. For,
He that would love life,
And see good days,
Let him refrain his tongue from evil,
And his lips that they speak no guile;
And let him turn away from evil, and do good;
Let him seek peace, and pursue it.
For the eyes of the Lord are upon the righteous,
And his ears unto their supplication:
But the face of the Lord is upon them that do evil" (I Peter 3:8-12, ASV).

"Blessed *be* the God and Father of our Lord Jesus Christ, who according to his great mercy begat us again unto a living hope by the resurrection of Jesus Christ from the dead, unto an inheritance incorruptible, and undefiled, and that fadeth not away, reserved in heaven for you, who by the power of God are guarded through faith unto a salvation ready to be revealed in the last time. Wherein ye greatly rejoice, though now for a little while, if need be, ye have been put to grief in manifold trials" (I Peter 1:3-6, ASV). Reserved in Heaven for you, my darling Pat.

Then I spoke of what we both shared in common, in addition to the deep love we had for one another. I had typed this prior to the service, and titled it, "PAT AND I – OUR COMMONALITIES." I wondered if I could possibly manage to get through reading this without breaking down. But the Lord gave me strength and confidence, and perhaps with moist eyes and some quiver in my voice, I made it. Here it is:

PAT AND I – OUR COMMONALITIES

WE BOTH...

1. Grew up on a farm. She picked cotton; I plowed corn.
2. Have blue eyes, and had brothers with brown eyes.
3. Were shy as children; she kept her shyness, I lost mine.
4. Had mothers whose name was "Beulah."
5. Were raised in Christian homes.
6. Attended Christian Service Camps, hers sponsored by Atlanta Christian College, mine by Ozark Christian College.
7. Confessed Christ as our Savior, and were baptized as youths.
8. Learned to cook; she from her mother and two years of Home Economics, and me, a teenager, how to boil water, peel potatoes, make cornbread, as well as 'look and cook' beans.
9. Played the piano and were in High School marching bands.
10. Have high voices; she sings 2nd soprano, and I, 2nd tenor.
11. Love the Lord, His work, and our wonderful kids and grandkids.
12. Endured many trials, with faith and an overcoming and joyful spirit.

In the ups and downs of our 66 years together, we have truly enjoyed the many ups, and together, faced and suffered through the downs. Pat had 15 or so years of occasional excruciating migraines, but at long last, was totally healed and enjoyed 20 fruitful and happy years as hostess of Gregg's Refuge Church. Braving courageously her stroke of September 17, 2009 'til her death, how incredibly happy she is now as a beautiful angel with her wings, flying all around in Paradise!

There was a joyful and "sunshine-like" atmosphere inside during the Tribute Service to Pat, but outside, a storm was raging with torrents of rain falling. One freeway had to be closed due to flooding and fallen trees, and many people on their way to the service had to turn around, while some didn't even try to brave the deluge of rain and stormy weather. But we still had a good crowd, and I was so pleased when my sweet and elderly cousin, Ruth Vernon Ray, along with her darling daughter Gail, came; also Joyce Flowerstown and Aracelli from the nearby nursing home where Pat had been for so long. And how good of our granddaughter, Jessica, to fly out, and for Carol Walker to come!

Of all the cards of love and condolence that we received, there are two that I have chosen to include in my book, which are representative of all the others. This one is from my oldest and very first, sweet niece born into our extended family, Sue Vernon Pike:

"Dear Bob, Becky, Gregg, and Debbie, We are celebrating sweet Pat's life with you! It is good to know that she is healed of the pain that held her for a time. And it makes Heaven all the more precious and real. A sweet memory I have of Pat, besides her beauty and hospitality, is the time she gave me sparkly gold slippers for Christmas at the farm. They were pretty special and 'grown-up!' We love you all and are thanking God for Pat's life! (signed) Sue and Bob Pike"

The next and last card came from the "other" Pat Vernon, darling wife of my 94-year-old brother, Dallas Vernon Jr., who has always been so exceedingly thoughtful and supportive of us Vernon Brothers in our lives and ministry. Pat wrote this loving message on the card in behalf of herself and Dallas:

"Dear Bob, How we wish we could be there with your family at this time of saying goodbye to Pat. There really is a special beauty in a funeral for a saint. It's so special to remember the good times and the trying times of a life lived for the Lord. No husband was ever more loving and caring for his wife than you have been to Pat. You have had a mighty witness and will continue to have. We love you. (signed) Dallas and Pat."

Finally, here is the loving tribute and descriptive obituary about the successful and victorious life of love and service that Pat lived. As my dear twin brother Bill read it, he put so much heart and soul in it, that you could almost feel her presence come alive!

PATRICIA ANN VERNON

"Patricia Ann Anderson was born November 17, 1932, and passed to be present with the Lord January 20, 2016. It was apparent to her parents and others that she was a very special child. Growing up on a large rice farm in the vicinity of DeWitt, Arkansas, she was privileged to be raised in a loving Christian home, and Gus and Beulah Anderson took their delight in Patricia who early manifested a meek and quiet spirit. But she always exhibited a joyful and optimistic outlook on life, which served her well in the challenges she faced later on.

"A popular and stunning brunette, with looks often compared to the actress Hedy Lamar, Patricia excelled in school, and was very dedicated in her faith and active in her church, the First Christian Church of DeWitt, Arkansas. At an early age, she confessed Jesus as her Lord and Savior and was baptized into Christ. In the summers, she loved attending Christian Service Camp, and had planned on enrolling in Atlanta Christian College after High School, until she caught the eye of Bob Vernon when he was in a college quartet from Ozark Christian College, singing at her church. It was love at first sight, and eight months later they were married.

"Patricia was talented in so many ways. From the two years of Home Economics in High School, she excelled in the art of home decorating and designing, as well as becoming gifted in crafts, cooking, sewing, and home-making. She was in the High School band, played the piano, sang with her crystal-clear soprano voice in the choir, and was later a chalk artist, which she eventually taught at Ozark Christian College in Joplin, Missouri.

"Pat sang second soprano in the Vernon Wives Quartet, as well as in the joint Vernon Octet of the four Vernon Brothers and their spouses, in which her husband Bob sang second tenor. The amazing circumstance is that the voices of all four of the wives corresponded with their husband's. Joy sang 1st soprano, her husband Bill, 1st tenor; Pat sang 2nd soprano, and her husband Bob, 2nd tenor; Carol, 1st alto, and her husband Don, baritone; Lodi, low contralto, and her husband B.J., deep bass! Surely God had something to do with that! Pat, along with the others, traveled widely in the country and abroad, singing and proclaiming the Gospel.

"Patricia, as well as the other girls, was an esteemed and natural actress in the *Homestead USA* television series, starring the four Vernon Brothers, their wives and kids, in addition to their parents. They pioneered in the first real life family 'reality' show on TV, filmed at the famed Universal International Studios, syndicated to some 200 television stations.

"Married to Bob Vernon in 1949, Pat and her devoted husband celebrated their 66th wedding anniversary in the nursing home where she had been in treatment for a stroke she suffered in 2009. To their union were born four children: Rebecca, a gifted singer, pianist, and worship leader, married to Stephen Walker; Gregory, a dedicated minister, musician, and writer; Deborah, a talented keyboardist, singer-songwriter, and worship leader, married to Randy Ballas; and Karen, who died of a rare, incurable disease when just a baby.

"Pat was a loving and devoted wife and mother, and a proud 'Grandy' to Jeremy, Jessica, Emma, Colton, Beau, and Baxter Drake. We, along with an innumerable host of relatives and friends, proudly celebrate Pat's many accomplishments, and the victorious life she lived.

"Her parents and her three brothers, Jim, Jake, and Ronnie have preceded her in the journey to 'the Great Beyond.'

"Though we mourn her passing, and Pat will be sorely missed, we look forward to that happy and eternal reunion when the last trumpet shall sound and we shall be caught up in the clouds to meet the Lord in the air. So shall we ever be with the Lord, and with those that have gone on before!"

CHAPTER 41

Reflections

I HARDLY KNOW how to close my book. I thought I would complete it with the Tribute and Obituary of Pat's life. But the story of her life is not over; it is just hidden from the view of us earthlings until our blinders are taken off at our Heavenly home-going! And my life, though frail and somewhat feeble since the middle of December of 2015, has not been wrapped up or winded down just yet! Lord willing, I have some miles to go before I sleep, and commitments I'd like to keep. Of course I will be 90 years old come January 4th, 2017, only a few months away. But my mind still tells me I am just 39, like Jack Benny of old! And though there have been challenges and periods of deep sorrow and trials, I have been so blessed and fortunate to live this long, and do so much far beyond what I could have imagined, thanks to God, His Spirit and power in my life. But I have to remember, "… we spend our years as a tale that is told. The days of our years are threescore years and ten; and if by reason of strength they be fourscore years, yet is their strength labour and sorrow; for it is soon cut off, and we fly away" (Psalms 90:9-10, KJV).

Throughout my life, I have tried to make my manner of treating people, teaching, and delivering the message of the Gospel of Love in the way Paul instructed Timothy:

"And the Lord's servant must not strive, but be gentle towards all, apt to teach, forbearing, in meekness correcting them that oppose themselves; if peradventure God may give them repentance unto the knowledge of the truth" (II Timothy 2:24-25, ASV).

Especially when I was in the Navy during World War II, I developed such love and respect for the Lord and His Word, I started memorizing Scripture and had a deep desire to share it with other people. Later, I committed the whole book of Ephesians to memory, along with many other portions of the Bible, for my own personal, spiritual, and devotional benefit, as well as for use in teaching and proclamation of the Gospel. What a blessing and help that was to me! I especially like the third chapter of Ephesians, and used it a lot for boundless confidence and optimism in the early days trying to get nationwide coverage for our television program. In my appearances at meetings and promotional rallies, I would always, toward the end of my appeal, quote Ephesians 3:20 and 21, "Now unto him that is able to do exceeding abundantly above all that we ask or think, according to the power that worketh in us, unto him *be* the glory in the church and in Christ Jesus unto all generations for ever and ever. Amen" (ASV). And with faith and passion, I added by quoting the great poem by Edgar A. Guest, "It Couldn't Be Done:"

> Somebody said that it couldn't be done,
> But he with a chuckle replied
> That "maybe it couldn't," but he would be one
> Who wouldn't say so till he'd tried.
> So he buckled right in with the trace of a grin
> On his face. If he worried he hid it.
> He started to sing as he tackled the thing
> That couldn't be done, and he did it.

Somebody scoffed: "Oh, you'll never do that;
At least no one ever has done it";
But he took off his coat and he took off his hat,
And the first thing we knew he'd begun it.
With a lift of his chin and a bit of a grin,
Without any doubting or quiddit,
He started to sing as he tackled the thing
That couldn't be done, and he did it.

There are thousands to tell you it cannot be done,
There are thousands to prophesy failure;
There are thousands to point out to you one by one,
The dangers that wait to assail you.
But just buckle in with a bit of a grin,
Just take off your coat and go to it;
Just start to sing as you tackle the thing
That "cannot be done," and you'll do it.

I have found it to be true that if you love and enjoy your work, whether it be spiritual or secular, and if you properly educate and prepare yourself for it, together with committing it to God, you will succeed as you do it with the utmost confidence and reliance on the Spirit of the Lord within you! You will be blessed and rewarded greatly, and doors will be opened to you.

All right! You've heard that I'm a confident person. An optimist, and a man of deep faith and passion. But these attributes came to me when I got out on my own in the Navy during World War II, and rediscovered God. As a child and young adolescent, I was quite shy, and certainly showed no signs of becoming a leader. But things changed when I was led to the new-found power in reading and memorizing the Word of God. I became a recipient of that which the Apostle Peter writes about in II Peter 1:2-4:

"Grace to you and peace be multiplied in the knowledge of God and of Jesus our Lord; seeing that his divine power hath granted unto us all things that pertain unto life and godliness, through the knowledge of him that called us by his own glory and virtue; whereby he hath granted unto us his precious and exceeding great promises; that through these ye may become partakers of the divine nature ..." (ASV).

But as I reflect on my life and do possess the "divine nature," I am a human being with feelings, flaws, and shortcomings, and have experienced deep sorrows and mysteries that have been difficult to understand and deal with. There have been periods of almost unbearable grief, loneliness, pain, and despair. But for the most part, I have hidden these emotions and times from the public, keeping them to myself and turning to the Lord for deliverance and strength. We Christians are an imperfect, but forgiven and redeemed people, cleansed by the "god-man" whose crucifixion and blood shed for our sins "saved" us when we reached the point of believing in Christ, repenting of our sins, confessing our faith, and being baptized "for the forgiveness of our sins." After Christ's resurrection and ascension, at the coming of the Holy Spirit, the preaching of the Apostles of the truth and proof of the messiahship of the risen Jesus, more than 3,000 hearing Jews reached deep conviction and belief, and were told to "... Repent, and be baptized every one of you in the name of Jesus Christ for the forgiveness of your sins; and you shall receive the gift of the Holy Spirit. For the promise is to you and to your children and to all that are far off ..." (Acts 2:38-39, RSV). On that great day of the Jewish Feast of Pentecost, the Christian Church was born, but it was composed only of Jews for the first approximately dozen years, until Cornelius, a Roman centurion, received the Gospel and was baptized, becoming the first Gentile convert. The great Hebrew steeped in the Law of Moses and a rabid persecutor of Christians, Saul of Tarsus, was confronted by the risen Christ, repented with great sorrow, and was told by a surprised but pleased minister, Ananias, to "… arise, and be baptized, and wash away thy sins, calling on the name of the Lord" (Acts 22:16, KJV). He, of course, became the famous Apostle to the Gentiles, establishing churches, and authoring most of the letters of the New Testament.

As I reflect on my life and my conversion and commitment to Christ, and relate how Christianity began, I am thinking not only of you who are Christians for whom this is just a review, but of my loving relatives and others who might be inspired to come to, or renew, their faith in Christ. We all need the encouragement and love of one another! I have been greatly benefitted by having been raised in a Christian home by godly parents, but as our society has become more secularized and our culture changes and crumbles, many have not been, nor are now, so blessed and fortunate.

We live in a world that is a fallen race, where as a result of rebellion and sin against God, there is disease, pain, death, hatred, lust, war, destruction, persecution, and even lack of decency and civility. None of this is God's doing. It is man's. God is a god of love, of mercy, and benevolence! He created a world that is spectacularly beautiful and good, and he created us in his own image, desiring the best for us. And as an antidote and cure for sin, of which we are all guilty, he loved us so much that he went even so far as to send his guiltless and only begotten Son to bear our sins on the cross, in order to make us blameless, just as if we'd never sinned! Oh! What love! It's almost too good to be true, but it's true, with proof aplenty! And the good news is, He raised Jesus from the dead so that we as redeemed and purified people could be resurrected at the last day, go to Heaven and be with our loved ones for all eternity! But to many the Good Book is merely a fairy story, a fable, or an ancient, time-worn document thought up, imagined, and authored by men, with no belief at all that it had been written by holy men under the inspiration of the Holy Spirit. Of course, if you don't even believe in God, that would naturally be the case, I suppose. However, there is such power and spirit in the words themselves, that just by reading the Bible has led people to come to deep belief in the integrity and divine inspiration of the Scriptures. Jesus said to his Apostles, "These things have I spoken unto you, while *yet* abiding with you. But the Comforter, *even* the Holy Spirit, whom the Father will send in my name, he shall teach you all things, and bring to your remembrance all that I said unto you" (John 14:25-26, ASV). And Peter said, "For no prophecy ever came by the will of man: but men spake from God, being moved by the Holy Spirit" (II Peter 1:21, ASV). The Apostle Paul wrote, "Every scripture inspired of God *is* also profitable for teaching, for reproof, for correction, for instruction which is in righteousness: that the man of God may be complete, furnished completely unto every good work" (II Timothy 3:16, 17, ASV).

I believe in the authenticity, accuracy, and the integrity of the text of the Bible as it has been copied, translated, and passed down to us. Why? Because having given careful and studious attention to researching the subject and history of how we got our Bible, it is unequivocally clear to me, and should be to every open, honest, and intelligent person, that it has been amazingly and reliably preserved, copied, and translated through the centuries. I studied two years of Koine Greek, in which the original letters of the writers of the New Testament were written on papyrus, or later, on parchment. There is no known original letter or book existent today of what we call the "New Testament." But there are almost 3,000 manuscripts of copies that have been preserved, some of which contain all, and some, portions, of the same New Testament that we have today.

What is called the "Syriac Palimpsest Version" of the New Testament was discovered in 1892 at Sinai. It is a copy of a translation made into Syriac about A.D. 150, within about fifty years of when the Apostles lived. This shows that the text we now have is substantially the same as the one used in the middle of the second century. Some argue that this version can't be trusted because of age. But works of Homer, Plato, and Aristotle are very ancient! There are Scripture quotations, many of them quite lengthy, from the early Church Fathers, one of whom was Polycarp, born in A.D. 69. He was a well-educated young man, becoming a noted theologian and learned disciple of the Apostle John. Polycarp not only became a lover of the Scriptures, a Christian, and a Church Bishop, but he accepted and faithfully taught others the writings of John, including these words: "Many other signs therefore did Jesus in the presence of the disciples, which are not written in this book: but these are written, that ye may believe that Jesus is the Christ, the Son of God; and that believing ye may have life in his name" (John 20:30-31, ASV).

There are in existence so many quotations of Scripture from early Church leaders, such as Justin Martyr, born in Israel at A.D. 100, who became a devout Christian follower, leader, and scholarly writer. Eventually moving to Rome, he wrote several strong, unrelenting but intellectual Apologies, still in existence today, to the Emperor, in defense of the Christians, who were being viciously persecuted. He died, being burned at the stake, as an early Christian martyr.

Other Christian writers quoting from the Scriptures were Irenaeus, Clement of Rome, Clement of Alexandria, Hippolytus, Origen, Chrysostom, Tertullian, Cyprian, and Novation. All constantly write and refer to texts of the various New Testament writings as not only being in existence, but as being the accepted sacred books of the Christian canon, which eventually was collected together at the Council of Nicea in A.D. 325.

All the books of the New Testament were written between A.D. 40 and 100, but contemporaneously, outside of these Scriptures, references to Jesus of Nazareth were made and written about by Josephus, a Jewish historian, as well as by Roman writers and historians Tacitus and Suetonius.

With my own eyes, I saw the caves in which were discovered just a few decades ago, the clay pots holding the Dead Sea Scrolls, one of which contained the scroll of the Old Testament book of the prophet, Isaiah! What a find! There, through all these centuries of two millennia, had been preserved this ancient and prophetic document of God.

For any who would like to do research and further study about the venerable and age-old manuscripts of which I have spoken, the six foremost are these: the Codex Sinaiticus, now in Russia; the Codex Vaticanus, now at Rome in the Vatican Library; the Codex Alexandrinus, probably a fourth century manuscript containing essentially the text of our King James Version of the Bible which was printed in 1611; the Codex Bezae; and the Chester Beatty Papyri, scrolls copied laboriously on papyrus, dating from the early part of the third century. The first three contain sixty out of 220 from the Gospels and Acts, twenty of Paul's epistles, and twenty pages of Revelation.

I hope I haven't bored you with these reflections about my faith in the Lord and the belief I have, based on accurate and historic evidence, about the integrity and reliability of the inspired Scriptures. But this is who I am and what I have been about, as well as loving life and people, being the very human, earthy, pensive, passionate, and ordinary person I am, continually thanking God for his mercy, his blessings, and his forgiveness of my weaknesses, my sins, and all the shortcomings of my life!

Now, some closing thoughts about the mystery of life on earth, the mystery of godliness, and the mystery of death. First, there are, and in my life I have experienced, mysteries and things I don't understand. That is part of the human dilemma. "Why did Karen have an incurable disease?" "Why did my darling wife, so beautiful, so caring, and so full of life and faith, have so many years of migraines and then more than a half-decade of impairment from a stroke?" "Why do the babes and innocents suffer and die?" "Why in our age do the Islamic militants up-root, persecute, and slaughter peace-loving Christians, obeying, as I have read in their Koran, the mandate to kill the infidels, Jews and Christians?" "Why the Holocaust?" On and on we could go. The only answer I know is that we live in an imperfect world, and we are a fallen people, in need of redemption, to live forever in a perfect Paradise where there is no disease, no death, no defeat, no fear, no hatred, no killing, and nothing but the very best of everything we could ever dream of!

Second is the mystery of godliness, spoken of by Paul in these words:

"And without controversy great is the mystery of godliness;
He who was manifested in the flesh,
Justified in the spirit,
Seen of angels,
Preached among the nations,
Believed on in the world,
Received up in glory" (I Timothy 3:16, ASV).

Whether a chorus by Paul, or a musical chant used by the Church of the first century, is immaterial. It was a beautiful summary of the life of the risen Christ that Paul included in his letter to the young evangelist, Timothy. Is God or godliness a mystery to you? If so, you can be assured that the mystery is cleared up and is solved by the revealed truth we see in the life of Christ. To the natural man, godliness is a mystery; to the believing, spiritual person, godliness is a discovered melody. The unbelieving natural man may be good and productive in his life, but the stain of sin remains, and God is foreign to his life. He robs himself of grace here on earth and glory in the hereafter. What a tragedy! I like the Phillips Version of this verse, because it puts the writing in such plain, understanding English that anyone can comprehend:

> "No one can deny that this religion of ours is a tremendous mystery, resting as it does on the one who showed himself as a human being, and met, as such, every demand of the Spirit in the sight of angels as well as of men. Then, after his restoration to the Heaven from whence he came, he has been proclaimed among men of different nationalities and believed in all parts of the world" (I Timothy 3:16, Phillips).

In very clear language, I want to "paraphrase" one more passage of Scripture from Paul about the mystery of Christ, as follows:

> By special revelation from Christ, when he appeared to me, it was made known to me the mystery, as I told you before in few words, how that when you read, you can perceive my understanding about the mystery of Christ. In other generations it was not made known to people, as it has now been revealed to his holy apostles and prophets in the Spirit, that is, that the Gentiles are fellow heirs with the Jews, fellow-members with them of the same body, and sharers of the promise in Christ Jesus through the Gospel. (My version of Ephesians 3:3-6.)

Plain and simple in that mystery, now revealed, is that the loving God of Heaven chose his beloved Son to be our messianic Lord and Savior, to come to earth to teach, to prove his messiahship through his compassionate deeds and miracles, to die for our sins and conquer death, and that everyone, through their faith and loving obedience to the Gospel, can inherit eternal life!

Third, and finally, as far as our earthly life is concerned, is the mystery of death. We call it "passing on," "going to the great beyond," "expiring," "crossing the bar," "the end," "sleep," and other such terms. Paul said, "Wherefore, as by one man sin entered into the world, and death by sin; and so death passed upon all men, for that all have sinned" (Romans 5:12, KJV). He also wrote, "The last enemy that shall be destroyed is death" (I Corinthians 15:26, KJV). To the Romans, Paul penned, "For the wages of sin is death; but the gift of God is eternal life through Jesus Christ our Lord" (Romans 6:23, KJV).

For the Christian, the exit of death is but the entrance into the Kingdom of our Lord Jesus Christ. That's why the aged Apostle John when banished to the isle of Patmos, wrote, "... Blessed are the dead which die in the Lord from henceforth: Yea, saith the Spirit, that they may rest from their labours ..." (Revelation 14:13, KJV).

My goal in life, although I have not always lived up to it, is still this, as expressed by Paul, "According to my earnest expectation and my hope, that in nothing I shall be ashamed, but that with all boldness, as always, so now also Christ shall be magnified in my body, whether it be by life, or by death. For to me to live is Christ, and to die is gain" (Philippians 1:20-21, KJV).

How comforting it is when a loved one dies, to read or hear these words, "Precious in the sight of the LORD is the death of his saints" (Psalms 116:15, KJV). Though it leaves one grieving and lonely, when a beloved spouse, a close friend, or a dear family member breathes their last as a Christian, there is peace and joy in the heart as teardrops fall. The pain and mystery of death fades when we hear these words:

"Listen! I will unfold a mystery: we shall not all die, but we shall all be changed in a flash, in the twinkling of an eye, at the last trumpet-call. For the trumpet will sound, and the dead will rise immortal, and we shall be changed. This perishable being must be clothed with the imperishable, and what is mortal must be clothed with immortality ... then the saying of Scripture will come true: 'Death is swallowed up; victory is won!' 'O Death, where is your victory? O Death, where is your sting?' The sting of death is sin, and sin gains its power from the law; but, God be praised, he gives us the victory through our Lord Jesus Christ" (I Corinthians 15:51-57, NEB).

As the signs of Christ's second coming are clearly being fulfilled with earthquakes, famines, false "christs," persecutions, wars, fear, faithlessness, the Gospel reaching all nations, and the Jews return to Israel, all this points to the reality that ours could be the last generation of life on the earth, and that Christ could come back at any moment. Even so, come, Lord Jesus! At that time, all questions, all puzzles, and all mysteries unanswered, will be solved.

I close my book now with these words of a poem I penned, and later put to music and recorded, when on a very dark night of a deep dilemma I was facing, light shone from Heaven bringing spiritual discernment and inspiration. I share it now with you, hoping and praying that it, as well as my book, will bless your soul.

BEAUTIFUL MYSTERY
By Bob J. Vernon

Oh Lord, I cry, the more I try
To live successfully,
It seems the way from day to day
Is a greater mystery.

But in thy Word we all have heard
Of Him who was so true.
Who came from Spirit to be flesh,
His life was a mystery too.

But Oh! What a beautiful mystery
Of light and life and love!
That blesses all the human race
With hope from high above.
As God, He took the form
Of fleshly man
To reveal the
Hidden plan,
And died, then rose!
That life might go on and on
When earthly life
Has gone.

So Lord I see thy majesty,
Thy beauty and thy love,
Revealed for me in history
When Thou didst come from above,
To bless the earth and show the worth
Of people just like me,
Who are unworthy and in need
Of truth that can set us all free.

CPSIA information can be obtained
at www.ICGtesting.com
Printed in the USA
LVOW03s1443050418
572436LV00011B/1279/P